Managing Risk
in the
New Economy

Dr. Dimitris N. Chorafas

NEW YORK INSTITUTE OF FINANCE

NEW YORK • TORONTO • SYDNEY • TOKYO • SINGAPORE

Library of Congress Cataloging-in-Publication Data

Chorafas, Dimitris N.
    Managing risk in the new economy / Dimitris N. Chorafas.
      p.   cm.
    Includes index.
    ISBN 0-7352-0217-6 (cloth)
    1. Electronic commerce—Management.   2. Risk management.   I. Title.

HF5548.32 .C48 2001
658.15′ 5—dc21   00-068374

Acquisitions Editor: *Ellen Schneid Coleman*
Production Editor: *Sharon L. Gonzalez*
Formatting/Interior Design: *Robyn Beckerman*

©*2001 by Prentice Hall*

Printed in the United States of America

10 9 8 7 6 5 4 3 2 1

This publication is designed to provide accurate and authoritative information in regard to the subject
matter covered. It is sold with the understanding that the publisher is not engaged in rendering legal,
accounting, or other professional service. If legal advice or other expert assistance is required, the services
of a competent professional person should be sought.

> *. . . From the Declaration of Principles jointly adopted by a Committee of the
> American Bar Association and a Committee of Publishers and Associations.*

ISBN 0-7352-0217-6

ATTENTION: CORPORATIONS AND SCHOOLS

Prentice Hall Press books are available at quantity discounts with bulk purchase for
educational, business, or sales promotional use. For information, please write to:
Prentice Hall Special Sales, 240 Frisch Court, Paramus, New Jersey 07652. Please
supply: title of book, ISBN, quantity, how the book will be used, date needed.

NEW YORK INSTITUTE OF FINANCE
An Imprint of Prentice Hall Press
Paramus, NJ 07652

http://www.phdirect.com/business

THE DOORS OF RISK AND OF RETURN
ARE ADJACENT AND IDENTICAL.

CONTENTS

PART THREE

RISK MANAGEMENT RESPONSIBILITIES   **205**
IN THE NEW ECONOMY

FOREWORD

GARP and the whole risk management profession were established in response to the growing importance of the risk management function within traditional financial institutions. In recent years, however, the risk management function, as we know it, is being challenged by the transformation grounded in the New Economy. Risks originating from businesses such as private equity investments and large-scale e-commerce projects now often dominate the financial risk landscape. Although these activities are not new, their breadth and scope has increased. Derivatives pricing gurus, regulators, and auditors are at a loss in trying to tackle these businesses as the more traditional Value at Risk modeling techniques have fallen by the wayside. There is no modeling to be done, no differential equations to be solved, and no data to be analyzed.

While we were developing GARCH models to make sure we could properly "manage" dollar-yen risk, our colleagues across the hall in the credit departments had trouble figuring out their exposure to hedge funds. Our audit friends were busy auditing those dollar-yen models instead of questioning the somewhat "difficult to deal with" bond dealer. And while Quants were improving the lattice of the Bermudan option model with a knockout feature, no one bothered to check the impact of a major emerging country defaulting on its obligations.

We could afford these luxuries in the past, but the days of funding fancy model development for risk management are over. The competitive landscape is changing quickly. The financial institution of the New Economy is an advisor, an opportunistic broker, a research company, an asset manager, and, most of all, an information technology firm. From General Electric to Enron to Ford, firms that traditionally depended on banks for financing and financial engineering advice are now running the show. These companies are well capitalized, far less regulated, and have a view that financial risk is as much about upside opportunity as it is about downside threat. These firms are now major players in the financing and investment game. They are making markets in swaps, issuing their own bonds, and even running a full set of financing and insurance services.

As the speed of change accelerates and a networked global economy creates opportunities of unprecedented scale, new risks are emerging. Pressures to cut costs are becoming immense and industries are consolidating and converging. Unseen competitors are challenging mainline businesses. Business models are becoming obsolete. And traditional barriers between companies are breaking down, along with the controls previously in place to reduce risk.

Stagnation is the biggest risk faced by many financial institutions today. Whether it is Charles Schwab and E-Trade squeezing out full retail brokers or low-cost independent B2B exchanges putting pressure on bond dealers and institutional brokers, the monopoly on pricing and dealing in financial products by large institutions has crumbled. Derivatives and commodities online exchanges are offering intermediation services recently available only from the most sophisticated of financial service firms. These services are performed at Internet speed and at a fraction of the cost previously charged by the "bricks-and-mortar" players.

Those institutions with high cost structures (including bloated risk management departments) must continuously search for new high margin-markets and take new types of risks, including investing in those same companies that are cutting into their business.

To add value to their institutions, risk management departments must become as dynamic as their new competitors. The focus needs to shift from Value at Risk calculations to the analysis of a firm's capital allocation and a search for concentrations of risk across the institution. Fierce competition, hot new businesses that everyone "has to be in," markets that are "truly different this time," and management's distaste for any warning signs are the things that often cause a buildup of risk concentration. The key is not to protect the company from this risk, but to detect the risk and to make sure this is what the firm and its shareholders want in the portfolio.

In this book, Dr. Dimitris Chorafas discusses this wave of change transforming institutions and their risk management practices. Dr. Chorafas tackles this topic with a broad, interdisciplinary approach, covering a number of practical issues illustrated by pertinent case studies. He sheds light on some of the more complex and controversial issues facing businesses today. As the New Economy engulfs the world of finance, the financial services industry landscape will change beyond recognition. For causes and clues to surviving the revolution, read on.

Dr. Lev Borodovsky
Co-Chairman, Global Association of Risk Professionals (GARP)

No new economy, no technology, no innovation, and no new product is worth anything if it does not create value. Therefore, the crucial questions are:

- How do we develop an economy that creates value for companies and consumers?
- What kinds of risks do we assume in this process?
- How do we identify and control these risks?

Born out of an intensive research project, which took place in the United States and Europe between June 1998 and October 2000, this book hits hard on two issues that currently dominate economic and financial thinking: *risk* and the *new economy*. One hundred sixty-one senior executives, working in 84 different organizations (roughly half in the United States and half in England, Germany, Switzerland, Austria, France, Italy, Sweden, Luxembourg, Hungary, Poland, and Iceland) contributed their insights. Participants included representatives of such regulatory authorities as the Federal Reserve Board, Securities and Exchange Commission, Office of the Comptroller of the Currency, FDIC and OTS; major investment banks like Merrill Lynch and Prudential Securities; well-known pension funds such as TIAA/CREF; and a select list of knowledgeable people expert in finance and technology.

The aim of this research, carried out in person-to-person meetings, was to understand the fundamental framework in which trades and investments in the new economy take place, and to locate where exactly the major risks lie—not only in a company or an industry, but in the economy at large, particularly the global economy.

The decision to divide the interviews equally between the United States and leading European countries was deliberate. The *new economy* is global, and, therefore, no one country establishes the laws and rules it must obey. The new economy is also to a significant degree deregulated, which means that boundaries that formerly separated one company from another and one industry from another no longer exist. As a result the market has taken upon

itself the Herculean task of imposing a sense of discipline, in trading as well as in the control of risk.

The new economy is leveraged, and this impacts greatly on the
way business is done, as well as on the financial staying power of the
different institutions. Leveraged companies must manage their exposure to all types of risks far better than they did in the past because
the risks they take are so much greater. They must also keep a careful
eye on:

- Nonperformance by counterparties,
- Exposure embedded in new financial instruments, and
- The amount of capital they must put aside to protect themselves
  in case of disaster.

Because financial institutions often make life difficult for themselves, important lessons can be learned from the study of why they
fail. One notable example, discussed in depth in this book is Long-
Term Capital Management (LTCM). Sadly, there is no lack of "good"
examples. In the last twenty years, we have witnessed several spectac-
ular examples of the effects of risk on financial institutions, among
them are the events leading to the demise of Drysdale, Kidder
Peabody, Barings, and Tiger Management to name a few.

Because the new economy is networked, it has led to real-time
innovative instruments, significant opportunities, and unprecedented
risks. Using the facilities provided by the Internet, the empires of the
21st century are those that operate in a virtual global space, not only
business-to-business and business-to-consumer, but also consumer-to-
business and consumer-to-consumer. This opens the new economy to
systemic risks, which, at this moment, we only partly comprehend, but
we can guess that they may create unheard-of consequences.

A problem senior managers commonly face when selecting
strategic solutions to systemic problems is how to choose one that
enhances both their short-term profits and their longer-term financial staying power. This is like trying to kill two birds with one well-
placed stone. It's a strategy that rarely, if ever, succeeds and, as
knowledgeable financial experts said to me, each option typically has
tradeoffs that can make any one no more desirable than any other.
No option can be assumed to be 100 percent secure. Therefore, it is
essential to choose strategic solutions that have as few side effects as
possible. This is every senior executive's dilemma.

Managing Risk in the New Economy is written for investment bankers, commercial bankers, traders, investors, treasurers, financial analysts, and risk management officers. It is divided into three parts: Part One focuses on the growing appetite for risk and the uncertainty that goes with it. It is illustrated with case studies from Daewoo, Sumitomo, Kidder Peabody, and Long-Term Capital Management.

All financial institutions face credit risk, market risk, operational risk, legal risk, and many other risks in most of their activities, but the intensity of these exposures increases with the type of instruments they trade and the leverage these instruments have. Other things being equal, the newer and more technical the instruments, the greater the potential exposure. Risks are manifested quite differently in derivatives than in traditional securities because:

- Several unknown factors are embedded in derivatives, and
- The amount of inverse leverage inherent in derivatives affects trading.

Part Two capitalizes on the lessons that have been learned from recent financial disasters. It brings to the reader's attention how some institutions, because of over gearing *and* inadequate risk control, find themselves at the edge of the abyss, unable to pull back without the help of the regulator's fire brigade. "I couldn't in my wildest dreams imagine that any responsible banker would want to take the risks LTCM was taking," suggested a senior financial executive who participated in the research leading to this book. But not all strategies go awry, and not all users of mathematical models twist them around and cut corners.

Part Three shows how we can apply the lessons learned from others' failures. If times of crisis are the worst of times for financial institutions, they are also the best of times for learning from the mistakes others have made. For this reason, it is essential to emphasize the responsibility and accountability for risk management in the new economy.

A central theme of this book is that while no one can claim to know everything about the management of risk, there is a body of knowledge on which we can and should capitalize. Therefore, my foremost goal is to present a wide range of information about risk management in the new economy, and to show how this know-how can be put into daily practice. The text is based on what is known and doable. As T. H. Huxley said, "The known is finite; the unknown is infinite."

I am indebted to a long list of knowledgeable people and organizations for their contributions to the research that made this text possible. Thanks also go to a number of company executives, technologists, and financial experts for their constructive criticism during the preparation of the manuscript. A complete list of the 161 people and 85 organizations that participated in this research appears in the Acknowledgments.

Let me take this opportunity to thank Ellen Schneid Coleman for suggesting this project and seeing it all the way to publication, Sybil Grace and Ruth Mills for their editing, and Sharon L. Gonzalez for the production work. To Eva-Maria Binder goes the credit for compiling the research results, typing the text, and creating the camera-ready artwork and index.

DR. DIMITRIS N. CHORAFAS
Valmer and Vitznau

ACKNOWLEDGMENTS

(Countries are listed in alphabetical order.)

The following organizations, through their senior executives and system specialists, participated in the recent research projects that led to the contents of this book and its documentation.

AUSTRIA

National Bank of Austria
Dr. Martin Ohms, Finance Market Analysis Department

3, Otto Wagner Platz
Postfach 61
A-1011 Vienna

Association of Austrian Banks and Bankers
Dr. Fritz Diwok, Secretary General

11, Boersengasse
1013 Vienna

Bank Austria
Dr. Peter Fischer, Senior General Manager, Treasury Division
Peter Gabriel, Deputy General Manager, Trading

2, Am Hof
1010 Vienna

Creditanstalt
Dr. Wolfgang Lichtl, Market Risk Management

Julius Tandler Platz 3
A-1090 Vienna

Wiener Betriebs—and Baugesellschaft mbH
Dr. Josef Fritz, General Manager

1, Anschützstrasse
1153 Vienna

FRANCE

Banque de France
Pierre Jaillet, Director, Monetary Studies and Statistics
Yvan Oronnal, Manager, Monetary Analyses and Statistics
G. Tournemire, Analyst, Monetary Studies

    39, rue Croix des Petits Champs
    75001 Paris

Secretariat Général de la Commission Bancaire—Banque de France
Didier Peny, Director, Control of Big Banks and International Banks

    73, rue de Richelieu
    75002 Paris

F. Visnowsky, Manager of International Affairs, Supervisory Policy and Research Division
Benjamin Sahel, Market Risk Control

    115, Rue Réaumur
    75049 Paris Cedex 01

Ministry of Finance and the Economy, Conseil National de la Comptabilité
Alain Le Bars, Director International Relations and Cooperation

    6, rue Louise Weiss
    75703 Paris Cedex 13

GERMANY

Deutsche Bundesbank
Hans-Dietrich Peters, Director
Hans Werner Voth, Director

    Wilhelm-Epstein Strasse 14
    60431 Frankfurt am Main

Federal Banking Supervisory Office
Hans-Joachim Dohr, Director Dept. I
Jochen Kayser, Risk Model Examination
Ludger Hanenberg, Internal Controls

    71-101 Gardeschützenweg
    12203 Berlin

European Central Bank
Mauro Grande, Director

    29 Kaiserstrasse, 29th Floor
    60216 Frankfurt am Main

Deutsches Aktieninstitut
Dr. Rüdiger Von Rosen, President

Biebergasse 6 bis 10
60313 Frankfurt-am-Main

Commerzbank
Peter Bürger, Senior Vice President, Strategy and Controlling
Markus Rumpel, Senior Vice President, Credit Risk Management

Kaiserplatz
60261 Frankfurt am Main

Deutsche Bank
Professor Manfred Timmermann, Head of Controlling
Hans Voit, Head of Process Management, Controlling Department

12, Taunusanlage
60325 Frankfurt

Dresdner Bank
Dr. Marita Balks, Investment Bank, Risk Control
Dr. Hermann Haaf, Mathematical Models for Risk Control
Claas Carsten Kohl, Financial Engineer

1, Jürgen Ponto Platz
60301 Frankfurt

GMD First—Research Institute for Computer Architecture, Software Technology and Graphics
Prof. Dr. Ing. Wolfgang K. Giloi, General Manager

5, Rudower Chaussee
D-1199 Berlin

HUNGARY

Hungarian Banking and Capital Market Supervision
Dr. Janos Kun, Head, Department of Regulation and Analyses
Dr. Erika Vörös, Senior Economist, Department of Regulation and Analyses
Dr. Géza Nyiry, Head, Section of Information Audit

Csalogany u. 9-11
H-1027 Budapest

Hungarian Academy of Sciences
Prof. Dr. Tibor Vamos, Chairman, Computer and Automation Research Institute

Nador U. 7
1051 Budapest

ICELAND

The National Bank of Iceland Ltd
Gunnar T. Andersen, Managing Director, International Banking & Treasury

    Laugavegur 77
    155 Reykjavik

ITALY

Banca d'Italia
Eugene Gaiotti, Research Department, Monetary and Financial Division
Ing. Dario Focarelli, Research Department

    91, via Nazionale
    00184 Rome

Istituto Bancario San Paolo di Torino
Dr. Paolo Chiulenti, Director of Budgeting
Roberto Costa, Director of Private Banking
Pino Ravelli, Director Bergamo Region

    27, via G. Camozzi
    24121 Bergamo

LUXEMBOURG

Banque Générale de Luxembourg
Prof. Dr. Yves Wagner, Director of Asset and Risk Management
Hans Jörg Paris, International Risk Manager

    27, avenue Monterey
    L-2951 Luxembourg

POLAND

Securities and Exchange Commission
Beata Stelmach, Secretary of the Commission

    1, Pl Powstancow Warszawy
    00-950 Warsaw

SWEDEN

Skandinaviska Enskilda Banken
Bernt Gyllenswärd, Head of Group Audit

    Box 16067
    10322 Stockholm

Irdem AB
Gian Medri, Former Director of Research at Nordbanken

19, Flintlasvagen
S-19154 Sollentuna

SWITZERLAND

Swiss National Bank
Dr. Werner Hermann, Head of International Monetary Relations
Dr. Christian Walter, Representative to the Basle Committee
Robert Fluri, Assistant Director, Statistics Section

15 Börsenstrasse
Zurich

Federal Banking Commission
Dr. Susanne Brandenberger, Risk Management
Renate Lischer, Representative to Risk Management Subgroup, Basle Committee

Marktgasse 37
3001 Bern

Bank for International Settlements
Mr. Claude Sivy, Head of Internal Audit
Herbie Poenisch, Senior Economist, Monetary and Economic Department

2, Centralplatz
4002 Basle

Bank Leu AG
Dr. Urs Morgenthaler, Member of Management, Director of Risk Control

32, Bahnhofstrasse
Zurich

Bank J. Vontobel and Vontobel Holding
Heinz Frauchiger, Chief, Internal Audit Department

Tödistrasse 23
CH-8022 Zurich

Union Bank of Switzerland
Dr. Heinrich Steinmann, Member of the Executive Board (Retired)

Claridenstrasse
8021 Zurich

UNITED KINGDOM

Bank of England and Financial Services Authority
Richard Britton, Director, Complex Groups Division, CGD Policy Department

Threadneedle Street
London EC2R 8AH

British Bankers Association
Paul Chisnall, Assistant Director

Pinners Hall
105-108 Old Broad Street
London EC2N 1EX

Accounting Standards Board
A.V.C. Cook, Technical Director
Sandra Thompson, Project Director

Holborn Hall
100 Gray's Inn Road
London WC1X 8AL

Barclays Bank plc
Brandon Davies, Treasurer, Global Corporate Banking
Alan Brown, Director, Group Risk

54 Lombard Street
London EC3P 3AH

Abbey National Treasury Services plc
John Hasson, Director of Information Technology & Treasury Operations

Abbey House
215-229 Baker Street
London NW1 6XL

ABN-AMRO Investment Bank N.V.
David Woods, Chief Operations Officer, Global Equity Directorate

199 Bishopsgate
London EC2M 3TY

Bankgesellschaft Berlin
Stephen F. Myers, Head of Market Risk

1 Crown Court
Cheapside, London

Standard & Poor's
David T. Beers, Managing Director, Sovereign Ratings

Garden House
18, Finsbury Circus
London EC2M 7BP

Moody's Investor Services
Samuel S. Theodore, Managing Director, European Banks
David Frohriep, Communications Manager, Europe

2, Minster Court
Mincing Lange
London EC3R 7XB

Fitch IBCA
Charles Prescott, Group Managing Director, Banks
David Andrews, Managing Director, Financial Institutions
Travor Pitman, Managing Director, Corporations
Richard Fox, Director, International Public Finance

Eldon House
2, Eldon Street
London EC2M 7UA

Merrill Lynch International
Erik Banks, Managing Director of Risk Management

Ropemaker Place
London EC2Y 9LY

The Auditing Practices Board
Jonathan E.C. Grant, Technical Director
Steve Leonard, Internal Controls Project Manager

P.O. Box 433
Moorgate Place
London EC2P 2BJ

International Accounting Standards Committee
Ms. Liesel Knorr, Technical Director

166 Fleet Street
London EC4A 2DY

MeesPierson ICS
Arjan P. Verkerk, Director, Market Risk

Camomile Court
23 Camomile Street
London EC3A 7PP

Charles Schwab
Dan Hattrup, International Investment Specialist

   Crosby Court
   38 Bishopsgate
   London EC2N 4AJ

City University Business School
Professor Elias Dinenis, Head, Department of Investment,
Risk Management & Insurance
Prof. Dr. John Hagnioannides, Department of Finance

   Frobisher Crescent
   Barbican Centre
   London EC2Y 8BH

UNITED STATES

Federal Reserve System, Board of Governors
David L. Robinson, Deputy Director, Chief Federal Reserve Examiner
Alan H. Osterholm, CIA, CISA, Manager, Financial Examinations Section
Paul W. Bettge, Assistant Director, Division of Reserve Bank Operations
Gregory E. Eller, Supervisory Financial Analyst, Banking
Gregory L. Evans, Manager, Financial Accounting
Martha Stallard, Financial Accounting, Reserve Bank Operations

   20th and Constitution, NW
   Washington, DC 20551

Federal Reserve Bank of Boston
William McDonough, Executive Vice President
James T. Nolan, Assistant Vice President

   P.O. Box 2076
   600 Atlantic Avenue
   Boston, MA 02106-2076

Federal Reserve Bank of San Francisco
Nigel R. Ogilvie, CFA, Supervising Financial Analyst, Emerging Issues

   101 Market Street
   San Francisco, CA 94105

Seattle Branch, Federal Reserve Bank of San Francisco
Jimmy F. Kamada, Assistant Vice President
Gale P. Ansell, Assistant Vice President, Business Development

   1015, 2nd Avenue
   Seattle, WA 98122-3567

Office of the Comptroller of the Currency (OCC)

Bill Morris, National Bank Examiner/Policy Analyst, Core Policy
Development Division
Gene Green, Deputy Chief Accountant, Office of the Chief Accountant

250 E Street, SW
7th Floor
Washington, DC 20024

Federal Deposit Insurance Corporation (FDIC)

Curtis Wong, Capital Markets, Examination Support
Tanya Smith, Examination Specialist, International Branch
Doris L. Marsh, Examination Specialist, Policy Branch

550 17th Street, N.W.
Washington, DC 20006

Office of Thrift Supervision (OTS)

Timothy J. Stier, Chief Accountant

1700 G Street Northwest
Washington, DC 20552

Securities and Exchange Commission, Washington, DC

Robert Uhl, Professional Accounting Fellow
Pascal Desroches, Professional Accounting Fellow
John W. Albert, Associate Chief Accountant
Scott Bayless, Associate Chief Accountant

Office of the Chief Accountant
Securities and Exchange Commission
450 Fifth Street, NW
Washington, DC 20549

Securities and Exchange Commission, New York

Robert A. Sollazzo, Associate Regional Director

7 World Trade Center, 12th Floor
New York, NY 10048

Securities and Exchange Commission, Boston

Edward A. Ryan, Jr., Assistant District Administrator (Regulations)

Boston District Office
73 Tremont Street, 6th Floor
Boston, MA 02108-3912

International Monetary Fund
Alain Coune, Assistant Director, Office of Internal Audit and Inspection

19th Street NW
Washington, DC 20431

Financial Accounting Standards Board
Halsey G. Bullen, Project Manager
Jeannot Blanchet, Project Manager
Teri L. List, Practice Fellow

401 Merritt
Norwalk, CT 06856

Henry Kaufman & Company
Dr. Henry Kaufman

660 Madison Avenue
New York, NY 10022

Soros Fund Management
George Soros, Chairman

888 Seventh Avenue, Suite 3300
New York, NY 10106

Carnegie Corporation of New York
Armanda Famiglietti, Associate Corporate Secretary, Director of Grants
Management

437 Madison Avenue
New York, NY 10022

Alfred P. Sloan Foundation
Stewart F. Campbell, Financial Vice President and Secretary

630 Fifth Avenue, Suite 2550
New York, NY 10111

Rockefeller Brothers Fund
Benjamin R. Shute, Jr., Secretary

437 Madison Avenue
New York, NY 10022-7001

The Foundation Center
79 Fifth Avenue
New York, NY 10003-4230

Citibank
Daniel Schutzer, Vice President, Director of Advanced Technology

909 Third Avenue
New York, NY 10022

Prudential-Bache Securities
Bella Loykhter, Senior Vice President, Information Technology
Kenneth Musco, First Vice President and Director, Management Internal Control
Neil S. Lerner, Vice President, Management Internal Control

1 New York Plaza
New York, NY 10292-2017

Merrill Lynch
John J. Fosina, Director, Planning and Analysis
Paul J. Fitzsimmons, Senior Vice President, District Trust Manager
David E. Radcliffe, Senior Vice President, National Manager Philanthropic Consulting

Corporate and Institutional Client Group
World Financial Center, North Tower
New York, NY 10281-1316

HSBC Republic
Susan G. Pearce, Senior Vice President
Philip A. Salazar, Executive Director

452 Fifth Avenue, Tower 6
New York, NY 10018

International Swaps and Derivatives Association (ISDA)
Susan Hinko, Director of Policy

600 Fifth Avenue, 27th Floor, Rockefeller Center
New York, NY 10020-2302

Standard & Poor's
Clifford Griep, Managing Director

25 Broadway
New York, NY 10004-1064

Mary Peloquin-Dodd, Director, Public Finance Ratings

55 Water Street
New York, NY 10041-0003

Moody's Investor Services
Lea Carty, Director, Corporates

99 Church Street
New York, NY 10022

State Street Bank and Trust
James J. Barr, Executive Vice President, U.S. Financial Assets Services

225 Franklin Street
Boston, MA 02105-1992

MBIA Insurance Corporation
John B. Caouette, Vice Chairman

113 King Street
Armonk, NY 10504

Global Association of Risk Professionals (GARP)
Lev Borodovski, Executive Director, GARP, and Director of Risk Management,
Credit Suisse First Boston (CSFB), New York

Yong Li, Director of Education, GARP, and Vice President, Lehman Brothers,
New York

Dr. Frank Leiber, Research Director and Assistant Director of Computational
Finance, Cornell University, Theory Center, New York

Roy Nawal, Director of Risk Forums, GARP

980 Broadway, Suite 242
Thornwood, NY 10594

Group of Thirty
John Walsh, Director

1990 M Street, NW
Suite 450
Washington, DC 20036

Broadcom Corporation
Dr. Henry Samueli, Co-Chairman of the Board, Chief Technical Officer

16215 Alton Parkway
P.O. Box 57013
Irvine, CA 92619-7013

Edward Jones
Ann Ficken, Director, Internal Audit

201 Progress Parkway
Maryland Heights, MO 63043-3042

Teachers Insurance and Annuity Association/College Retirement Equities Fund (TIAA/CREF)
John W. Sullivan, Senior Institutional Trust Consultant
Charles S. Dvorkin, Vice President and Chief Technology Officer
Harry D. Perrin, Assistant Vice President, Information Technology

730 Third Avenue
New York, NY 10017-3206

Grenzebach Glier & Associates, Inc.
John J. Glier, President and Chief Executive Officer

55 West Wacker Drive, Suite 1500
Chicago, IL 60601

Massachusetts Institute of Technology
Ms. Peggy Carney, Administrator, Graduate Office
Michael Coen, Ph.D. Candidate, ARPA Intelligent Environment Project

Department of Electrical Engineering and Computer Science
Building 38, Room 444
50 Vassar Street
Cambridge, MA 02139

Henry Samueli School of Engineering and Applied Science,
University of California, Los Angeles
Dean A.R. Frank Wazzan, School of Engineering and Applied Science
Prof. Stephen E. Jacobson, Dean of Student Affairs
Dr. Les Lackman, Mechanical and Aerospace Engineering Department
Prof. Richard Muntz, Chair, Computer Science Department
Prof. Dr. Leonard Kleinrock, Telecommunications and Networks
Prof. Chih-Ming Ho, Ph.D., Ben Rich-Lockheed Martin Professor,
Mechancial and Aerospace Engineering Department
Dr. Gang Chen, Mechancial and Aerospace Engineering Department
Prof. Harold G. Monbouquette, Ph.D., Chemical Engineering Department
Prof. Jack W. Judy, Electrical Engineering Department
Abeer Alwan, Bioengineering
Prof. Greg Pottie, Electrical Engineering Department
Prof. Lieven Vandenberghe, Electrical Engineering Department

Andersen Graduate School of Management, University of California, Los Angeles
Prof. John Mamer, Former Dean
Prof. Bruce Miller

Roundtable Discussion on Engineering and Management Curriculum (October 2, 2000)
Dr. Henry Borenstein, Honeywell

Dr. F. Issacci, Honeywell

Dr. Ray Haynes, TRW

Dr. Richard Croxall, TRW

Dr. Steven Bouley, Boeing

Dr. Derek Cheung, Rockwell

>Westwood Village
>Los Angeles, CA 90024

University of Maryland
Prof. Howard Frank, Dean, The Robert H. Smith School of Business

Prof. Lemma W. Senbert, Chair, Finance Department

Prof. Haluk Unal, Associate Professor of Finance

>Van Munching Hall
>College Park, MD 20742-1815

PART ONE

Emerging Industries, the Internet Economy, and the Need for Redefining Management Control

Managing risk in the new economy promises to be a much more complex and demanding task than the one we know from the old economy. Chapter 1 brings to the reader's attention the fundamentals underpinning the concepts of risk and leverage.

CHAPTER 1

The Impact of Risk and Uncertainty on Financial Institutions

Risk is no alien concept in finance. Today, more than ever, bankers, treasurers, traders, and analysts appreciate that transactions made and positions taken by an institution (or any other entity) must be controlled steadily and effectively. *Credit risk* is ever present (the growing number of defaults being a worrying development), while volatility and liquidity combine to increase *market risk*.

With the 1999 New Capital Adequacy Framework by the Basle Committee on Banking Supervision, the attention of financial institutions has also been brought to *operational risk*, which in the past was often treated as an afterthought. Operational risk covers a whole environment in which the management of credit, market, and other risks takes place. In fact, it pervades all other areas so that credit and market exposure necessarily exist in a landscape of operational risk and its control.

Credit risk, market risk, operational risk, and other risks facing an institution are amplified because of globalization, deregulation, innovation, and technology, which together help to define the new economy characterizing the beginnings of the 21st century. Experts today worry that in the middle of many risk calculations there are often one or two mythical assumptions—for instance, the hypothesis that money will always be available in case adversity hits.

New economy is the name given to those industries benefiting directly or indirectly from the latest revolution in information and communications technologies, the extensive use of the latest electronic systems, advanced software, digitalization, and the Internet. The new economy contrasts to the old economy, which refers to those companies that are still embedded in decade-old business models, whether these be product innovation, paper-based supply chain, wanting inventory management, expensive modes of financing, slow-going sales practices, and other aspects of distribution.

The new economy has teething troubles. The disruptions and uncertainties the new economy experiences since the late March/early April 2000 major corrections of the NASDAQ and of the New York Stock Exchange have sent organizations scrambling for professional guidance. This is not forthcoming because major financial institutions as well as the technology companies responsible for the changes taking place are themselves struggling to make right guesses on the course they should follow.

There is, however, convergence of opinion that in the new economy creativity is the best source of growth and wealth. Therefore, the value of education rises exponentially particularly when it focuses on conceptual solutions and analytical thinking. To a large extent, training people in a way that increases their conceptual skills is novel to the educational establishment and the politicians.

Money is the raw material of banking and of the financial industry at large; and it must come from somewhere. The ability to attract credit depends on many factors: your products, your markets, the quality of your management, and the rating of your institution. The curse but also the opportunity in lending, investing, and trading is uncertainty. Here are two key points to keep in mind:

- **Risk characterizes the uncertainty of a certain planned or expected outcome.**
- **Banks that manage uncertainty well will always have deposits and credits, while those that don't perish.**

Management skills and quality of service are key ingredients in business success stories. Yet, it is surprising how often in financial institutions, as well as in industrial organizations, improvement in management means that by and large mediocrity replaces ineptitude. Uncontrollable risk is a testament to the shallowness of many management functions. By contrast, an able administration manages risk well by doing the following:

- It constantly monitors the total performance of operations under its control at any time, anywhere;
- It steadily watches the efficiency, profitability, cash flow, and exposure of each of its important clients; and
- It puts in place a system of warning signals for all activities and it acts decisively as soon as an out-of-control condition is detected.

RISK AND RETURN IN THE NEW ECONOMY

A financial institution—be it a retail bank, commercial bank, investment bank, or any other—has a *commercial presence*. Commercial presence means that a company has established itself in a territory (local, national, regional, or global) for the supply of financial services. Its activities may include wholly or partly owned subsidiaries, joint ventures, partnerships, sole proprietorships, franchising operations, branches, agencies, representative offices, or business units operating on a network (e.g., the Internet).

A financial institution may be engaged in an innovative or a classical type of financial service. A new financial service may be related to existing or new products in terms of their conception, their production, and their delivery. An institution has an edge if the type of service it offers is not supplied by any other financial services provider in its territory (though it might be supplied in another territory) or if its competitors are inefficient.

The Impact on Risk Factors in a Truly Global Economy

Even institutions with a competitive edge within their own local territory might not maintain this edge for long because they need to think *globally* (be concerned about business beyond their domestic marketplace). This is necessary both for competitive reasons and for identifying opportunities for growth for their products and services. And globality makes it necessary to account for different cultures and business environments, possibly alien virtues and moral values, and surely contradictory regulatory rules and laws. Globality forces moving and trading across time zones and country borders, so one can work literally around the clock.

Formerly sacrosanct national frontiers are becoming transparent for trade as regional trading blocs, such as the North American Free Trade Agreement (NAFTA) and the European Union (EU), move forward and as global money flows know no national boundaries. This is, in principle, an advantage because it enables businesses with diverse forms of organization to operate in multiple countries. But it is also a challenge because it involves many unknowns as well as new and old risks.

The Impact on Risk Factors in a Virtual Economy

Another challenge with economic social and cultural overtones is the change in the relative weight of the *real economy* of manufacturing and agriculture versus that of the *virtual economy* of financial and other services (described in detail later in this chapter). Figure 1.1 compares income from productive labor to that from capital gains.

Figure 1.1
Productive Labor Income and Realized Capital Gains in the 1955 to 2000 Timeframe in the U.S.

Source: Based on statistics by EIR, February 11, 2000.

The new global economy requires monetary exchange standards. The integration of national payment systems, through which people and companies can execute foreign operations and make payments in different currencies, or between residents of different countries, is very important to the global economy. Transborder trades have the potential to change government regulations, the way people view money, and the banking industry as a whole.

The financial system faces other great challenges as well. John Walsh, director of the Group of Thirty, suggests one is the risk inherent in increasingly complex instruments and institutions as well as in strategies undertaken by sophisticated financial organizations. Under what were once called normal circumstances, we could fairly accurately define and price risk. But the new economy has many unknown factors and (as the late 1990s showed) is sensitive to shocks and crises anywhere in the world.

Because of the growing number of unknowns, it is not surprising that pricing methods in nearly all economic sectors start to resemble insurance policies, moving away from the traditional industrial equilibrium, which is a simplified model, to a complex price-setting mechanism that is able to account for risk.

People with experience in the pricing of products and services appreciate that, for any practical purpose, *risk is a cost.* Costs occasioned by the utilization of instruments, systems, and other resources require a judgment that comes close to the way an insurance underwriter thinks. Here are the key points to bear in mind:

- **Future events that are even remotely probable will affect the cost of any economic performance.**
- **Hence, pricing must incorporate the likelihood of future events.**

The future performance of products and services is a key factor in calculating the costs of production and distribution. Beyond that, the new economy has another crucial characteristic. Whereas classical industrial economics more or less aim at a perfect equilibrium for prices, given adequate information, in the new economy the notion of *uncertainty* is an integral part of theory and practice. Risk and return increasingly reflect a probabilistic judgment on (1) the future costs from the utilization of current products and services and (2) the outliers and extreme events that may turn your institution belly up.

Another critical characteristic of the new economy is that products and processes produce positive results, in the sense of economic value, when they are correctly priced and they function properly. This forward-looking concept of functioning requires consideration of the dynamics of real life; the degree of uncertainty that impacts any human decision becomes a central issue.

By and large, the old economy did not work that way because the economic thinking of the 19th-century Industrial Revolution largely relied on the fiction of a perfect theory that was largely outside time and duration; and it was based on the assumption of certainty.

In classical economics, the monetization of risk and the notion of perpetual uncertainty have been legitimate subjects of concern only for financial historians and some sociologists, but not for bankers. This has greatly changed. The new economy will be merciless to any person or legal entity that disregards the message conveyed by these two concerns.

The Impact of Technology on Risk Factors

There is also another key issue to consider: the cutting edge of high technology, which can be friend or foe. Its elements range from real-time operations for data collection, monitoring, command, and control to mathematical modeling, simulation, and the analysis of the pattern of patterns.

Technology can help to achieve the goal of constant monitoring and rapid action. But technology is rarely well used in spite of vast sums of money spent on it. Properly employed models and real-time solutions permit us to detect and control risks that in large measure are inherent in the way we do business, but also are snowed under lots of irrelevant data. Technology makes it feasible to do all of the following:

- Span continents and bring exposure to risk into a single space where risk can then be controlled;

- Map the market and its moves into our intelligent network through knowledge-enriched software; and

- Provide an exceptionally good decision tool by means of steady experimentation.

As long as you steadily keep up your know-how and your instruments, you can use technology to enrich your operations, gain competitive advantage, and help yourself in both the short term and long term. On the other hand, networks and computers will be of little help unless you have a clear concept of risk proper, of the polyvalence of your exposure, and of what precisely you wish to control, which is discussed in the next section of this chapter.

A COMPREHENSIVE DEFINITION OF RISK AND UNCERTAINTY

Dictionaries define *risk* as the chance of injury, damage, or loss; a hazard. In insurance and banking, risk is expressed quantitatively as the degree or probability of an adverse effect and its financial aftermath. The computation of this probability is not a matter of pure mathematics, though statistics and analytics are necessary to measure it. Rather, risk and its likelihood are a function of the type of loss that is covered, the prevailing market conditions, and the amount of leverage behind the transaction.

Exposure in volatile markets comes from changing exchange rates, interest rates, equity indices, and other commodities, as well as from default risk concerning the counterparty with which you are dealing, and from this party's willingness to perform. No wonder regulators aim to make bankers, traders, treasurers, and investors more sensitive to the inequalities of borrowers and other parties with whom contracts are drawn.

In mathematical terms, risk is the measure of variance around an expected value. Algorithmic formulas try to pinpoint the target (expected) value and to calculate the probability of reaching this goal. A valid approach would differentiate between expected risks, unexpected risks, and extreme events. This concept is illustrated in Figure 1.2, where the frequency of losses from loans is divided into three major areas:

- *Expected risks*—these are typically covered by profit and loss resulting from current operations, reflected in end-of-year financial reporting.

- *Unexpected risk*—this is lower in frequency than expected risks but represents a higher level of losses per event and must be faced through reserves and equity.
- *Extreme events*—these can result in very large losses. To face catastrophes we must be able to tap capital markets in a way that will be credible to investors.

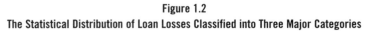

Figure 1.2
The Statistical Distribution of Loan Losses Classified into Three Major Categories

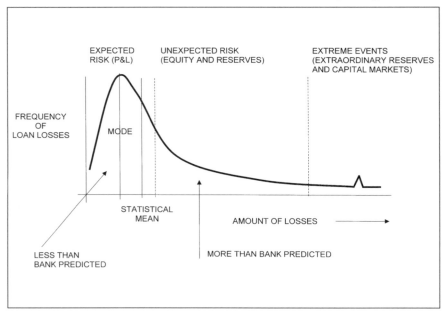

Through mergers and acquisitions, some companies try to enlarge their business base and balance their risks. As we will see in Chapter 11, they capitalize on deregulation and globalization through intra-industry and interindustry acquisitions (which may be national or international). The targeted outcome is economies of scope, and economies of scale. Rarely are both attained at the same time, if they are reached at all. When such an outcome is feasible, its achievement depends a great deal on management's ability to get results as well as to face the unknowns. It also depends on the extent to which the law of unexpected consequences comes into play.

Recognize Your Institution's Appetite for Risk

Rare or extreme events come in spikes. Few bankers truly appreciate that these spikes multiply with leverage and their amplitude increases. When assessing risk factors, consider the following:

- **Typically, the transactions that you do and the positions you take reflect the type of bank you are; they also map the economic factors under which you operate and the exposure you assume.**

Are you primarily addressing the real economy or the virtual economy in your transactions? As noted earlier in this chapter, the *virtual economy* is the world of finance, which more and more gets uncoupled from the *real economy* of manufactured goods and agricultural products. The virtual economy's main channels are shown in Figure 1.3. The clients of these channels are shopping not only for financing and execution skills, but also for expertise, price, and value. Historically, *quality of service* has not been a buzz word in banking; however, this is changing.

Figure 1.3
Real and Virtual Economy Products Offered by a Universal Bank

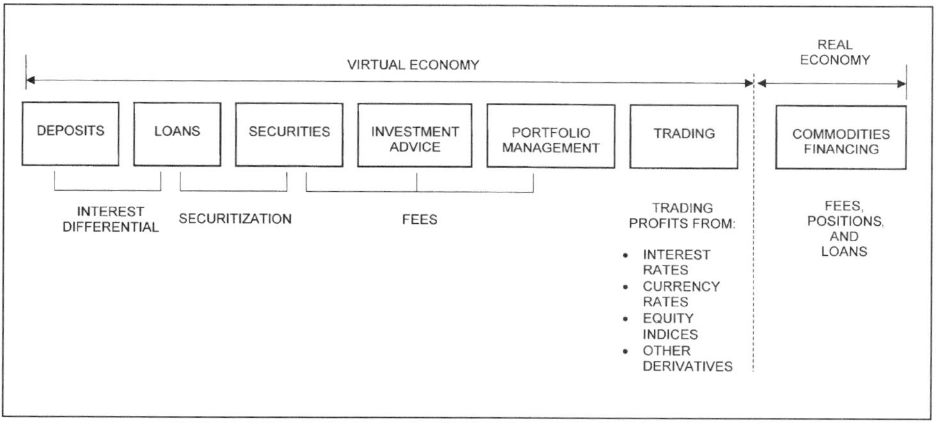

Quality of service and the price(s) we charge correlate. In classical economics, prices are typically established on the basis of one's own costs of production and distribution. But globalization, deregulation, and the assumption of significant risks invert this process.

Prices must be established while accounting for globalization (hence the cost of other vectors), integrating into pricing decisions the risks we are assuming, and considering future events that are uncertain.

This is the basic reason why pricing increasingly resembles the nonlinear process employed in insurance. Rather than the old industrial model of a demand/supply equilibrium (the foundation of classical economics), we deal with an environment whose dynamics are understood by only a few of the players. The most critical factor in this environment is its nonlinearities, which increase the uncertainty of an outcome.

Managing Risk Using Knowledge Management

According to a knowledgeable central banker in New York, because uncertainty has become a cornerstone notion of the new economy, regulators face the nightmare of a blowup in a world where no clear rules apply, at least as we have conceived them so far. In today's interconnected environment, business risks are multiplying at an alarming rate. The solution is knowledge management, which includes:

- Real-time information flows, at any time, from any place,
- The ability to map the market into a computer in a dynamic way,
- Limits to act as guidelines and safeguards,
- Statistical charts broken down by attributes and by variable to track quality of business partners and the behavior of the instrument(s),
- High-order support functions allowing quick but poised response to events.

An approach that includes knowledge artifacts able to account in some way for uncertainty is more comprehensive than classical studies focusing on what people understand by the term *risk*. Crucial questions that should receive valid answers are:

- Is the uncertainty embedded in markets only an expression of other, more fundamental risks?
- Is risk really recycled between credit, market, and operational types of exposures?
- Or, once assumed does risk accumulate?

Risk is no alien concept in banking. However, today more than ever, bankers, traders, and investors appreciate that the position taken by their institution must be controlled all the time for credit risk, market risk, operational risk, legal risk, reputational risk, and other risks. There are plenty of reasons for what I say. One of the worrying developments is the increasing number of defaults; another is the growing amount of market volatility. Still another source of worry is that in the middle of many risk calculations there are often one or two mythical assumptions.

The proper definition of the risks we are taking is inseparable from the fact that for those who participate in financial markets such risks are created remarkably easily. With deregulation, globalization, innovation, and rapid technological advances that affect the pricing of instruments as well as market sensitivity and subsequent behavior, uncertainty zooms. Increased volatility reflects this. Keep in mind these suggestions on managing risk more effectively:

- **Because risk can easily be underestimated, the concepts and tools of risk management must get increasingly sharp.**
- **Models help, but at the core of prudential risk management is independent oversight of markets, products, and clients.**

There is one more prerequisite to note. Because the nature of risk changes, our culture in studying uncertainty should be significantly upgraded. Traditionally, the computation of different levels of risk is done algorithmically in a procedural way. But while algorithmic solutions are necessary, they are not enough. There is also a need for heuristic approaches to risk, which account for varying levels of uncertainty. A heuristic solution is more applicable with trading, particularly with leveraged deals; an algorithmic approach is more appropriate with principal and interest applicable to classical loans.

With this in mind, top-tier financial institutions now appreciate that risk management increasingly resembles pretrial preparation by criminal law attorneys. This is a cultural change, not just a matter of creating another department or service aimed at keeping ill-defined risks under control. The functions of investigative risk management include the following:

- Thorough preparation;
- Detailed investigation;
- Examination and cross-examination; and
- Distillation and summation.

Figure 1.4 presents the steps for studying and evaluating real-world situations (which in most cases are too complex for one person to conceive and solve). An analytical methodology permits the idealization and simplification of prevailing conditions, which are subsequently mapped into the computer through modeling. This is followed by experimenting on the outcome of different scenarios, leading to optimization and conclusion.

Figure 1.4
Evaluation of Complex Real-World Situations and
Optimization of Decision and Action Through Technology

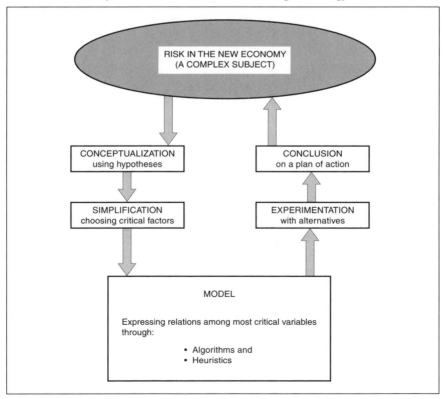

RISKS OF LEVERAGED DEALS

Leverage is what a person, a company, or a nation does by living beyond its means; and it is endemic in the new economy. Typically, somebody is financing somebody else's leveraging up, or gearing, by extending credit, thereby assuming counterparty risk. Leveraging is done by means of loans and trading: Derivative financial instruments are, in principle, geared. The relatively recent practice of giving loans to an entity at 10, 20, or even 50 times its capital (as was the case with LTCM) is another worrisome development. The more leveraged an entity is, the less the likelihood that it can face up to its financial obligations, in case of crisis.

To explain the sense of leverage, Wall Street analysts use the paradigm of cracking a whip. A force applied in the snap of the wrist results in multiples of that initial effort being discharged at the whip's end. In a similar manner, as derivative financial instruments exploded in the 1990s, two things happened:

- **Leverage conjured vast amounts of virtual value; and**
- **This resulted in a higher rate of growth than could otherwise be possible.**

A leveraged nation, a leveraged company, or a leveraged person can survive as long as the environment continues to grow in the virtual world. Indeed, a geared entity's biggest fear would be a long period of calm and stability in the markets, which would lull companies and investors into slowing their trading activities.

The worst of all worlds for those who are geared is a marketplace where nothing happens. The Number 1 risk is not that a high volatility will hit the market, but that the market will be calm and stable, an environment where customers are less susceptible to continue entering into risky contracts. High volatility is the Number 2 risk. When adversity hits, a leveraged entity leads itself into *reverse leverage,* a vicious cycle of disposing assets at fire-sale prices to face margin calls or the demand to repay loans that have become due.

Reverse leverage is dangerous because gearing means debt. Speculators assume an inordinate amount of debt to capitalize on projected changes in securities and commodities prices. But the doors of risk and return are adjacent and identical. Paraphrasing Mao, "The market is the sea. We are only the fish in it."

A bloated capital structure and imaginary cash flows are among the means often used for leveraging. Typically, the capital structure of a company will include different financing schemes—e.g., the use of ordinary share capital, preferred stock, reserves, or long-term borrowing in the form of debentures. Companies also rely on short-term borrowing (e.g., bank overdrafts) and short-term credit such as commercial paper and bankers acceptances. An inordinate amount of risk comes from the fact that derivative instruments are extensively used for leverage and/or to hide major losses. Bear in mind:

- **A 12th-hour fire-brigade approach to salvage the leveraged institution, industrial company, or nation creates moral hazard.**
- **Its failure leads to outright bankruptcy.**

Reverse leverage and salvage by fire brigade is the story behind the meltdown explained blow-by-blow in the case study on Long-Term Capital Management (LTCM, discussed in detail in Chapters 5 to 10) as well as the more silent but just as deep troubles faced by Tiger Management (see Chapter 10). There is also the case of Daewoo, which was mired in $58 billion of debt (see Chapter 2) and narrowly escaped what could have been the largest insolvency in South Korea's history, after its creditors granted fresh loans and rescheduled 12.4 trillion won ($10.3 billion) of debt falling due in 1999. In return, Daewoo pledged to speed asset sales and overhaul its debt payment plans, but in the end Daewoo Motors failed.

Until the day of truth arrives, leverage helps to hide an ugly balance sheet. In Daewoo's case, in 1996 (only three years prior to its virtual crash), bankers considered this South Korean conglomerate to be as solid as the rock of Gibraltar—the very model of Asian capitalism with 90,000 employees on its payroll. Alain Jupé, then French prime minister, was ready to sell it Thomson Multimedia for a symbolic one French Franc.

Daewoo had been a highly leveraged company which went bust. In July 1999, the Bank of Korea (the reserve institution) spent $15 billion to save Daewoo (the country's third largest conglomerate) from outright bankruptcy.

Investment bankers in Paris spoke of another case, Crédit Lyonnais, salvaged with taxpayer money thrown down a bottomless pit. As disaster never comes alone, in August 1999 in neighboring Japan, badly wounded Mitsubishi Motors decided to consolidate its production facilities and sell land (in a depressed market) to help slash its debts which stood at 1.77 trillion yen ($15.5 billion) at the closing of the financial year (end of March 1999). Finally, Mitsubishi Motors sold itself to Daimler-Chrysler.

Japan's and South Korea's debacles help to demonstrate that in the short term—but only in the short term—superleveraging can be a motor of growth hiding ugly balance sheets. But in the long run, the debts come due and there are no liquid assets to face the entity's financial obligations. This radically changes the pattern of rare events as Figure 1.5 shows.

Figure 1.5
Superleverages Turn the Tables on the Economy, Increasing the Frequency and Magnitude of Spikes

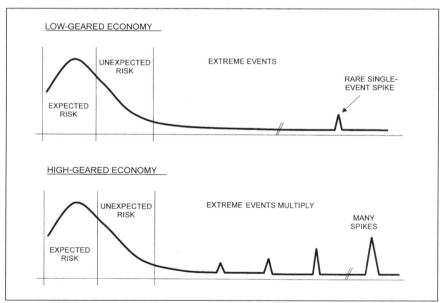

The upper half of Figure 1.5 shows the behavior of a normal economy, with extreme events far away from one another. But in the lower half of Figure 1.5, because of high leverage, both the frequency and magnitude of extreme events increase.

In the aftermath of uncertainty and with plenty of outliers around, the economic system becomes a lottery (an allotment or distribution of something by fate or chance). The foreground might be perceived as a fair enough game of chance in which tickets are sold and some number(s) drawn up as winner(s). But in reality this is an investment plan where uncontrollable factors play a key role in the outcome, and the process itself, and its expected results, have features of an uncertain choice.

Prognostication is of no great value either because the prognosticators themselves are uncertain. For instance, in early 1999, in Merrill Lynch's weekly financial report, the chief economist advised the brokers' clients that in that year the stock market would underperform so those who wanted double-digit gains should invest in bonds. PaineWebber agreed: "Looking ahead over the rest of 1999, by year-end the 30-year T-bond yield should retreat as low as the mid-5's as overall economic growth stays moderate."[1] Instead, the 30-year Treasuries advanced to the upper-6's.

FINANCING THROUGH EQUITY AND DEBT

Leverage brings the economy away from the principle that all financial obligations must be served by cash flow. Cash flow is normally produced by the way an entity capitalizes on its assets, using them for productive reasons. In classical business economics, when a firm issues both debt and equity, as is usually the case, it needs to split the cash flow into two streams: a relatively safe one that goes to debt holders and a riskier one that goes to stockholders.

Because tax laws and other incentives tend to favor debt over equity, companies traditionally have been inclined to borrow. Economists have long debated whether it is better to finance through share capital or bought money. In 1958, Dr. Franco Modigliani and Dr. Merton Miller demonstrated that the market value of a company does not depend on its capital structure. As a result, management cannot increase the firm's value by changing the mix of instruments used for financing.

One way to look at this finding is that no matter what type of capital structure is being used, the underlying value of assets cannot

---

[1]PaineWebber, *Portfolio Manager's Spotlight*, August 17, 1999.

be appreciably beefed up through traditional financial instruments. To get more bang for the buck, companies get geared. Modigliani and Merton, however, pointed out that leverage increases financial risks, leading shareholders to demand higher returns to cover the greater exposure they take. This leads to a vicious cycle:

- **Year after year, the more a company wants to impress with its profits, the higher its leverage tends to be.**
- **And the more geared a company is, better and better profit figures are demanded by investors to compensate for gearing.**

Modigliani and Merton have also documented that the higher the debt-to-equity ratio, the higher the return on equity asked by shareholders. There are, of course, certain simplifications in this theory, which is fundamentally abstracting the effects of taxation. Based on rather shaky assumptions, these simplifications suggest that:

- Investors are rational, and information is free and readily available.
- The capital market operates perfectly. There are no transaction costs.
- All firms in the same sector have the same degree of business risk.
- And the probability distribution of expected earnings is the same as present operating earnings.

Because in real life, such assumptions are rarely if ever satisfied, there is scope for optimization in capital mix always keeping the leverage factor in perspective. This task becomes more demanding when the model includes (as it should) credit risk, interest rate risk, currency exchange risk, equity risk, operational risk, and other exposures. Some of these factors, such as currency risk, are fundamental to all multinational companies and to those firms that depend a great deal on imports or exports.

Wall Street analysts have the opinion that because in the new economy the optimization of capital structure necessarily brings into the picture the issue of gearing, one should ask many critical questions before overleveraging one's assets.

- Should we really take advantage of financial leverage, or is this counterproductive in the long term?

- How much of our financial flexibility do we lose with leverage?
- By how much do we increase the risk of a downturn?
- What is the amount of risk embedded in leverage by 10-to-1? 20-to-1? 50-to-1?
- Given the dilution of equity, how much gearing is too much or too little?

There are no right or wrong answers to these questions. Only rigorous study and experimentation can tell. Analytical studies, however, require high technology, which leads to a paradox the careful reader should note.

The large amount of leverage by financial institutions and other entities is made even more vicious (rather than less so) by the use of risk management models such as value-at-risk (VAR). If markets become more volatile, current models typically require traders to either cut their positions or increase their capital to keep the same overall risk level. So bear in mind:

- **Forced selling tends to drive markets against themselves, ending in even more fire sales.**
- **And in turmoil, markets become more interlinked, canceling the perceived effects of diversification.**

The essence of risk management models (described in the following chapters) is to look at a firm's overall risk—so that institutions are not obliged to sell what they can when the market turns against their top assumptions on which they based their bets. This leads to disasters because, due to leverage, the risk-taking parts in the balance sheet of commercial, merchant, and investment banking are huge.

There is another paradox. Many financial institutions went into derivatives trading because the risk-adjusted returns were thought to be much better than could be found elsewhere (for instance, in lending). Now there is evidence that, to the contrary, the risks are much greater than originally thought, particularly because of these trends:

- **Volatility is significantly higher than in years past.**
- **And the projected diversification benefits are much lower than expected.**

There is also a lag in the recognition of changes in volatility. Most models, including VAR, are based on how markets have moved in the past. A normal distribution has no room for extreme events. Even stress tests with five standard deviations assume that extreme movements are rare, representing rather trivial probabilities.

If markets are becoming more volatile, then these extreme events affecting the distribution tails may be much fatter than our models can accept. If the probability that we may face adversity increases, then institutions should hold a lot more capital. On the other hand, if banks keep much larger reserves to better their financial staying power, their financial products will be more expensive or, alternatively, it will oblige them to reconsider why they are in business and to reset their goals while downsizing their level of leverage.

Long-Term Capital Management did not do this until it slid nearly into bankruptcy. How often should a well-managed institution reevaluate its exposure in the most rigorous terms and, when necessary, reinvent itself? This is one of the most basic queries you serious readers should ask as you read the chapters on the LTCM case (Chapters 5 to 10)—always keeping in mind that 90% or more of all accidents are man-made.

FACTORS THAT AFFECT FINANCIAL POLICIES AND RISK CONTROL

While some companies are digesting what has happened in the recent past and trying to derive a lesson that might be helpful in the future, others continue as if nothing has taken place that alters age-old habits that have been instrumental in shaping their policies and decisions but are now out of tune with reality. Yet, success and failure in business are heavily governed by new rules and involve uncertainties which may upset even the most carefully laid out plans or have unintended consequences.

For example, consider a study done by private parties in 1999 in the UK that demonstrated that two British banks—NatWest and Barclays—which in the late 1990s dropped their investment banking arms (respectively, NatWest Markets and BZW) and subsequently suffered an attrition of their personal banking activity. The likelihood of this loss of clout was not taken into account when the disinvestment was decided, but it became particularly acute for both institutional clients and high–net-worth individual clients of NatWest and Barclay. This study suggested that the major reason for such attrition was that by eliminating their investment banking activities, the two financial institutions deprived themselves of the skills of professionals who design and market imaginative new products—specifically the products rocket scientists develop for correspondent banks, high–net-worth individuals, and institutional investors.

Rocket scientists are engineers, physicists, mathematical economists, artificial intelligence (AI) experts, psychologists, biologists, and applied mathematicians who came into banking from aerospace, missiles, other weapons systems, computers, and communications industries. Their presence serves a triple purpose:

- Develop new, imaginative financial instruments
- Help to open up new business opportunities, and
- Assist in the control of risks of different origins and kinds.

The new economy needs rocket scientists because of their background and training. They provide the know-how necessary to establish "lenses" to focus on gains and losses in the banking business. They also develop prognosticators and analyze the nature of patterns in a cross-market sense. Rocket scientists help as well to define how the institution can control its transition from one equilibrium to another.

The work of rocket scientists today addresses investments, derivatives, and personal banking. Indeed, there is a significant overlap between investment banking and personal banking, which was not clearly perceived in the past but now is of particular interest to the more imaginative investors who go for innovative financial instruments. This common ground is embedded in an envelope of risk, which is more important in investment banking but also infiltrates personal banking.

Alan Brown, Group Risk executive at Barclays Bank, believes that what happened in September 1998 with LTCM has helped in understanding better the risks the bank's clients are taking on. "The problem," says Alan Brown, "is that correspondent banks did not know enough about their book." This is a good lesson on the importance of transparency which is promoted by the 1999 New Capital Adequacy Framework by the Basle Committee of Banking Supervision.[2]

---

[2]Dimitris N. Chorafas, *New Regulation of the Financial Industry* (London: Macmillan, 2000).

According to the same opinion, another aftermath of the LTCM debacle is that institutions now appreciate that they need to do a significant amount of stress testing, a process contingent to the need to know more about the counterparty's trading book and banking book. "The market learns from this experience," Alan Brown suggests, and he also points out that while in the summer of 1999 interest rate risks widened like in the summer of 1998, there were no blow-ups of 1998 type vintage.

In the opinion of Arjan P. Verkerk, director of market risk at MeesPierson, the LTCM meltdown "is not necessarily affecting our present way of dealing, but it has changed the way of how we analyze the financial power of the counterparty." MeesPierson has a long experience in this domain but (correctly) it never stops learning from new earthquakes. The sense of the references made by Alan Brown and Arjan Verkerk converge. Institutions now look beyond the balance sheet and into all of these factors that can affect exposure to extreme risk:

- The counterparty's senior management
- The company's quality track record
- Ethics and performance in dealing, and
- Clues regarding systematic risk

CONCLUSION

Whether we talk of the new economy or the old, the question of limits and boundaries is fundamental. There are moments in business practice when limits and boundaries appear relatively well defined but far off. There are other periods when limits are approached and then exceeded. Therefore, keep in mind these key points:

- **The board, the CEO, and senior management must always be willing and able to take corrective action when the limits risk being breached.**
- **Such action has to be studied well in advance through analysis, appropriate scenarios, and evaluations of its possible aftermath.**

Corrective action cannot just be an immediate liquidation of trades, because a bank's derivatives portfolio is not a one-day holding business. No institution can sell off or replace the positions in its portfolio in just 24 hours, particularly in the case of a leveraged portfolio with over-the-counter (OTC) bilateral trades whose fair value changes constantly and is subject to extreme events and the whims of counterparties.

Precisely because inventoried positions have no self-evident fair value, John Hasson at Abbey National Bank underlined the need for rethinking collateralization, adding, "The big challenge is to manage collateral efficiently." This is not easy, given that the frontier between credit risk and market risk is blurred. Collateral is usually priced at market value so repricing should be done at least on a daily basis; even better, intraday. In decreasing order of acceptance, banks consider collateral to be:

- Cash,
- Exchange-traded instruments, and
- Bilateral agreements based on the International Securities Dealers Association (ISDA) standard contract.

Financial products described by the last two instruments should be reined in. Cash is king. Clearers accept for margin reasons any equitable collateral and convert it to cash. The problem is that some counterparties tend to pledge their collateral with different deals. This poses legal risk. One issue that has not yet been tested in court is who has priority on collateral.

One lesson taught by the LTCM meltdown is that with hedge funds, problems associated with collateralization can be particularly complex. Senior commercial bankers' reactions during my research meetings in New York and London can be distilled in this statement: "Hedge funds are very good business. We cannot cut them off altogether, but we need a more rigorous way of collateralization and greater transparency."

Cognizant financial analysts on Wall Street and in the City did not fail to notice that without outright support by regulators, commercial banks don't have much clout either in asking hedge funds to be transparent or in pressing them to effectively document their collateral. At the same time, competition sees to it that counterparties cannot take a big haircut with pledged securities. As hedge funds have come back into grace after the financial hurricane of 1998, they have tended to tighten the margins, which increases the assumed risk. This too is a characteristic of the new economy.

CHAPTER 2

The First Big Shock of the New Economy: Meltdown in East Asia

Reviewing the economic and financial earthquakes in East Asia is important because they have been the opening shots of the painful transition to a new economy. The story of Thailand, Indonesia, South Korea, and others is also one of failures in risk control that only the blind could ignore, a painful mismatch of policies that proved to be unsound.

BACKGROUND: THE RAPID RISE AND CRASH OF THE EAST ASIAN ECONOMY

During the 1980s and early- to mid-1990s, the East Asian economies experienced extremely high growth. Key reasons were huge loans from Western banks, a rapidly rising population, high rates of savings and investment, a monetary policy that was able to hold down inflation, and the mirage of exceptional returns of investment (ROI), which also characterized other emerging markets. Low inflation prevented the flight of capital, while the expectancy of fast riches by Western investors pumped up local economies beyond sustainable growth.

No less an authority than Joseph Stiglitz, former chief economist of the World Bank, said, "In East Asia it was reckless lending by international banks and other financial institutions, combined with reckless borrowing by domestic financial institutions" that may have precipitated the crisis.[1] Companies in East Asian countries, particularly the so-called tiger economies, were eager to attract capital flows and grow fast to conquer global markets for two reasons:

* Western banks, hedge funds, and other nonbanks were eager to lend to meet their high ROI targets.
* Reckless credit policies created the huge boom and bust that would not have been possible through domestic savings alone.

On the surface it was good that these emerging countries benefited from a strong influx of foreign investments. But this created a huge indebtedness of their corporate sector and led to overvalued local currency rates. Gearing through foreign money inflows finally led to unacceptable current account deficits. The current account deficit for 1990–96 amounted to:

* 7.0% of GDP in Thailand,
* 5.7% in Malaysia,
* 4.1% in the Philippines, and
* 2.4% in Indonesia.

Money was no problem for the East Asian tigers in the 1990–97 time frame. Governments and multilateral institutions did not give many handouts, but, as Figure 2.1 shows, lending to emerging countries by private capital rose year after year. Then, when the crisis hit in 1997, it dropped precipitously while the fire brigade of the IMF tried to do damage control.

Indeed, the day of reckoning did not take long to come. After the skepticism of foreign investors about the validity of highly leveraged East Asian economies manifested itself on the Thai currency market in June and July 1997, the U.S. dollar rose 30% against the baht within three months. Subsequently, Indonesia, the Philippines, and Malaysia had to devalue their currencies to bring some market reality into the picture.

The crash wave propagated itself, lasting almost four months, from August to November 1997. The following year was dreadful for

---

[1] *International Herald Tribune,* January 10, 2000.

East Asian economies. While the tigers felt the brunt, China announced that in first-quarter 1998, industrial output slowed from double digits to about 8% because its exports were significantly curbed. In other East Asian countries industrial output reached negative values compared to a year earlier: minus 16% in Thailand and minus 10% in South Korea.

As Dr. Stiglitz suggested, "The costs, in terms of soaring unemployment and plummeting wages, were borne by the workers." But Western banks and other investors too lost a great deal of money (see later in this chapter the discussions of Peregrine and Daewoo). In the aftermath of the 1997 crash, numerous parties have been licking their wounds. Many investors, however, have short memories and the IMF is again forecasting higher net flows to the region in year 2000.

Figure 2.1
Loans to Emerging Markets by Banks and Other Private Investors
versus Support by Governments and Multilateral Institutions, 1990–99

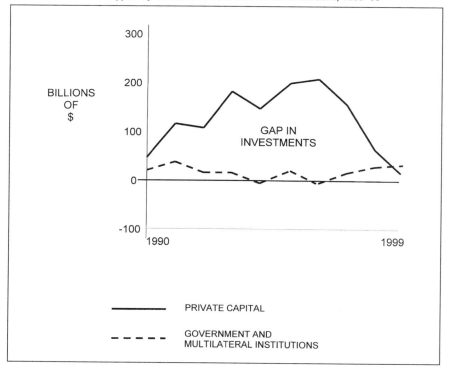

OVERINVESTING AND OVERLEVERAGING
IN EMERGING MARKETS

Some Wall Street analysts believe that many foreign investors failed to properly appreciate that exchange rate corrections in Asia, following the mid- to late 1997 meltdown, were less dramatic than those seen from mid-December 1994 to mid-January 1995, when the Mexican peso plunged 55% against the U.S. dollar. One senior executive pointed out that in the first quarter of 1998 Japan's industrial output too fell by 4%—the inference being that negative growth is not necessarily associated only with emerging markets.

Neither argument holds water. Japan was a sick economy for the better part of the 1990s, as market reality caught with the high leverage of its financial industry. This is an interesting case because it shows the new economy's low points and its risks. By 1990, when the long economic winter set in in Japan and it eventually became the weakest link in the world's economy, this country was a paradox:

- On paper, rich beyond belief,
- Mismanaged more than any other place,
- Stuck in a vicious slump, and
- Sinking fast, led down by its financial industry.

Mexico, was another case of an economy inflated through massive foreign investments that had no relationship to the local economy's ability to absorb them in a way commensurate with expected return. The lesson to be learned from the East Asian tigers and the on-and-off crises in Central and South America is that the consequences of big jumps to virtual riches can be severe and can lead to catastrophes. Even in the best cases (those that avoided outright drops in GDP), growth remained anemic in the years after the crisis.

To better appreciate East Asia's plight as well as to derive some lessons for the new economy, we should go back to the fundamentals. One of the origins of globalization has been the conversion of half the world—some 3 billion people—from a communist system to a free market with the metamorphosis of capitalism into the new economy. The fall of communism happened as the 1980s came to a close. Nearly at the same time, world economies experienced these two trends:

- **Global trade barriers were reduced and capital flowed more freely in a global sense.**
- **Less-developed emerging markets attracted huge flows of foreign capital in search of fast profits.**

These two trends show cause and effect. East Asian countries boomed because of the influx of capital, and their boom attracted even more capital. Then emerging markets became victims of their own success because of:

- Overinvestment in competing projects,
- Relaxed lending standards by foreign banks,
- Government corruption and waste, and
- Sudden outflow of foreign capital.

People, companies, and countries are greedy to publicize the success of their efforts, but reluctant to make known their blunders and their failures. But capital markets are not forgiving. Overgearing and blunders led to currency devaluation, debt defaults, and stock market collapses throughout the emerging markets. Another consequence was deflated economies as the many excesses from the boom were cleared up.

At the Western investors' end there was a rotation of star performers well before the 1997 Asian crash. The prima donnas of 1990–94 no longer received the same degree of reverence. For example, George Soros became famous after cracking the British pound in 1992, but the 1994 bloodbath with rising U.S. interest rates left him (and most other hedge funds) with a bloody nose—both financially and regarding his reputation. For example, in the late January 2000 World Economic Forum in Davos, Soros did not attract the attention of the 1,500 global participants; the star was Bill Gates and his Windows 2000 (W2K) press conference as well as the other whiz kids.

With a steady interest rate in dollar-denominated securities and Mexico out of the way as the land of rising profits, East Asian filled the speculators' appetite for risk. But the East Asia meltdown and then the Russian earthquake in 1998 showed that hedge funds can be notorious in making the wrong bets. The markets took notice.

REKINDLED INTEREST AND RENEWED INVESTMENT

But speculators did not lose their resolution to succeed. In the shadow of big globalization events and their media blitz, the artists of finance are saying that a disaster may present just as good business opportunities as a boom time. The opportunity is in bargain hunting among the wreckage. Practically all economies in East Asia went through a vicious cycle from 1990 to 1999, although some suffered more than others and they did not fall flat at the same time. During the first six months of 1997 the Japanese economy weighted negatively in the East Asia average. After the Japanese economy improved somewhat, Thailand, Indonesia, South Korea, and others fared worse than Japan.

This is one of the ironies of the new economy and the Epicurean philosophy (based on the teaching of Epicuros, ancient Greek philosopher 341–270 B.C.) that underpins it—a statement valid not just for Asia but worldwide. In 1999 Brazil got (and in 2000 it is rated to get) new commitments for an estimated $52 billion in foreign cash, with not a dollar of it coming from IMF. Instead, the money will flow from global capital markets and private investors, just as did the subscriptions to a $3 billion Eurobond that floated in April 1999.

East Asia, of course, is not forgotten in this Eldorado of renewed hopes for big fortunes. Goldman, Sachs and General Electric Capital are working together to restructure $7 billion in Thai consumer and corporate loans. In South Korea, venture capitalists Hambrecht & Quist led a group that took over Ssangyong Securities; and Daewoo is up for grabs (which will be discussed in more detail at the end of this chapter).

The hypothesis underpinning these investments is that the highly leveraged, featherbedded, and mismanaged big conglomerates (chaebol) will deconsolidate. They would hopefully put themselves together to pay down debt, restructure, and begin to view equity as a means to more prudently finance expansion. Another not so far-fetched hypothesis is that the cost of equity will hopefully encourage more responsible investments both by local capital and by foreign investors who again get interested in Asia.

In the background of this rekindled interest three short years after the debacle is the fact that, on a global basis, Asia can compete. It is rare to find so many globally oriented players and plays in emerging markets. There is as well a reasonably high quality of labor, and the level of technological penetration makes Asia one of the better locations for both consumption and production while the financial crisis seems to encourage the following scenarios:

- Open the markets for foreign investment, and
- Encourage more transparent operations.

Some analysts think that the 1997 cataclysm and beginning of a rebirth in 2000 lift the curtain to a new global monetary system, in which the markets rule and bodies such as the IMF take a back seat. While academics, bankers, and policymakers shower each other with ideas, arguments, and plans, private investors and lenders have sent a total of $1.2 trillion to major emerging economies. This is six times the $200 billion that came from all official sources.

Transborder money flows indicate that while waiting for the wounded emerging markets to get back on their feet, investors are not standing still. The slack in investments in emerging countries after the 1997–98 events has been compensated by cross-border flows with the Group of Ten (G-10) countries themselves.

The pattern suggests that investors might no longer need the emerging market for growth. They can find opportunities in their own backyard or at least in the backyard of the developed world. But, are capital movements toward G-10 countries and toward emerging markets really exclusive of one another?

One opinion I've heard in the City is that recent rallies in the Asian markets are, at least in part, the reflection of funds flowing back into these countries and they are evidently helping the recovery as much as they benefit from it. Asia has historically been a volatile place to invest. By now foreign capitalists appreciate that the tight family-controlled conglomerate of East Asia has made huge loans and investments a bet based more on economic growth and demographics than on fundamentally sound financial policies.

The silver lining, as analysts and policymakers see it, is that the private sector in these countries proved remarkably adept at seeking out opportunities to restructure. Forward-looking leaders in Korea and Thailand have let the market process work and invited in private parties to aid in reform—thereby helping to do it faster and maybe better than would have been the case otherwise.

According to a growing number of experts, a possible new blueprint for the global financial architecture is emerging out of the Asian crisis. In it, the IMF is using its limited funds as seed money to attract private money. This is not yet a sure bet, but there is a distinct possibility that such a trial-and-error approach will work. It's up to the new head of the IMF to form a policy that is new-economy compliant.

OTHER RISKS: PRIVATE MONEY FLOWS AND CRONY CAPITALISM

One characteristic of huge money flows to East Asia and elsewhere, prior to the 1997 crash, is that these were mainly private-sector lending. In terms of source, the capital that poured into Asia was different from the capital that ran to Latin America. Therefore, ill-studied investments have reflected a failure of analysis by industrial lenders as opposed to sovereign lenders. Private capital travels fast to find better gains, but sometimes it stumbles. Up to the crash of July 1997, brokerages in western countries were awfully bullish about the Asian economic miracle, which was characterized by:

- High-growth rate,
- Tireless workers,
- Devoted savers,
- Born capitalists,
- High-rise buildings and industrial parks, and
- Can't-lose stock markets.

But the can't-go-wrong East Asian economic miracle suddenly became the debacle characterized by:

- Funny money,
- Dispirited workers,
- Phony earnings,
- Sluggish growth rates,
- Cronyism in government,
- Greed artists in boardrooms, and
- Can't-win stock markets.

A key problem for Asia has been that most of the countries are saddled with huge debt burdens in terms of both domestic and foreign currencies. To service those debts, the firms need to concentrate on their debt obligations, but it is difficult for many Asian firms to generate the revenue needed to service these obligations, partly because they don't have skill and experience in doing so.

The East Asian countries and most other emerging markets cannot buy their way out by devaluation. Foreign investors are not stupid. They lend in dollars, and devaluation worsens the chances of repaying the loans. Foreign currency debt ratings are usually capped by the sovereign ceiling for the nation in which a company is domiciled.

In a well-functioning credit screening system, the country rating is intended to map the likelihood that during a currency crisis the sovereign may choose to limit all foreign currency payments by entities subject to its legal jurisdiction. This is essentially the probability that a borrower facing the obligation to make a payment in foreign currency might not be able to convert its own domestic currency cash flow into foreign exchange in a way that would meet its obligations. Known as transfer risk, this event may also occur not because of country risk but because of a liquidity crisis in the international currency markets. This has led rating agencies to differentiate between international and local currency ratings. Consider the contrast to foreign currency:

- **Local currency ratings are not specifically capped by the sovereign ceiling.**

- **Therefore, ratings tend to be higher for borrowing in local currencies than in international currencies.**

These basic facts of financial life should have made both lenders and investors much more careful than they proved to be. Normally, a prudent fund manager would place no more than 3% of total assets in any closely linked group of smaller countries, and diversify the rest in the big markets. To the contrary, the different funds caught in the turmoil were found to be up to their ears in Asian debt and stocks—about 12% of total portfolio, or four times the normal percentage. When adversity struck, all sorts of G-10 funds paid dearly for their Asian tiger euphoria of past years. Investment managers bought all they could get their hands on, as if the growth boom was there forever.

They also failed to heed other sound investment advice: Know the quality of management of the company you are investing in. There is a crazy school of economics, some call it neoclassical, that says you can fire in all directions at once and the market will ensure that you hit the target. That's not a serious line of reasoning, and it can lead to major debacles—particularly in the conjunction with other distortions of free markets, such as crony capitalism.

Crony capitalism is not a part of the new economy but of the old. If anything, it is the antithesis to whatever the new economy stands for because it merges two disciplines that are keen to conceal their blunders:

- Ordinary capitalism marred by corruption, which is grossly inefficient economically,
- While communism, socialism, and dirigism are masquerading as "free economy."

Let's face it. What makes a market economy, first of all, are the six freedoms: freedom to enter the market, to engage in competition, to exit the market, to set prices, to make profits, and to fail. Other just as important characteristics of the free economy are:

- Market sensitivity
- Customer orientation
- Rapid research, development, implementation
- Hire and fire of employees

There are also three preconditions for a market economy to work properly: First and foremost, a legal system supportive of individual accountability and corporate responsibility. The old legal system of the former communist countries and former colonies did nothing of the kind. Soft laws or fuzzy laws do not support the new economy.

Second, there must be a new culture of ethics and a well-defined personal responsibility. It is not possible to transit to the market economy without cultural change in the government and in the business community. Third, there must be a thorough revamping of regulatory rules and of supervisory procedures. This presupposes an independent regulatory authority, which simply does not exist in many of the emerging countries.

This is not happening under crony capitalism which has much to do with authoritarian regimes, typically characterized by absence of public accountability. Shielded from peer and public scrutiny, the top brass feels great temptation to hide shortfalls, distribute false information, favor industries in which they or their families have an interest, divert other people's monies to companies or individuals they prefer, and conceal favors by all possible means.

All this is a breeding ground for disasters. As Asia's economic "miracles" came to an end, in late June 1997, Thailand's reported foreign reserves of over $30 billion were found to be a myth. In fact they had dwindled to $1.4 billion, equal to just two days of imports. In the face of such official distortions and deceptions, it is not surprising that money lenders and investors got panicky and all tried to exit from the same door.

This and plenty of other examples demonstrate that a factor that investors often overlook in emerging markets is the worrying vulnerability to nonconventional risks that have been very poorly researched. These include cronyism, corruption, organized crime, ripoff, and physical violence.

Product and process pirating too exemplifies how some countries, companies, and people try to leapfrog at the expense of other parties.

Here's just one brief example of how companies investing in emerging markets expose themselves to unexpected risks. In its drive to expand into China, Kimberly-Clark opened its Handan Comfort and Beauty facility in 1994, producing sanitary products worth about $10 million a year. This remote plant was one of 12 owned by the group.

Things seemed to go well until in early 1997 a nearby factory started making a very similar product. The head of this rival operation was the man selected by Kimberly-Clark's partner, Xingha Factory Company, to manage the joint venture factory. To make matters worse, swinging doors came into play as raw material from Kimberly-Clark's own operation was diverted to the copycat factory.[2] The least that can be said about this story is that Kimberly-Clark did not help itself with its choice of allies.

CASE STUDY: THE BANKRUPTCY OF PEREGRINE INVESTMENTS

On January 12, 1998, Peregrine Investments Holdings, one of East Asia's largest and more dynamic investment banks, locked its doors. This was the biggest casualty up to that time in the financial crisis

---

[2] *The Sunday Telegraph*, UK, May 10, 1998.

sweeping that region. However one considers the fate of Peregrine, it was a disaster that combined superleveraging, bad judgment, and crony capitalism in one act.

The rise and fall of Peregrine, inside a decade, from a small niche player to Asia's number 1 underwriter of stocks makes an interesting case study. Philip Leigh Tose founded Peregrine with the backing of billionaire property developer Li Ka-shing, of Hong Kong. Peregrine's list of shareholders read like a "Who's Who" of Hong Kong's rich including Li's Cheung Kong (Holdings); the Beijing-backed Citic Pacific; and Templeton Investments, a part of the U.S.-based fund manager Franklin Resources.

Tose cultivated the firm's reputation for ruthlessness. He was proud of having made Peregrine "a company people love to hate." But when the crisis came, Tose failed to find investors after a plan to sell a big chunk of the firm to the Zurich Group fell through on Friday, January 9, 1998. While Peregrine's shareholders lost their equity, banks too had to lick their wounds. The list of losers included Deutsche Bank, Standard Chartered Bank, Australia and New Zealand Bank, and Grindlays Bank.

Only 40 days before the Peregrine crash, the December 1, 1997, issue of *BusinessWeek* had published an article essentially praising Peregrine Investments and its prospects. This interesting piece of business news started by saying that for nearly a decade Peregrine had been one of Asia's most controversial but also bolder investment vehicles. From his Hong Kong base, Chairman Philip Leigh Tose, a former Formula 3 race car driver, combed Indonesia, Burma, Bangladesh, and Vietnam in search of deals. Peregrine bet that the Sukarno regime in Indonesia was eternal, while the other three countries would catapult rapidly from poverty to affluence, the way Thailand had done.

The East Asian currency crisis of 1997 changed all that by sweeping across the region's economies, shaking investor confidence and overwhelming the Hong Kong stock market. Rumors suggested that Peregrine had suffered $1 billion in trading losses and was in danger of going under. Peregrine played its part in stockholder and market deception when, on October 26, 1997, it took out a newspaper advertisement denying any substantial losses or distress. For the period ending October 24, 1997, the ad stated that Peregrine had reserved $60 million against bond losses as it saw profits at its stock- and bond-trading operations drop by more than half, to $35 million. But then

Peregrine claimed that its shareholders' equity had increased during the year, and in a show of financial staying power it was buying back 10.3 million shares.

Peregrine being able to provide such misinformation and get away with it proves the thorough overhaul necessary for East Asia's legal system and supervisory rules. Some analysts fell into this trap. ABN-Amro Hoare Govett analyst Anne Gardini estimated that Peregrine's earnings would rise from $82 million in 1997, a fiscal year with 11 months because of the reporting change, to $115 million in 1998.

It is human to err, but *BusinessWeek* should not have misinformed its readership. Any professional intelligence operation should look for evidence, such as reports from other sources confirming the information to be published. The magazine should have either double-checked the news it got or kept such information on the back burner.

BusinessWeek also stated that on November 16 of that same year, with "its stock down 64 percent from its June high, it [Peregrine] found a deep-pocketed savior. Zurich Group, the acquisitive Swiss financial giant, is buying 24.1 percent of Peregrine for $200 million. At 73 percent of book value, the deal was 'very attractive,' says Steven M. Gluckstern, CEO of Zurich Center Investments, the private equity arm of the Zurich Group."[3]

If a well-managed company such as Zurich made a $200 million investment in Peregrine, as *BusinessWeek* wrote, then the Hong Kong company's assets must have been worth a good deal more than analysts had thought. Zurich was also supposed to contribute at least $50 million to a new Asian venture capital fund that was expected to total between $350 million and $500 million. Nothing of that sort was the case. The news item was smoke and mirrors—and it was misleading. In fact, Peregrine's failure to obtain the $200 million in Swiss money in January 1998 turned the company belly up.

Peregrine ran into trouble after the plunge in the Indonesian rupiah made it all but impossible for Indonesian companies to repay their U.S.-dollar loans. The toxic waste was a series of loans in the form of promissory notes to the Indonesian taxi company PT Steady Safe, which earned $9 million in 1997. PT Steady "Un-"Safe owed Peregrine about $265 million with practically no collateral—so there goes the claim of altogether under 10% asset exposure in Indonesia.

---

[3] *BusinessWeek*, December 1, 1997.

Since one piece of misinformation does not seem to come
alone, shortly after the aforementioned article in *BusinessWeek,* the
Financial Times published the asset allocation chart shown in Figure
2.2. Theoretically at least, this chart was double-sourced: from
Morgan Stanley Capital International (MSCI) for the All Country Far
East Free (except Japan) allocation, and from Peregrine regarding its
recommended weightings. Subsequent events have shown that either
Peregrine did not follow its own advice on asset allocation or these
statistics too were misinformation. It is simply unbelievable that
Peregrine had 24% of its assets in cash in late October 1997, when
two and one-half months later it crashed because of being starved for
cash. If its liquidity had been that high, it would not have fallen victim to a plunge in Indonesia's rupiah, after it lent money to a shaky
taxi company with great plans to expand into ferries.

Figure 2.2
Asset Allocation Advice by Peregrine Investment Holdings: Misinformation?

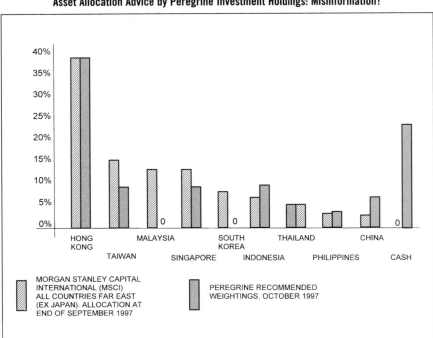

With the crash of Peregrine Investments Holdings, Hong Kong's
Securities & Futures Commission restricted the firm's trading activities
"in the interest of the investing public" to essentially closing out exist-

ing trades for clients. The company was barred from transacting new business. In a last ditch effort to save itself from bankruptcy, Peregrine tried to separate its profitable equity brokering and equity capital markets from a fixed-income department that had been sitting on millions of dollars of next-to-worthless Asian bonds. When this strategy too failed, the investment bank's fate was sealed.

CASE STUDY: THE DAEWOO BUBBLE BURSTS

When the Daewoo bubble burst in mid-1999, evidence that became available suggested this company had borrowed inordinate amounts of money as banks used lower and lower credit risk criteria for their lending spree. Other South Korean firms had also jumped on the debt bandwagon, but Daewoo borrowed much more than the other firms. It had also converted a good deal of the loans into entropy: a rumored $85 billion in debt, against less than $65 billion in assets, some of which were questionable.

Clear-eyed analysts had seen the signs that the Daewoo bubble would burst. The writing on the wall came from Standard & Poor's rating, from Goldman, Sachs, and from other careful watchers of financial business, which began issuing harshly negative reports on Daewoo. The debacle came to the public eye on July 19, 1999, when Daewoo announced that it could not pay some $6 billion in domestic loans.

With this news, the headquarters of every major foreign creditor in New York, London, Frankfurt, Tokyo, and elsewhere began demanding all their money back. The foreign banks wanted all $15 billion in foreign loans to be paid first, with Daewoo to declare bankruptcy, be carved up, and be sold to foreigners.

However, on July 30, the South Korean government said that it would not bail out the $15 billion foreign banks had loaned to the Daewoo conglomerate. The government's position was that foreign lenders could not have their cake and eat it too. They had been foolish in giving unsecured loans and had done a bad business; then the moment of truth arrived. For its part, Daewoo (Korea's second-largest conglomerate) was trying to avoid default, which would bring down Seoul's six major banks and threaten several New York banks on top of that.

After the debacle, the government mandated that Daewoo's domestic Korean creditors organize the company's restructuring. It also vowed to remove a freeze on Seoul's dozens of Investment Trust

Companies (ITCs), which held a major share of Daewoo's bad loans, with the possibility that investors with money in the ITCs would rush to pull out their assets. The fear was that if the ITCs went bad, that could add another $8 to $10 billion in bad ITC debt on the books of Korean commercial banks, compounding the bad Daewoo debt already there.

Holding foreign creditors off, the Kim Dae Jung government arranged for South Korea's four largest banks to loan Daewoo the $6 billion to roll over its domestic loans. In exchange, the Korean banks received $9 billion in collateral, essentially consisting of stock in Daewoo and its subsidiaries. The government said domestic banks could sell this collateral as they wished. Foreign banks, however, were told to wait for their money, at least $5.5 billion of it was to come due in December 1999.

Foreign banks were furious because of this treatment. Analysts suggested that the government's decision to take charge of the overhaul of Daewoo rather than selling it off was a sign of backsliding against the IMF reform package negotiated in 1997 and 1998, as well as a reminder of the old order. In that environment where cronyism was king, government bureaucrats directed lending, and market forces were not permitted to determine winners and losers in the economy.

South Korea's government refused foreign bank demands on the basis that this was a company debt, not a country debt. Therefore, it was not up to the taxpayer to come up with the cash when the foreign private companies made a bad investment decision. But in the opinion of foreign creditors, Daewoo's debt was the size of a small country's.

"We do not plan to provide any government backing for a particular private entity," a government spokesman told reporters on September 30, 1999, in Seoul. "We made it very clear not just to the IMF and to [Treasury Secretary] Summers, but to all others that there is no bailout program."[4] Foreign banks were also concerned that the Daewoo bubble was signaling the presence of a serious infection in the South Korean economy that was not yet quite visible.

One has to look back to 1997 to appreciate the government's position. Almost from the moment he came to power in the 1997 elections, president Kim Dae Jung has been fighting to restructure the giant South Korean conglomerates (which in a single generation helped to transform a poor country into the world's 11th-largest

---

[4]*EIR*, October 22, 1999.

economy and to thrust it ultimately into a major debt crisis). After three decades of crony capitalism, Daewoo's bubble was the reality test for the South Koreans.

Daewoo's rapid rise to stardom mirrored the seeming miracle of South Korea's ride up the economic ladder. In the late 1960s, this Asian nation was still emerging from the 1950–53 war with North Korea. It had no manufacturing and there were no banks worth talking about. In trying to get the economy moving, practically everything was done in a hurry with very little in terms of controls.

As Daewoo narrowly escaped what could have been the largest insolvency in South Korea's history, foreign creditors were not inclined to accept reorganization of the company's debt without special conditions that give them some leverage. They demanded that the South Korean government provide guarantees in regard to rescheduled loans, and that they be granted preferential treatment, including a first choice at Daewoo's assets.

This was not exactly what the government had in mind in trying to save Daewoo from outright bankruptcy. The August 1999 government-brokered plan quietly ordered the company to comply with a debt repayment program that effectively stripped it of control over its own finances. But while government intervention eased the credit risk woes, an inordinate amount of credit risk, compounded by operational risk, remained at the side of every player.

Many Daewoo subsidiaries, such as Daewoo Motors, froze operations awaiting the reorganization, and idle factories meant no incoming cash while debts continued to mount. In late 2000, when Daewoo Motors finally failed, the risk was that bad loans at South Korea's financial institutions might snowball.

Because of this background with failed former high-flyers, one can understand financial analysts and investors when they say that they want to know when Amazon.com and its ilk in the United States will turn a profit. They like the dot-coms as consumers, but don't want them anymore as investors.

What the Daewoo Debacle Illustrates About Operational Risk

As far as operational risk is concerned, the case of Daewoo deserves special attention because it shows how lenders, debtors, and investors can let down their operational defenses. Investors and lenders may do so if a company is considered to be too big to fail. Debtors may accumulate exposure without clear plans for repayment. (Mitsubishi Motors illustrates this problem too. Both it and Daewoo show the perverse aspects of operational risk.)

At the junction of credit risk and operational risk are wrong estimates about the size of indebtedness. Before the $85 billion black hole hit the news, financial analysts guessed Daewoo's debt to be about $57 billion. Even that would have been more than the entire national debt of Poland or Malaysia. Yet, none of the big banks that found themselves exposed in this bubble took the required operational measures in time.

With the effective demise of the Daewoo Group, and with similar restructuring plans being forced upon its sister conglomerates—internationally familiar names such as Hyundai (the largest), Samsung, LG, and SK—many South Korean and foreign investors began to say that the twilight of the chaebol was finally at hand or, at least, there would be some prudential supervision to take care of the black sheep.

The changes sought by the Kim Dae Jung government include the breakup of the huge enterprises into a collection of much smaller business units that must be run for the first time as totally separate companies. This means ending the subsidization of weak industries by strong ones as well as changing the pattern of borrowing in which companies within the chaebol that have healthy balance sheets obtain capital on favorable terms for those that are chronically losing money.

As far as operational risk is concerned, this government-induced change means an eventual end to the days when the conglomerate's chairman wielded total decision-making power over his sprawling empire, even though he sometimes controlled as little as 5% of the stock. Also, in the majority of cases, these decisions were made in total secrecy so it was nearly impossible for lenders, investors, and government authorities to exercise operational control.

Operational risk can be reduced further if all companies take on outside directors, gradually raising their number until they form the majority of each corporate board. This is what the South Korean government wants to do. The new measures would also prohibit companies from sharing executives or directors. But other operational problems remain, ranging from poorly established brand names to a reputation for stodgy design and spotty quality.

A key reason that operational risk boomed in South Korea is that the growth of conglomerates was made possible only through heavy protectionism and continuous borrowing. This necessitated a supportive, even pliant, government and a favorable international economic environment. Eventually, extreme paternalism led the South Korean companies to the precipice. Extreme paternalism, the alter ego of crony capitalism, is a raw demonstration of political power. As Lord Acton said, "All power corrupts, and absolute power corrupts absolutely."

GETTING CORRUPTION OUT OF THE SYSTEM IN INDONESIA

"With every new market, every new emerging opportunity, you have another set of public officials to be paid off," says Christopher Whalen of Legal Research International.[5] To prove Whalen right, in an admission that underlines the extent of corruption in Indonesia and the difficulty of eradicating it, a senior minister said on February 3, 2000, that the three-month–old reformist government of President Aburrahman Wahid of Indonesia was still uncertain of its ability to bring to justice those who misused huge amounts of public money.

The message by Bambang Sudiblyo, the finance minister, was simple: To nail someone who did wrong deeds, the government must be powerful and have the power to catch, bring to justice, and punish. Anything less is mere theater. Sudiblyo was speaking to a parliamentary panel investigating reports of financial fraud after a decision by the government of then-President Suharto to provide emergency liquidity support of rupiah 164.5 trillion ($2.16 billion) to local banks during the 1997–98 Asian currency crisis. Corruption is promoted by laxity (and sometimes outright support) at the top and also by substandard or nonexistent auditing procedures. Starting at the level of the authorities themselves, consider these questions:

- **Are the books of the central bank audited at all?**
- **If so, are they audited by reputable certified public accountants?**
- **Is the auditing system valid, or are accounts kept in a local, secretive manner with no real transparency?**

---

[5] *Time,* September 16, 1996.

A December 1999 audit of Indonesia's central bank revealed that $7 billion earmarked for emergency loans had disappeared.[6] This was the first independent audit of the reserve institution. Auditors suspected some of the money was rerouted to an affiliate bank in Amsterdam and from there to different beneficiaries.

The independent audit was indeed a laudable initiative. It was part of a new agreement with the International Monetary Fund to ensure that loans first pledged in 1997 keep coming. Dakarta had finally agreed to come clean on past government financial wrongdoing, not only at the central bank level but also within the military and at state-owned companies, such as oil giant Pertamina.

Not that the private financial sector fared better in terms of lust, greed, and secret funding. The public release in November 1999 of the audit of Bank Bali revealed that senior officials of the then-ruling Golkar party served themselves with some $80 million from the bank after it was nationalized in 1998. When the audit hit the public eye, it upset the government's plan to sell Bank Bali to the Standard Chartered Bank.

After its independence (particularly in the aftermath of the 1960s military takeover), Indonesia experienced the worst of cronyism. But with the Wahid government some new economic principles might be taking hold. A call for greater transparency has been part of what is described as a new economic program. This is good for Indonesia's future, but there is little hope stolen money will be returned. Official investigators say that a large portion of this money may never be recovered. And rupiah 237 trillion ($3.11 billion) in bad loans made by state banks during the Suharto regime may also have to be written off.

The Wahid government seems to appreciate that while it cannot change the past, transparency is a good initiative even if many other problems connected to Indonesia's economy and credibility remain. In all likelihood the government believes that getting all the bad news out is the only way to regain investor confidence as well as the support of Western governments.

Under crony capitalism, it is not unusual for large amounts of credit to be given to favored borrowers without their having to provide any collateral if, and only if, they have the right political connections. By agreeing to disclose audits of state agencies and even the private finances of officials, the government of President Wahid has con-

---

sented to air more of the country's laundry in return for badly needed new loans. This is the result:

> • **Despite receiving $11 billion of the $12.5 billion in loans pledged by the IMF since 1997, Indonesia remains in a desperate condition.**
>
> • **By January 2000 public-sector debt in Indonesia was as large as its GDP, and the government found itself obliged to issue another $85 billion in bonds to clean up its banking mess.**

The Indonesian Bank Restructuring Agency (IBRA), which is responsible for recapitalizing the country's six biggest banks, needs new money to carry on its job. New loans aside, it is raising $10 billion by selling seized assets of deadbeat corporate borrowers to foreign companies.

Some analysts suggest that the cleansing may backfire, as public probes could discourage Indonesian businesspeople with funds hidden offshore from bringing them home, out of fear that they would be investigated and their holdings seized. Foreign investors may also choose to put their money in safer havens until they are confident that they can once again hit the fast bucks with impunity.

A first-quarter 1999 survey by Political and Economic Risk Consultancy of over 450 foreign business executives working in Asia showed that of 12 countries whose practices were examined, Indonesia was regarded as the most corrupt.[7] Corruption is like the mythical hydra; you cut off one head and two new heads spring up. Unfortunately, western companies haven't shown exemplary behavior—as should have been the case.

Quite often the leaders of former colonies and of formerly communist countries don't help themselves with their choice of allies and of assistance. They often team up with corrupt individuals, or choose people who may be nice but are regarded as lightweights. Postmortem, we have come to appreciate that not only the miracle of Asian growth oversold, given the quality of political leadership, but also the skill of corporate management in planning and controlling business operations. This is documented by the case study on the huge losses at Sumitomo Corporation, in Chapter 3.

---

[7]*International Herald Tribune,* February 4, 2000.

CHAPTER 3

The Breakdown of Internal Controls: Sumitomo Corporation

In modern times, Sumitomo Corporation was widely seen as the most conservatively managed and financially sound of Japan's powerful trading houses. It also provided the nucleus of a conglomerate, including one of Japan's top banks, its most important computer company, a leading chemicals firm, as well as mining and machinery businesses. It has been an imposing conglomerate *(keiretsu.)*

The company traces its origins to Kyoto in early 17th century when Masamoto Sumitomo, a samurai turned Buddhist priest coming from a family with merchant skills, created the world's largest copper export house and a mighty trading company. By the late 17th century, the House of Sumitomo prospered from a huge copper deposit on the island of Shikoku. In a few decades it had become the most important Japanese refiner of copper and the official purveyor to the Tokugawa shogunate, which ruled Japan until 1868. Obviously, copper has long been a Sumitomo core business.

But like practically everybody else, the Sumitomo Corporation did not want to miss the derivatives revolution. In the name of hedging, derivative financial instruments led to massive trading losses in mid-June 1996 with initial estimates reckoned at a minimum of $1.8 billion—a number that kept creeping up as months passed and more was revealed about the magnitude of the gamble.

Heavy losses from copper hedging greatly increased anxiety in the interbank market over the reliability of Japanese financial institutions at large, as Sumitomo losses steadily mounted to a rumored $5 billion. "People just started to sell everything," a dealer was to suggest in the aftermath of the Sumitomo debacle. Consider the price decline:

- On June 1, 1996, copper stood at £114/ton against a yearly high of £126/ton.

- On June 14, when the crisis hit, the copper price had dropped to £92/ton, though it rebounded to £95/ton.

Some believed that Sumitomo's huge exposure in copper might cause liquidation in the gold market to pay for the losses. This was reinforced by the fact that copper prices in premarket trading on the London Metal Exchange fell to two-year lows. "The gold and silver markets are following the copper market," said Roy Friedman, a broker with Rudolf Wolff & Co., in New York.[1]

The copper meltdown did not happen overnight. The Sumitomo losses due to derivatives transactions with copper had been building up for several years. Since at least 1991 London Metal Exchange (LME) officials reportedly had been aware of illegalities in the market for copper and copper derivatives, but had done nothing. Also, there was a precedence involving senior losses with derivatives in Japan:

- Showa Shell had lost over $1 billion in 1993 as a result of massive foreign exchange deals done through derivative financial instruments.

- The Japanese Postal Savings Bureau (KAMPO) was also reported to have lost several billion dollars in currency exchange during 1992 and 1993.

- In 1994, Japan Airlines (JAL) declared a huge loss—yen 45 billion (475 million)—on foreign exchange hedging.

- And Nippon Mortgage, which specialized in lending money to property developers, had collapsed with liabilities of more than yen 518 billion ($5.5 billion).

The year 1995, just prior to the copper market meltdown, was also not kind to companies that had overleveraged themselves:

- In 1995, Daiwa Bank was forced to report a $1.5 billion derivatives trading loss.

- There was also the failure of the Japanese Shin Kyoto Shinpan credit institution with debts of almost $4 billion, which signaled that massive bad debt problems at smaller regional banks might be just emerging.

---

[1]As reported by Bloomberg.

Not that the situation in other Asian countries was much better. There were big losers all over. Figure 3.1 shows the top 10 cases of red ink in the Asian banking industry in 1995, ranging from the huge $3.36 billion lost by Sumitomo Bank with assets of $524 billion, to the $124 million lost by Indian Bank, whose assets were only $4.7 billion. These were mainly losses from bad loans and mismanaged assets, not from derivatives. But they were a mighty blow.

DERIVATIVES, HEDGE FUNDS, AND THE PRICE OF COPPER

On June 6, 1996, the copper market was in for some surprises as the price of the world's most heavily traded metal plummeted 15% in just two hours of hectic activity on the London Metal Exchange. This followed an earlier 10% drop and led dealers to increase the spread between the prices at which they were willing to buy or sell copper to $50 a ton.

Figure 3.1
The Biggest 1995 Losses Among Asian Banks: Six Japanese and Four Indian Banks

	Losses	Assets
1. Sumitomo Bank	$3.36 billion	$524 billion
2. Nippon Trust	1.64 billion	17 billion
3. Nippon Credit	1.10 billion	N.A.
4. Bank of India	347 million	8.8 billion
5. Bank of Osaka	296 million	21.6 billion
6. Central Bank of India	227 million	6.0 billion
7. United Bank of India	197 million	2.7 billion
8. Ucu Bank (India)	174 million	4.0 billion
9. Hanwa Bank (Japan)	158 million	524 million
10. Indian Bank	124 million	4.7 billion

A \$50-a-ton spread was a level previously unheard of, but it did not quite calm the frantic activity. For its part, the board of the London Metal Exchange took action to calm the market by doubling to \$400 a ton the initial cash that would have to be provided by anyone buying or selling copper. LME's anteing the bets helped the copper price to recover somewhat in late trading. But the speed and size of the price fall had already done serious financial damage to some market participants.

All told, copper lost 25% of its value and came down \$800 a ton in just six trading days. As the hectic selling died down, the price recovered to close at \$2,105 a ton. This was still \$610, or 22.5%, below the 1996 peak of \$2,715 reached early in May. Figure 3.2 presents the pattern of this movement.

Figure 3.2
The 25% Drop in the Price of Copper in Early 1996

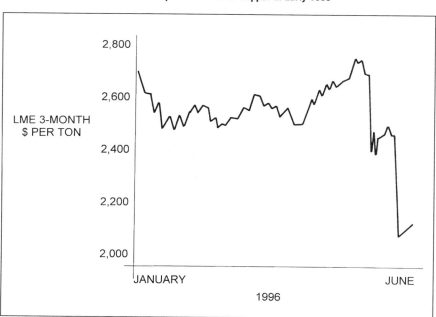

The base metal market was at the edge of a panic. As this message passed to investors and arbitrageurs, it further depressed copper prices. By contrast, shares in leading copper producers were relatively unscathed because the market feeling was that this particular debacle was a huge speculation, for example:

- RTZ, the world's biggest mining group, was down only 2.4%,
- Asarco shares were down $1 3/8 at $29, while
- Phelps Dodge shares were down only $1/4 off at $65 3/4.

Experts subsequently said that derivatives played a key role in copper's drop down the cliff. Copper producers were not immune to the meltdown because they had hedged extensively against lower copper prices through options. This contributed to the speed of the base metal's precipitous price fall.

Cognizant financial analysts subsequently suggested that copper's rout was not a one-tantum phenomenon. The price drift in reality started on June 4, when two American hedge funds sensed the time was ripe to force copper down for speculatory reasons. The two funds considered to be the motors of the move were George Soros's Quantum Fund and Julian Robertson's Tiger Fund.

This inference by financial analysts was partly based on the fact that both funds have a policy of capitalizing on large price movements that they help to produce. Their objective was to drive copper down to below $2,424 a ton, at which point the investment banks and market makers that had written put options to the copper producers would panic and start selling.

An article in the *Financial Times* suggested that Soros and Robertson were not alone in the copper game. They seem to have had a partner: Herbie Black, president of American Iron & Metal, a Montreal scrap business. Black allegedly helped copper's debacle by entering LME's copper market and selling short.[2]

Quantum and the Tiger Fund are widely thought by copper traders to have profited from Sumitomo's copper plight. The precise role of hedge funds in the Sumitomo case is not clear, as they are secretive about their positions, but dealers believe that betting on a fall in the market was helped by establishing short positions ahead of the 15% collapse in copper futures on June 6, 1996.

The Sumitomo Corporation lost heavily here because (contrary to the hedge funds) it had an opposite, long position. This meant

---

[2]*Financial Times,* June 18, 1996.

that the hedge funds' selling exacerbated the Japanese company's losses. In the aftermath of this event, one investment bank active in the copper market suggested that the main questions were:

- Did Quantum and its allies have any indication of what was to happen when they established their positions?
- And did they know of the hidden losses and the vulnerability of Sumitomo and try to make a killing in the copper market?

Neither did the financial market forget that Quantum profited at the expense of the British government when sterling fell out of the European Exchange Rate Mechanism (ERM) in 1992. Also fresh to the market's memory was the fact that the main hedge funds joined other investors in driving Barings to the wall on the Nikkei futures market in February 1995.

The funds had sold Nikkei futures, linked to the Japanese stock index, knowing that Barings or one of its clients had a loss-making and vulnerable long position. This is in line with what Sun Tzu has suggested in his famous book, *The Art of War.* The genius of specula-tors (and great generals) is not found in looking at the market at large but in being able to put themselves into their opponent's mind and discover its true position. Then they make their next move.[3]

The downfall of Barings, Sumitomo, and the other major losers of the mid-to-late 1990s took place at the dawn of the new economy. "Kings had always been involving and impoverishing their people in wars pretending generally, if not always, that the good of the people was the object," Abraham Lincoln once suggested.[4] The new kings of finance see something similar to the kings of old: They plan and exe-cute their moves for the benefit of their investors.

BEHIND THE SUMITOMO DEBACLE

Careful analysis of the events that led to the June 6, 1996, debacle suggests that this was not just a Sumitomo derivatives scandal but a more widespread disorder, whose extent was concealed by the tactic of over-revealing the Sumitomo side. Knowledgeable people suggest

---

[3]Sun Tzu, *The Art of War* (New York: Delacorte Press, 1983).
[4]Emil Ludwig, *Lincoln* (New York: Grosset & Dunlap, 1930).

the target of such strategy was to lead attention away from what was a systemic cash crunch throughout the global financial system.

As the dust started to settle, some indicators pointed to the fact that there was far more going on than the billions of trading loss by a large Japanese company. The hypothesis of a systemic cash crunch was sustained by the fact that over the weekend of June 16, the heads of the Bank of Japan, the Federal Reserve, and the Bank of England activated emergency crisis management procedures.

For their part, different government officials went on record to show how to prevent a potentially disastrous drop in the base metal's price that could have financial repercussions around the globe. This wide expression of concern took place despite the fact that Sumitomo's chief executive had announced on June 14 that the trading company had the financial staying power to make good any losses and that there was nothing to fear from a firm that had annual turnover in excess of $152 billion.

Sumitomo was not alone in a torrent of red ink. Investment banks affected by the Sumitomo copper scandal included leading dealers in commodity derivatives such as Bankers Trust, J.P. Morgan, Lehman Brothers, Merrill Lynch, and Goldman, Sachs. Competitors speculated that J.P. Morgan and Merrill Lynch lost $100 million each and Bankers Trust a further $30 million.[5] These amounts, however, did not put these institutions in peril.

The top City of London clearinghouses (including Barclays, NatWest, HSBC, and Lloyds) financially backed the London Metal Exchange market. Also in the Sumitomo copper game was (Winchester Commodities) a British commodities firm and Global Minerals & Metals of New York. In addition, there were unconfirmed reports that the Dutch ING Bank, which a year earlier had taken over the bankrupt Barings Bank, might have had dealings with Winchester and Sumitomo along with the chronically troubled French bank, Credit Lyonnais.

Below the surface there was a different sort of information. In London it was said that the Bank of England had been directly controlling, trading on the London Metal Exchange for a week. Added to this was a decision on June 12 by the all-powerful Japanese Ministry of Finance (MOF). Two days before the Sumitomo scandal was made

[5]*Financial Times,* April 19, 1996.

public MOF had decided to join—and therefore expand—the monetary reflation efforts of the Bank of Japan. Since June 12, the Ministry of Finance had been visible in buying Japanese government bonds and injecting large sums of liquidity into the Japanese financial system. Analysts saw this to be a big reason for the steady rise of the Tokyo Nikkei stock index, as added liquidity hit the market.

Experts suggested that beefing up liquidity was a defensive move justified by a possible meltdown in an already destabilized Japanese financial industry. The vast problem in Japanese banks—together with the fragility of the international banking system—created what many analysts considered to be a scary situation.

In America, the Federal Reserve had been covertly intervening to stabilize the falling U.S. bond markets. Evidence pointed to an effort by G-7 countries to take attention away from the details of the copper market's woes and try to come up with a solution that would avert a larger system-threatening crisis. One expert in London said the financial community approved these measures, because increasing liquidity was the only possible, reasonable, and logical answer to the crisis.

But other analysts believed that the Sumitomo debacle was covering up a far larger crisis in the international financial system. An indicator of this was the flimsy story Sumitomo issued to explain its losses. The idea that one of the world's best-known commodities experts, which had been a senior trader in Sumitomo copper trades since 1975, could hide billions of trading losses, which Sumitomo claimed were run up over a period of more than 10 years, was laughable.

Also, claims that Yasuo Hamanaka, the former trading head, acted alone as a rogue dealer as Baring's Nick Leeson allegedly had done were not credible. Japan is known for producing a hierarchical consensus culture which takes time to build up and involves successive senior management strata. This is exactly the antipode of lone individual culture commonly found in some Western financial institutions.

The regulators don't seem to have doubted that this was not a one-man act and that the senior management of Sumitomo Corporation was on the hook. In mid-May 1998, the Commodity Futures Trading Commission (CFTC) announced that the Japanese Group would pay a record $133 million to U.S and UK regulators. The CFTC also explained how and why Yasuo Hamanaka allegedly manipulated the international copper market.

According to this account the web of deception stretched back several years. Just before Hamanaka was appointed head of the copper team and senior copper trader, in 1987, Sumitomo had suffered large losses in speculative futures trading as well as actual copper losses. With this background information in mind, it seems that the new executive did not enter his trades in the normal bookkeeping system; instead, he recorded them in personal notebooks—a sort of double bookkeeping.

The CFTC said that back in 1993, Yasuo Hamanaka had agreed to buy copper from a new New York copper merchant on a monthly basis for three years. Such agreements contained an unusual minimum-price provision, which allowed both sides to profit from any rises in the market over the established minimum—giving both firms a financial interest in higher prices. But Sumitomo Corporation claimed that this was not the case; the copper purchases were made to satisfy customer demand.

Acting on behalf of Sumitomo, Yasuo Hamanaka and the merchant bank put up several special accounts, which made it possible for the New York firm to trade in Sumitomo's name and use its credit in futures trades. The plan was to push copper prices artificially high by purchasing both physical metal and futures contracts and then profit by liquidating their positions. A hedge fund could not have done better than that.

Yasuo Hamanaka: Rogue Trader or Scapegoat?

Yasuo Hamanaka was allegedly the lone wolf whose copper deals cost the company somewhere between the $2.6 billion finally officially admitted and the rumored $5 billion. While the torrent of red ink came to light in June 1996, not until late March 1998 was Hamanaka sentenced to eight years in prison for fraud and forgery.

As the miracle of Asian growth was oversold, so seem to have been Hamanaka's sins. His sentence capped a narrowly focused year-long trial in Tokyo that left many questions unanswered. No matter how one considers its outcome, it was a disaster for Sumitomo. The court found that the former star trader forged documents to do deals off the books and to hide massive losses.

It is difficult to believe that just one person was behind all these allegations, and nobody exercised management control over the whole debacle. Evidence that became available suggests that in his high times Yasuo Hamanaka was not a man who stood out in any way other than his influence on the copper market. He was not known for extravagant ways, unusual habits, or fraudulent activities. No particular pattern of fraud seems to have been present except the following incident.

One piece of the puzzle used in his conviction is that in October 1991, Hamanaka made a highly unusual special request to a London trader. In a handwritten note, he asked the trader to issue a back-dated invoice for a fictitious copper deal worth about $225 million, promising not to cause any trouble, any damage, or any loss at all.

The London trader who received this request is said to have voiced concern about such an unorthodox approach to LME. Subsequently, a meeting took place with regulatory authorities to discuss the matter. Questioned about the note, Sumitomo said Yasuo Hamanaka was supposed to match his buy-and-sell orders for copper. The hypothesis therefore was that the star trader might instead have gambled on the copper price going wholesale in one direction or the other by option trading. Even with Sumitomo's powerful presence helping to push prices in the desired direction, this was a high-risk strategy potentially involving big financial losses. Furthermore, Hamanaka's master position in the copper market came from the fact that Sumitomo was handling about 750,000 tons a year—some 5% of the global total. For this reason, he was known as "Mister 5%."

Indeed, other traders had complained in years past that Sumitomo had control of most of the copper stocks in London Metal Exchange warehouses and was refusing to release the base metal.[6] This caused prices for immediate delivery to rise, and also poses the puzzling question of whether in this case too Hamanaka acted as a lone wolf.

There is of course nothing illegal about cornering the market. Many people are doing it. In copper's case, traders protested because of huge inventoried positions that seem to show that Hamanaka always was making sure Sumitomo's clients would have the copper they needed delivered on time—regardless of a market squeeze in the base metal. Analysts in London suggested it was precisely this market squeezing by limiting supply that led to his downfall.

---

[6]*Financial Times,* June 19, 1999.

There is also another fact associated with the Sumitomo/ Hamanaka story. During the Tokyo trial, prosecutors produced evidence that Hamanaka held a secret Swiss bank account in which he received millions of dollars for helping third-party dealers benefit from copper trades. But the trial did not answer two key questions:

- Did Hamanaka manipulate global copper prices and, if so, how and for how long?
- Was Sumitomo senior management involved with or know of these trades?

The court decision seems to have implied that Hamanaka acted alone. "If there was a bigger conspiracy of market manipulation, we probably will never know exactly what happened," said Hidesato Sekine, chief of the three-member team that defended Yasuo Hamanaka. "This is it. There will be no more full-fledged inquiry into the Hamanaka copper scandal, at least in Japan."

Sekine added that his client, who pleaded guilty to both forgery and fraud, had no plans for appealing. But analysts in other Group of Ten capitals said prosecutors had misplaced their thrust. Hamanaka should not have been prosecuted alone. Cognizant metals traders wondered just how it was possible for Hamanaka to have concealed losses totaling the official admitted $2.6 billion over 10 years. And they concluded that it was near to impossible to hide such big losses for so long.

If it was not the board who backed up the deals, then at least someone at Sumitomo's top management was presumably signing all the checks that had to be sent to cover the losses. It is simply unthinkable that the back office had not noticed sums of that size and had not reported them to the auditors, the chief executive officers, and others in senior management. In the last analysis:

- **Even if Sumitomo's internal controls were abysmal, it is simply not possible that this torrent of red ink went on undetected.**
- **By delaying action, Sumitomo worsened its position as it continued to trade in copper.**

After Sumitomo officially released Hamanaka's confession, it added that the only other employee aware of the unauthorized trading had left eight years ago. Big deal. The gap in management control was not 10 years long; it had lasted "only" eight years according to the company's own admission.

The allegation that senior management had been inattentive for eight years was of no great help to the investigators or, for that matter, to the markets. In the wake of the copper earthquake, both regulators and traders suggested that if the market was to remain stable, three important questions needed to be answered in a factual and documented manner:

- How big was Sumitomo's remaining long position?
- Were there any hidden copper stocks?
- How large were the non-Sumitomo long positions that might influence the market?

To my knowledge no answers have been provided to these queries. The only thing that can be said with confidence is that there has been a bottoming and less bad than expected market response in the sense that there was no panic. The market stabilized, but recovery was not around the corner. As for Yasuo Hamanaka, many analysts think he was no more than the scapegoat. He was dispensable.

WHEN INTERNAL CONTROLS FAIL

To say the least in the Sumitomo copper case, losses as high as Mount Fuji helped to prove the company's internal controls were substandard if they existed at all. Therefore, even if Hamanaka was guilty, senior management should have been prosecuted along with the trader for a notoriously defective internal controls system over 10 years and an associated total absence of personal accountability.

Let me explain what lies behind this assertion. In intensive research that I did in 1998–99 in the United States, United Kingdom, and continental Europe, nearly 100 talented people from central banks, commercial banks, investment banks, brokers/dealers, and trade associations expressed the opinion that the board, CEO, and top management are directly accountable for the company's internal control system. These opinions converged to the definition of internal control presented in the following five points:

- Internal control is a dynamic system covering all types of risk, addressing fraud, assuring transparency, and making possible reliable financial reporting.

- The chairman of the board, the directors, chief executive officer, and senior management are not just responsible, but are personally accountable for internal control.

- Beyond the control of risks, internal control goals are the preservation of assets, account reconciliation, and compliance. Laws and regulations affect the internal control system.

- The able management of internal control requires policies, organization, technology, open communications, real-time, access to all transactions, steady quality control, and corrective action.

- Internal control must be regularly audited by internal and external auditors to ensure its rank and condition and see that there is no cognitive dissonance at any level.

(This last point is covered in more detail in the next section of this chapter.)

One sign that internal control at Sumitomo was lacking is that if top management's allegations are right, then Yasuo Hamanaka enjoyed a degree of freedom unheard of in a well-run organization. He was known to appear without notice in London and there had been persistent rumors about what seemed to be extremely speculative trades. According to copper traders, Sumitomo was known as a company that does not take risks, but Hamanaka seemed to be given liberties uncharacteristic of a Japanese firm.

Amid widely circulating reports about Hamanaka's activities and their impact on the market, Sumitomo suggested that it did not have any grounds to suspect that anything unusual was taking place. The company's confidence had led to a lapse in the "strict controls" in which the Osaka-based trading firm so prides itself. One Sumitomo official was rumored to have said, "We have the normal controls. Other than that, all we can do is trust our employees."

What was the reason for this overconfidence by top management? Does a $5 billion scandal occur when internal control breaks down because an employee has many years with the company? Commenting on what appeared to be a blank check by Sumitomo that made a star trader out of Hamanaka, a London analyst brought to mind the words of King James I, who, when asked by one of his nurses if he could make her son a gentlemen, replied, "A gentleman I could never make him, though I could make him a lord."

Other London analysts said that if one sets aside the fact that disclosure of billions in losses caused misery to Sumitomo Corporation, these losses had a positive aftermath because they brought to the fore the need for better controls elsewhere. Metal trading may finally fall inside the regulatory domain of government supervisors; there has long been a lack of adequate control procedures and a base metals industry watchdog.

In Britain, the Securities and Investments Board's primary concern with copper was to ensure that the price formation process for quotes on the LME is fair and transparent. Activities that distort the true level of demand for copper could cause losses for investors and undermine confidence in the LME and, generally, the UK markets.

At the time, the other key watchdog in Britain was the Securities and Futures Authority (FSA, now Financial Services Authority), a regulatory body whose authority covers those who trade commodity futures. According to its charter it must ensure that participants are fit and proper and that the financial resources of firms trading commodity futures are sufficient to cover the financial risks they take on.

The majority opinion in both New York and London, however, has been that as long as Sumitomo comes up with the money, no major harm was done. Unlike Barings and Daiwa, the Sumitomo Corporation was not a bank. Therefore, no depositors' money was at risk, and it was not inviting public investments with diverted money.

But the regulators had no reason to be pleased with themselves for not having supervised some of the goings-on in the copper market, particularly because this market was working less well than it should. The backwardation alone should have alerted the regulators. Besides that, keep in mind that:

- **A sensible supervision starts with investigation of the largest player in the market.**

In copper trading, Sumitomo was much bigger than any of its immediate competitors, and it should have been investigated earlier. My words about regulators in England are just as valid for regulators in Japan. After the fact, Japanese regulators admitted that one factor in the failure to detect the buildup of Sumitomo Corporation's billions in losses over the past decade was that no single organization in Tokyo is responsible for regulating trading companies. Japanese government agencies are often criticized for being a patchwork of turf battles. In the case of Sumitomo, though, the battle was for avoidance of embarrassment rather than turf per se.

No one in the various regulatory agencies and branches of government with an interest in trading companies was prepared to admit being in charge. This too is evidence of lack of internal control but at a higher level: that of government regulation and supervision. Internal control in commodities trading does not seem to be an energizing central theme—and as long as this is true, the market will be exposed to all sorts of risks—particularly when its heart beats at Internet time, as it does in the new economy.

PRESCRIPTION FOR DISASTER: WEAK INTERNAL CONTROL AND SPLIT RESPONSIBILITY

As noted, the Sumitomo Corporation is a global trading company, not a bank. However, part of the Sumitomo Group is a major money-center bank (one of Japan's largest) which must follow the directives of the Basle Committee. Conglomerates that own major financial institutions should be subject to strict supervision. The trouble is that regulators of commodities trading have no clear definition of internal controls, so top management can always plead the excuse "it did not know about their need."

In a nutshell, here is the definition of internal control by the Basle Committee on Banking Supervision:

- **Internal control is a process effected by the board of directors, senior management, and all levels of personnel.**
- **It is not solely a procedure or policy that is performed at a certain point in time, but rather it is continually operating at all levels within the company.**

The Basle Committee also makes the point that while historically the internal control process has been a mechanism for reducing instances of fraud, misappropriation, and errors, today's economy needs much more than that both in the breadth of subjects that it covers and in the depth of their coverage. It recommends these practices:

> - **No senior management can escape its internal control duties and yet perform its functions in an able manner, with accountability.**
> - **The auditors (internal and external) of the internal control system should always bear in mind that their own resolution to succeed in uncovering exposure is more important than anything else.**

In the new economy, where the risks multiply and the unknowns are a legend, any trading company needs a first-class internal control system to ensure that senior management is in charge. For financial institutions, Basle also advises that globalization requires that the internal control process must become more extensive than in a local economy, addressing all risks faced by an organization. This is true of all five interrelated elements defined by the supervisors of the Group of Ten:

- Management oversight and the control culture,
- Risk assessment,
- Other control activities,
- Information and communication, and
- Monitoring and measurement.

The effective functioning of all of these elements is essential to achieving a company's operational, information, and compliance objectives—any company's, not only a bank's. But it is just as true that there should be a regulatory authority to oversee if internal controls are in place and they are properly functioning. Central banks and other bank supervisory authorities now focus on internal control, though authorities whose domain is regulation of trading organizations do not necessarily.

Technically, Sumitomo should have been governed by different departments of the Ministry of International Trade and Industry (MITI), which is responsible for international trade, mining, and commodities. This reflects split responsibility. MITI also supervises Japan's commodity exchanges, from aluminum to gold, an area where trading interests verge on the financial.

The irony in connection to commodity exchanges is that Tokyo has no copper market despite the fact that Japan has the world's second largest copper smelting industry. This dilutes the supervisor's role in the specific case under discussion—a fact reflected in MITI's opinion that Sumitomo had broken none of the laws and regulations that came under this ministry.

For its part, the Japanese Finance Ministry (which usually lets it be known that it is in charge of almost everything) has repeatedly pointed out that trading companies are not regulated by any single Japanese authority. One Tokyo financier said that it should have been the UK authorities' responsibility, not the Japanese authorities', to police any illicit commodity dealings since the unauthorized trades occurred in London.

As for the Bank of Japan, its responsibility was said to be limited to ensuring that any fallout from the Sumitomo loss did not damage the economy in any significant way. Theoretically at least, the central bank is there to ensure that the financial industry remains afloat and there is no systemic collapse. As these examples show, with what might have been the three major players in regulation and supervision of a king-size global trading company keeping in the sidelines, we can draw these conclusions:

- **There was not much left of an authority in Japan to ensure logical and reasonable limits to exposure.**
- **And the case of Sumitomo Corporation was passed from ministry to ministry with nobody in charge.**

One result of the Sumitomo affair is that it did turn the spotlight onto the London Metal Exchange. Copper is the biggest element on the LME, yet the supervisory practices seem to have been inadequate and incomplete, giving commodities trading companies a free hand. But as the market turns against the speculator, the same commodities companies may find themselves to be the nearest thing to damaged goods.

Critics say that the LME board is dominated by dealing members of the exchange, who make their money from volatility. Because of conflicts of interest, these critics suggest that only the chief executive sees the trading records, which greatly reduces internal control accountability. In organizational terms, this results in a concentration of responsibility that would be unthinkable inside a modern bank or securities firm, and it also provides further evidence of lack of internal control, this time at the level of the exchange.

But something may be changing in this regard, at least in a global setting. Following the Sumitomo affair, questions were raised in Chile, the world's largest copper producer, about the suitability of the London Metals Exchange as the main stage for setting the world copper price.

For its part, in London, the Serious Fraud Office (SFO) started investigating Yasuo Hamanaka's dealings on the London copper market. The Securities and Investments Board called in the SFO. The Bank of England also got involved in the damage containment efforts of the LME because some members of LME are owned by banks (and for a number of other reasons, some of them having to do with systemic risk).

All trades on the LME are guaranteed by the London Clearing House, which is owned by big banks: Barclays, Lloyds, Midland, NatWest, Royal Bank of Scotland, and Standard Chartered. Together they provide financial backing of £150 million ($245 million) for counterparty risk. As a result of the Sumitomo earthquake, the London Clearing House that matches trades on the metal market announced that traders in copper will need to increase deposits by 50% from $400 to $600 a ton. At the same time, international regulators heightened their surveillance of copper trading.

In the United States, the Commodity Futures Trading Commission (CFTC) had already increased its monitoring in November 1995 in cooperation with UK regulators, based on an inordinate market volatility. The crevasse at that side of regulation is that while CFTC's jurisdiction can extend to supervision of trades in the underlying physical commodity, the U.S. regulator has no direct oversight of trades made on the London Metal Exchange. The new economy has not yet tied together its loose ends.

THE CASE OF THE NIPPON CREDIT BANK TALKS VOLUMES ABOUT WEAK INTERNAL CONTROL

The torrent of red ink at Sumitomo Corporation and the failure of several big Japanese banks, particularly long-term credit institutions, in the years that followed the heavy copper derivatives losses in the Sumitomo Corporation affair are by all evidence independent events.

What these happenings have in common is the evidence about nonexistence of internal controls that can ring alarm bells well before the point of no return.

After the Sumitomo Debacle: The Crash of Nippon Credit Bank

Adding to a negative psychology in a Japanese economy under stress for many years were a number of well-publicized events following the Sumitomo debacle. In May 1997, Nippon Credit Bank (NCB), one of the largest Japanese institutions, announced losses for 1996 of yen 367 billion (about $3.20 billion), over and above the 1995 losses of yen 126.5 billion ($1.1 billion). With a capital adequacy ratio of 2.99% versus the 8% capital adequacy requirements defined by the Basle Committee, the Nippon Credit Bank withdrew from the international financial market.

NCB's woes have been a telling story about the fragility of the international financial system, as the new economy searches its ways, its rules, and its base. It reveals how overexposed some companies can be as risks mount. Many try to keep afloat up to a certain time, but in the end reality catches up with them and they have to deposit their balance sheet.

The case of Nippon Credit Bank is interesting because it was once one of the stars of Japanese finance, providing a golden horde of companies with long-term credit to launch themselves in international competition. But stars fall from the sky; they don't stay in the constellation forever.

By January 2000, NCB was a bankrupt nationalized lender about to be purchased by a consortium led by superleveraged Softbank, a service firm increasingly presented as a "New Japan" company. Apart from Softbank, this consortium originally featured Orix (a leasing company), Tokio Marine & Fire (an insurer), and Ito-Yokado, a supermarket chain.

As negotiations proceeded, Ito-Yokado dropped out from the syndicate, allegedly being unimpressed with Softbank's thinking about what to do with NCB. This led to an interesting dilemma. If Softbank took Ito-Yokado's share, its stake would rise from 40 to 65%. However, according to Japanese law, if the share of one of the partners rises above 50%, that partner will have to consolidate the bank together with the proportion of NCB's (many) doubtful loans. Yet these are the loans the Japanese government declines to underwrite on its balance sheet, and reportedly they are so large that they could topple superleveraged Softbank.

Softbank can hardly afford to take upon itself and include in its financial report such huge exposure, since on its own balance sheet $2 billion worth of debts lurk already. For a company whose portfolio of Internet investments yields precious little cash flow, that huge leverage is virtual suicide.

Neither are the future plans for Nippon Credit Bank something to crow about. These call for turning the bank into a lender to the sorts of high-technology start-ups in which Softbank likes to invest— i.e., into Software clones that will themselves be superleveraged and, by all evidence, lack internal controls to keep their risks under lock and key.

Softbank talks about an Internet version of zaibatzu, a sort of reincarnation of the giant pre–World War II Japanese holding companies that combined financial and industrial interests in huge conglomerates and were widely considered to be responsible for pushing Japan into World War II. Interestingly enough, the *zaibatzu* were the predecessors of the keiretsu, which dominate the financial and industrial landscape of Japan today.

The concept of an Internet *zaibatzu* is, to say the least, puzzling because the currency of venture capitalists is equity, not bank loans. Also Internet start-ups are notoriously bad at making money day to day and so have little free cash to service debt. But the foremost problem in my mind is that small Internet start-ups lack a rigorous management control structure. This makes them very flexible and, when they fail, the venture capitalists lick their wounds.

Having failed once in the recent past in a big way, and having been salvaged at the 12th hour through nationalization, the Nippon Credit Bank can ill afford to fail again. Yet, bankruptcy is the sure trillion-dollar thing when it takes upon itself and its unstable balance sheet the losses that will most likely result from a myriad of superleveraged little but blown-up firms trying to make their fortune in the new economy.

One of the things eager beavers should learn is that if they want things to go well for them, they should not play games with the new economy. In the case of Softbank/Nippon Credit Bank as in many others, common sense seems to have taken a leave, and with it the fundamentals of internal control and management accountability.

SOGO AND SEIYO: THE JAPANESE GOVERNMENT ADOPTS A HANDS-OFF ATTITUDE

During the week of July 13, 2000, the large Japanese retailer SOGO filed for protection from its creditors with almost yen 1,900 billion ($17.6 billion) of debts. That same week, Seiyo, a property group, filed for liquidation with yen 517 billion ($490 million) debts. With the Japanese government adopting a new, hands-off attitude, the question analysts have been asking is whether Japanese banks have adequate reserves against these big, bad loans.

The Japanese banks insist they do, and as evidence have already written off more than yen 50 trillion ($475 billion) of bad loans in recent years, out of the estimated yen 70 billion ($660 billion) of problem loans inherited after the bursting of the 1980s bubble. But analysts are not convinced, even if SOGO's main creditors, including Dai-Ichi Kangyo, Industrial Bank of Japan, Sumitomo Trust, and Mitsui Chuo Trust, say that the year 2000 results will not be affected because they had written off most of their loans to the fallen retailer.

What has also fueled investor concern is that Japanese banks have been over-optimistic about their bad loans. At Shinsei Bank, where transparency has improved since its sale to U.S. investors in 1999, it was rumored that managers recently admitted that their reserves were inadequate to cope with the poor quality of loans in its books. The old policy has been that the Japanese banks tended to keep large ailing companies going by debt-forgiveness programs.

The case of SOGO's bankruptcy is interesting because it represents a switch in the fire-brigade policies of the Japanese government. The latter seems to have been undecided about letting SOGO go bankrupt. Just days before filing for protection from creditors, the government had announced plans to forgive a huge amount of bank debt issued to SOGO. This sent the wrong signal to both domestic and international investors.

Postmortem, financial analysts pointed out that if market forces had been allowed to act, chances are that SOGO would have gone bankrupt years ago. Many other Japanese companies are in the same situation. In Seiyo's case, its woes were well known for some time, but the former paternalistic policies of the Japanese government had led people to believe that failure has its reward.

The good news is that, finally, the SOGO and Seiyo bankruptcies seem to be subtly different from the previous pattern. Both companies were refused new concessions because the Japanese banking system can no longer absorb such large shocks and survive. Three other factors making Japanese banks less willing to forgive debt are:

- A new Japanese law making it easier for a company to file for bankruptcy,

- Tighter accounting standards that put a ceiling on creative accounting practices, and

- The fact that the government has become less willing to use public funds to keep private companies alive.

There is as well a higher level of public awareness, both in Japan and abroad, about the cost of fire-brigade solutions. If the government is still trying to protect the banks, but not SOGO and Seiyo, this implies that reserves had not been set aside for the two companies' loans, nor were the loans written down. How many more billions of bad debt are out there, weighing heavily on bank balance sheets?

The bad news is that concerns about transparency are arising all over again, and Japan's promises about financial reform are being questioned, and worries about the extent of unreserved loans on the books of Japanese banks seem to be the talk of central bankers around the world.

Undisclosed and unreserved loans may be one reason why, after so many years, Japanese banks are still not making many consumer loans, thereby implying the credit system does not work. This has an aftermath. The lack of strong consumer demand has been a major factor in the country's stop-go type of recovery. Extending credit to consumers is essential to simulating public demand and economic growth.

At the same time, SOGO's bankruptcy sends a signal that the long-held perception that major Japanese companies are too big to fail is no longer valid. As a result, SOGO and Seiyo might signal the start of a wave of failures for which neither the Japanese government nor the banks are properly prepared. The silver lining is that this wave of failures might help to prune the Japanese banking system of many of its bad debts.

CHAPTER 4

Creative Accounting and Lax Auditing: Kidder Peabody

In 1994, Kidder Peabody alleged that one of its traders, Joseph Jett, cheated his company of $350 million by exploiting the inefficiency of its accounting system. According to the company's management, Kidder's accounting permitted a person to create bogus profits by buying a STRIP and then booking its sale at a much higher price. This accounting twist was handy, because it also led to high commissions for traders.

The window of opportunity for nonexistent profits but real commissions and real potential losses was opened by the fact that STRIPs are sold with face value of the original bond from which they are torn off. In reality, because they represent only a piece of the original bond, their value is much less than that of the whole bond, but there seems to be no sure formula to give the exact value. Into this crevasse came the fake profits.

Kidder's poor accounting system made matters worse by failing to disclose the $350 million of losses from skewed STRIP trading. Neither was Kidder Peabody the only investment bank to pay for this sort of accounting failure. It appears that prior to unearthing such creative accounting practice, some of the $350 million had miraculously migrated to Credit Suisse First Boston (CSFB).

As of mid-April 1994, senior executives at Kidder Peabody had a problem on their hands they could ill afford to ignore. Their investigation of who was behind the two-year $350 million phony government bond trading scheme led to an organizational earthquake implicating different parties. Regarding senior management's responsibilities in this affair, the CEO suggested that Kidder's risk management is good, but no system is foolproof.

Michael A. Carpenter, the chief executive of the brokerage firm, said he and his top lieutenant, fixed-income head Edward A. Cerullo, were victims of a sophisticated rogue trader named Joseph Jett, who headed the firm's government bond desk. But Jett answered that he was singled out and discriminated against because he was black. In the wake of the controversy, both Jett and another trader, Neil Margolin, were dismissed while six other employees were suspended from their jobs.

According to what I was told at Wall Street, Carpenter described this very costly failure by saying that the altimeter said they were flying at the right altitude, and the compass said they were flying in the right direction. Then they banged into the mountain. So the altimeter simply had a kick, and the mountain suddenly moved into their way. But after the dismissal of Joseph Jett, an internal review of trading practices found some gaping holes. Jett had allegedly conducted an elaborate trading scheme that permitted him to create the $350 million in fake profits and to conceal some $100 million in real losses.

During the time this trading scheme occurred, nobody at Kidder Peabody seems to have sensed (let alone questioned) how Joseph Jett was generating "profits" of $20 million to $40 million a month. Or, alternatively, if somebody had noticed, he simply did not bother to report it and top management did not move to straighten the balances.

In my opinion, senior management should have been more aware. This does not seem to have happened because of the prevailing internal culture, which is found in many brokerages and other firms: the push to do more and more in guestimated profits and commissions without accounting for "toxic waste" left behind. Who is to blame for building such a culture at Kidder that bent the rules to favor superstar traders?

It is no secret that inadequate accounting, "creative" bonus practices, auditors who don't challenge the obvious, defective internal controls, twisted cultures, and lax management lead to debacles and eventually to catastrophes. Kidder Peabody was a well-known brokerage firm. After this bogus affair, it disappeared from the constellation of investment banks. This should be a lesson to others, as well as a case study of management risk.

COLLATERALIZED MORTGAGE OBLIGATIONS: ONE SOURCE OF "TOXIC WASTE"

In 1993, Kidder Peabody underwrote $94 billion of collateralized mortgage obligations (CMOs). These deals had given it a respectable 20% market share. But the party did not last long. In October 1994, General Electric announced that its subsidiary GE Capital was taking over $6.7 billion of Kidder's inventoried positions prior to the firm's merger with PaineWebber.

Kidder Peabody had been unwinding its positions through 1994, from over $15 billion in the first quarter to about $6.7 billion. On Wall Street, analysts said that $6.7 billion represented the instruments that were toughest to sell and therefore remain in the issuer's portfolio. This, too, is a sort of toxic waste. In December 1994, GE Capital disclosed that this portfolio had shrunk a bit more to $5.9 billion, but the statement also left open the possibility of other piles of toxic waste still held at other underwriters.

For General Electric, this represented another $800 million loss, over and above the $1.5 billion lost with the sale of Kidder to PaineWebber. Experts said at the time that most likely, losses from toxic waste were far from over but they also praised Jack Welch, chief executive officer of General Electric, for cleaning house. Substantial losses would continue for two reasons:

- Because the dealers may face such heavy losses if they sell the positions in reference, they tend to keep them in the books at highly distressed levels.
- But there are always bogus profits and real losses because of twisted accounting methods used when the system is lax.

Kidder Peabody had two distinct problems: the huge write-offs due to the Jett trades (which eventually reached $210 million) and the aftermath of its inordinate exposure to the mortgage-backed securities business. The latter derived from rumored large losses during the abrupt collapse in bond prices in March 1994, which battered the mortgage-backed portfolios of many Wall Street firms and individual investors.

Kidder Peabody was very big in the CMO market because its management was willing to assume bigger risks than other financial companies. Never slow to criticize a firm that mismanaged its investment, Wall Street analysts did not seem to accept at face value a

Kidder statement that the company had no big hits because it operated on a hedged basis "for the most part."

Quite to the contrary, experts said that Kidder Peabody was thought to have the largest mortgage-backed portfolio in the marketplace. From January to early May 1994, the company had issued $28 billion in mortgage-backed securities, for a huge 24% percent market share. This had been more than the total of the next two positions, respectively held by Lehman Brothers and Bears Stearns at just less than $12 billion each—and it came over and above the $81 billion in mortgage-backed financing the company had issued in 1993.

While Kidder wouldn't say how much of its end-of-1993 $72 billion balance sheet consisted of mortgage-backed paper, Wall Streeters suggest that this amounted to a significant portion. Much of the company's $439 million in 1993 operating earnings was thought to have come from its mortgage securitization deals, with all this meant in terms of risks taken down the line as the market reversed itself.

A crucial issue in estimating the riskiness of Kidder Peabody's mortgage-backed financing was how much of it consisted of high-risk mortgage derivatives. The rub is that the latter's value can fluctuate radically with a big move in interest rates, because this move affects the market's psychology. Two instruments highly sensitive to market twists are inverse floaters and interest-only securities.

Just as important was the exposure of Kidder Peabody's clients and losses associated with this exposure. Several customers of Kidder's, such as Askin Capital Management and Piper Jaffray, had been badly burned by rising interest rates' impact on the values of their portfolios of mortgage derivatives.

Because Kidder Peabody was thought to be a big owner of these securities, the rate rise was believed to have sparked serious losses of its own. Therefore, despite the company's statement that it did not take any major hits and that its bond portfolio was accurately priced, Wall Street experts (particularly mortgage-backed traders) remained skeptical.

Available evidence suggests that at Kidder Peabody, management control was absent and an analytical approach to profitability was not part of the company's culture. In a nutshell, an analytical approach to profitability requires these management controls:

- Strategic planning and budgeting must be structured along the framework of a value system.
- Competitive advantages are often determined by the quality of management control.

- The information system constituting the infrastructure must be in full evolution.

- The bankers' ability to adapt themselves is subordinate to the existence of profitability measurements.

- The risks and rewards system should permit multidimensional analyses and prognostication.

Creative accounting practices obviously work to the detriment of such a well-structured solution. Instead, reliance at Kidder Peabody was placed on word of mouth and hearsay. A daily calculation of profits at risk and capital at risk would have been instrumental in informing GE's CEO and the board about exposure, but such a solution seems to have been alien to this investment bank (and many others).

Granted, the big interest rate hike from February to May 1994 made it very difficult to estimate prices for mortgage-backed financing and other collateralized mortgage obligations. This was true particularly for CMO derivatives, which are often very illiquid. This was true not only for Kidder Peabody, but for every player in a market hit by rapidly rising interest rates. But until then, marking-to-market was feasible if one was not afraid to look at the red ink.

When all hell broke loose in the CMO market, some companies were burned more than others. Steinhart's hedge fund was thought to have lost $1 billion and then called it quits. In the opinion of market insiders, Kidder's mortgage-backed portfolio was worth between 10 billion and $15 billion, and Wall Street sources speculated that if it was marked-to-market to reflect current values, losses could be several hundred million dollars. This is hardly the case of a company "flying in the right altitude" whose pilot kept it "in the right direction."

THE ROOT PROBLEM: COMPLETE LOSS OF MANAGEMENT CONTROL

As is often said, "Two wrongs don't make a right." At Kidder Peabody, the two things that were wrong were creative accounting and the lack of management control. The mortgage-backed obligations debacle and the dry hole of STRIPs added to Wall Street's opinion that this investment bank's management was an unmitigated disaster. Stated simply, there was no evidence that anybody was in charge.

Very timely and accurate means for management control are particularly important to the new economy because the rapid pace of innovation—and the need to manage unknown situations—may well bring up a twist in the rules and a bypass of prudential barriers, if such rules and barriers existed in the first place. Without such control, two scenarios can easily arise:

- **Lust and greed can cause a trader, a desk, or the whole institution to overexpose itself and its fortunes wholesale in one instrument (in Kidder's case, CMOs).**

- **And steady manufacturing of traders' commissions creates its own penalties to the company, particularly when combined with substandard accounting and inefficient internal controls.**

The scheme Joseph Jett put into motion was not unheard of in trading. It involved arbitrage trades between the value of pieces of Treasury bonds (the STRIPs) and the recombined bonds. The trouble was that Jett's desk was not generating any significant profits from the slightly greater value of the reconstituted bond. The game plan was that using forward contracts in the STRIPs, he could create much larger bogus profits by exploiting flaws in the wounded company's accounting system.

Because such game plans are not uncommon, senior management at Kidder should have been aware of their likelihood. In business there is sometimes considerable speculation on when various accounting "twists" will happen, but no one doubts that they will happen again—therefore, top management and the auditors must always be alert.

What Kidder Peabody Could Have Learned from Bankers Trust

Let me take a more recent and more serious example that proves that Kidder was not alone in this misfortune. On March 11, 1999, Bankers Trust pleaded guilty to federal criminal charges arising from a scheme in which it allegedly misappropriated some $19 million in funds belonging to its customers. The bank reportedly employed those funds to create a slush fund, which it then used to overstate its earnings.

"Pursuant to its agreement with the U.S. Attorney's Office, Bankers Trust will plead guilty to misstating entries in the bank's books and records and will pay a $160 million fine to Federal authorities," the bank announced in a remarkable March 12 press release. "Separately, Bankers Trust will pay a $3.5 million fine to the State of New York."[1]

When an institution's own management and its auditors are not vigilant at all times, the next thing that happens is the supervisory authorities step in. Vigilance is no one-tantum affair, and to a large extent, the regulators' involvement should be welcome because no matter what the penalty is, it constitutes a reality test that is better than bankruptcy.

Let me bring this concept to the Kidder Peabody environment. At that time of the debacle, Wall Street experts told me that trading Treasury STRIPs is generally a very low margin area of the fixed-income business. From this fact came their hypothesis that Jett's immediate supervisors did not really *understand* Treasury STRIPs trading—hence they could not control what was going on!

One expert suggested that in all likelihood, Kidder Peabody management felt its traders were running a low-risk, high-margin business—a sort of financial paradise. Even more curious is the fact that nobody questioned how these profits were made when it became evident that while Jett's desk produced king-size profit figures, adversity never hit. Other people said that Kidder's top management was in full conflict of interest—in other words, they knew what Jett was doing but ignored it because Jett's bogus profits served them as well because they could show their owner (General Electric) skyrocketing profit. But they eventually paid for this conflict of interest and creative accounting practice with their jobs.

Knowledgeable readers will observe the similitude between this Kidder Peabody case and that of the Barings Bank disaster, which came to the public eye a year later in February 1995. At Barings, an incompetent top management could not see that it was simply not possible that Nick Leeson generated only profits. If accounting suggests there are no losses to be seen, then management should understand that they are submerged somewhere. The nearest paradigm to the STRIPs case is that of someone who invested $1,000 and made $100,000 in profits out of it.

---

[1]*EIR*, December 24, 1999.

Joseph Jett's Defense Also Points to Poor Management Oversight

Every misfortune evidently yields different viewpoints. As Joseph Jett saw it, the whole mess was largely about race. Two and a half months after he was sacked from Kidder Peabody following his unprecedented trading scam, the trader gave every sign that he wanted to fight back, painting himself as the victim of a smear campaign. "They depicted me as being an urban black criminal," Jett said of Kidder and its parent, General Electric. "That is something I rail against. I have never in my life attempted to use my race as an advantage. I cannot allow it to be used as a weapon against me—and that is what Kidder and GE's public relations blitz was."[2]

Comparing himself with Mike Vranos (the Kidder Peabody mortgage bond chief whose bonus in 1993 topped even his own $9 million—more on Mike Vranos in Chapter 9), Jett said, "If you look at Vranos', progress and you look at mine, there is no difference—except that I'm older and better educated." If Jett sounds rather big-headed to you, consider the alternative. This is the only possible, reasonable, and logical answer from people who are paid millions of dollars each year in bonuses for exploiting accounting soft spots and generating big losses.

Jett did not seem to be ready to discuss the specific allegations that Kidder had leveled against him, but it was clear that he tried to implicate senior executives of the firm with which he worked. Referring to management oversight of his trading activities, he said, "Kidder is one of the flattest organizations on the street. The management is direct, it's right there. The things that made Kidder strong—the flatness of the organization—meant that management had to be involved."

Or, alternatively, this flat management structure is what made Kidder weak. It is good to have direct management, but direct management too must be controlled. If the top executives don't want to have anybody (for instance, the auditors) looking over their shoulders, if they maintain scanty accounting, if they put the back office under their thumb, and if they give internal control a leave, this creates a situation of no management control. It means that:

* They are mismanagers.
* They keep conflict of interest within easy reach.

---

[2]*Financial Times,* July 4, 1994.

- And they have an internal company culture that leaves much to
  be desired.

According to many Wall Street observers, the rise and fall of
Joseph Jett is a story with a moral about what happens when an ambi-
tious securities firm with lax controls gives too much power to a
trader with a checkered past. Joseph Jett was made redundant from
two previous trading jobs, yet was appointed head of Kidder's government bond desk after only two years with the firm.

THE PRICE OF MISMANAGEMENT: KIDDER PEABODY CEASED TO EXIST

As a result of the issuing losses, General Electric (the parent company
of Kidder Peabody) took a $210 million charge on $1.07 billion in
first-quarter 1994 earnings. But GE chairman Jack Welch implied that
the mess could have been avoided. "Clearly this man [Jett] couldn't
do it all alone. People either knowingly made errors or didn't see red
flags. No question, when Gary Lynch is through with this investigation, there will be findings."[3]

Joseph Jett, who claimed he was innocent, was being investigated by the Securities and Exchange Commission and the U.S.
Attorney's Office. These investigations as well as Lynch's finding
aside, Welch was absolutely right by any management standard. How
was Joseph Jett, a rather obscure government bond trader, able to
rack up $350 million in phony profits over a three-year period before
the firm found out about it? Kidder Peabody needed to answer these
questions:

- Why was management not more vigilant concerning the trader's
  deals?
- Who is to be held responsible for portfolio losses that add to
  dramatic write-offs?
- How did it happen that other major gaps also existed in the
  internal control armory, such as the CMOs overexposure?

---

[3] *BusinessWeek*, May 2, 1994.

Jack Welch was also proved right by the SEC when in early January 1996 it was officially announced that (after about two years delay) the Securities and Exchange Commission planned to file civil administrative charges against not only Joseph Jett but also two other former senior executives of Kidder Peabody (Edward Cerullo and Melvin Mullin), though Kidder, the company itself, was not formally charged with wrongdoing.

The SEC charges marked the most significant regulatory action resulting from the bond-trading scandal that triggered Kidder's demise after a long time on Wall Street. Slowly, it became known that the Joseph Jett story and the toxic waste from mortgage-backed financing were not Kidder Peabody's only scandals.

In another incident due to mismanagement, a trader on the interest rate swaps desk had been mispricing holdings of index-amortizing notes. That trader was fired, but his mispricing had cost the firm $12 million, and management decided to check every department for other hidden irregularities, accounting snafus, and auditing slippages.

For instance, in early March 1994 an auditor had concluded that Jett's positions showed a loss of about $3 million. Officially, this was reported as a profit distortion rather than a malpractice. Probably top management did not want to bother with a discrepancy of "only" $3 million, or somebody down the line did not think the $3 million was a big loss. But by the end of March 1994, adding accrued interest on Jett's forward sales, the auditors decided that Kidder's past profits had been inflated by about $300 million—a figure that grew subsequently to $350 million. It is indeed difficult to believe that a creative accounting figure of $3 million grows to $350 million within a couple of weeks. It is also difficult to accept that any serious manager would dismiss a $3 million loss as "profit distortion" rather than use it as an alarm signal.

And an alarm signal it was. The scandal that broke because these alarms were not followed up immediately by corrective action swallowed the once-proud brokerage firm. On December 16, 1994—the same year these findings came to light—PaineWebber took its pick of Kidder's assets and staff at a net cost of $170 million—a bargain basement price.

In late 1994, I heard on Wall Street that Kidder management not only did not sanction the malpractice when it was time to do so, but it seems management felt that Jett had brought a new dimension to the broker's low-key government desk. Within 18 months of his arrival, he was apparently by far the most profitable STRIPs traders on Wall Street. His bonus rose from just $5,000 in 1991 to $2 million in 1992 and $9 million in 1993. Also in 1993, Jett won the chairman's award for achievement—no minor deed.

Let me add this postmortem. In its report on the Jett affair, New York law firm Davis Polk & Wardwell claimed that Jett produced his stunning figures by taking advantage of a quirk in Kidder Peabody's accounting systems. Wall Street insiders said that in Jett's heyday other brokers, Kidder's rivals, would have paid almost anything to learn Jett's secret trading formula. Little did they know that the "formula" was a quirk.

To rub some more salt into the wound, it was widely discussed among financial analysts that Jett's $9 million bonus for 1993 had become a worldwide news item. The anticlimax came when Kidder froze the funds held by Jett in his company's cash management account.

But others took the money and ran. The $350 million of nonexistent profits had brought big bonuses for hundreds of other Kidder managers and employees. Curiously enough, from what I learned, none was asked to return all or part of the bonuses that had been paid out of creative accounting gimmicks and the resulting fictitious profits. This raises a number of other critical questions regarding management control—or the extreme lack thereof.

A BETTER MANAGEMENT STRATEGY: USING STATISTICAL QUALITY CONTROL CHARTS

Winston Churchill once said that the human donkey would not move unless it sees a carrot in the front and feels a stick in the back. Commissions like those awarded at Kidder Peabody are without any doubt a golden carrot. But what about the stick? Why should not there be a system of demerits, a reverse reward for short-term and long-term negatives associated with the dealer's behavior—like in the Kidder example, which blew up the firm?

Following the investment bank's senior losses, General Electric was fed up with the demerits and the money it had to pay as the broker's owner. The decision was not unexpected. On Sunday, October 16, 1994, it was announced that Kidder Peabody would be broken up, with its most attractive businesses transferred to Wall Street rival PaineWebber.

The official announcement made a day later ended GE's eight-year ownership of Kidder Peabody and the troubled record associated with it. The events we have seen in this chapter were not the only ones that rocked the boat. In the late 1980s, for instance, there was an insider trading scandal and loss-making junk bond holdings but, unlike the 1994 events, corrective action had followed swiftly.

Something had changed in Kidder's culture in the 1990s. Companies typically call managers on the carpet when their results fall below expectations. Yet, whether out of negligence or for other reasons, most chief executives never ask apparent "superstars" such as Joseph Jett to explain results that far exceed normal returns. Let me bring in perspective a lesson taught in industrial engineering on this very subject of outliers.

The reason why Frederick Winslow Taylor developed time study at Bethlehem Steel in 1912 is that workers' output varies and to plan production (as well as to institute an incentive system) one needs to know what constitutes a fair day's work. Nearly nine decades of experience demonstrate that in industry the ratio of higher to lower productivity tends to be 2.2. This ratio holds no matter what the absolute level of productivity is, and no matter how much the average grows, because of increasingly sophisticated technology.

Quantitative approaches to work measurement have given exceptional results in manufacturing, yet these approaches only now find their way into banking. General Electric Capital and J.P. Morgan have been the first financial institutions, to my knowledge, to implement GE's Six Sigma methodology for rigorous cost control and for significant improvements in quality assurance. To bolster performance, the Morgan Bank implemented Six Sigma through 300 projects that are squeezing costs out of everything. Channels under scrutiny range from distributing research results to selling derivatives.

Thousands of managers at J.P. Morgan attended "black belt" and "green belt" classes to learn how to slash costs while increasing sales. Signs were posted on a board in the training center's hallway. They read: Build Morgan, Enable Morgan, Kill Morgan. Douglas A. Warner, the Morgan Bank CEO, says these sessions helped to save $1.1 billion in 1999.[4]

---

[4] *BusinessWeek*, September 18, 2000.

At GE Capital, Six Sigma helped to significantly improve service quality. Business customers told GE Capital that for them a critical quality issue was how often a salesman could answer their questions directly, without delay.

Adhering to the Six Sigma data-gathering discipline, each salesman now keeps a meticulous diary, noting each time a customer asked him/her a question, and whether he or she was able to answer it immediately. Prior to Six Sigma, immediate answers took place only in 50% of all cases. Therefore, the effort was to deduce:

- Which types of questions salesmen are unprepared for,
- What training would fill that gap, and
- Which persons were best suited to the job of salesperson.

High quality of service and cost control correlate. Through another project on Six Sigma, GE Capital Mortgage identified the branch that best handles the flow of customer calls. Then, management used that model to redesign all processes in all other branches.

As Jack Welsh, General Electric's CEO, puts it: "Customers once found the mortgage corporation inaccessible nearly 24 percent of the time. Now they have a 99 percent chance of speaking to a GE person on the first try. And since 40 percent of their calls result in business, the return for GE Capital is already mounting into the millions."

The Contribution of Statistical Quality Control Charts to Sound Management

Statistical quality control charts, such as the examples in Figures 4.1 and 4.2, are a case in point. They help us to control the output of traders, investment advisors, and other banking professionals over time. They can also be linked to measurements of risk and return or any other crucial business factor that is quantitatively expressed.

The chart in Figure 4.1 is by variables. It plots the mean of the means $\overline{\overline{X}}$ of successive lots and the mean of the ranges $\overline{R}$ comparing the results to tolerances and upper/lower control limits.

This engineering concept can be applied in banking in a very rewarding way. The upper tolerance may be market risk or credit risk limits, depending on the domain in which the statistical quality control chart is applied. Or it may be quantitative metrics the bank develops to keep exposure under control for each individual trader.

The P chart in Figure 4.2 is by attributes. It plots the percent defective of a process. Alternatively, we may plot defects per unit of work. This is known as the C chart.

Figure 4.1
X̿ and R̄ Quality Control Charts for Mean and Range

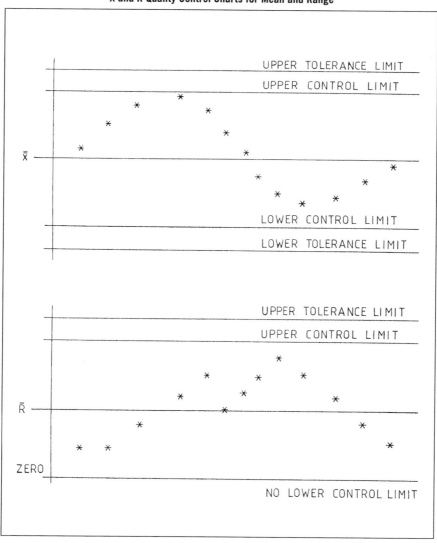

Figure 4.2

p̄ % Defective Chart: Monthly Performance in a Large Back-Office Operation

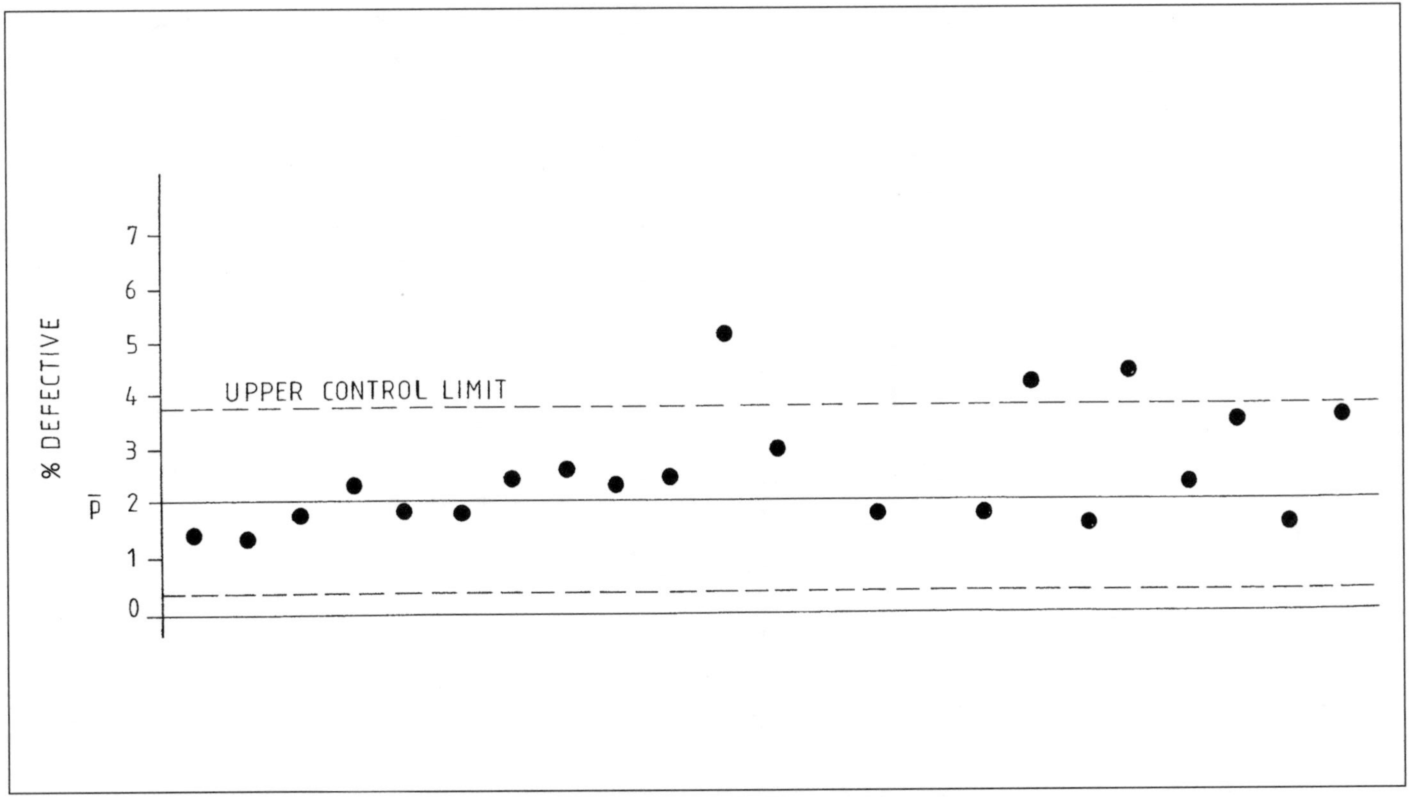

Control by attributes is of a go/no-go type. It can be successfully used in financial operations where continuous measurements are not feasible. In my meetings in the City and on Wall Street I heard many examples characterized by the parties I was talking to as "fouled up beyond any recognition" (FUBAR), which can be straightened up through percent defective controls.

One important implementation area of statistical quality control charts is that they permit top management to follow up on operations: plotting realizes (but does not yet recognize) benefits and associated exposures. Even if this were the only important implementation domain (and there are many others), statistical quality control charts would have an eminent role in finance. The trouble is that most institutions don't know them and therefore don't appreciate them.

Statistical quality control charts make it feasible to follow up on events intraday down to the level of each individual and desk in a way no other tool makes possible. For this reason, they are eminently fit to answer challenges associated with the new economy.

- **Senior management has a professional obligation to be tough, because showing mercy to one person's excesses opens the gates for other people's misfortunes.**

- **The tools we use must lend credibility to the saying that most frauds are picked up by people who ask knowledgeable and cutting questions and see through the aftermath of current actions.**

The first bullet is the message one gets by the fact that after General Electric sold its investment banking firm to PaineWebber, the latter significantly reduced Kidder's work force. One man's pleasures became a pain to thousands of people. As for the second bullet, cutting questions are always assisted through the analysis of pattern. This is part of the mission of GE's Six Sigma and of the statistical quality control charts.

THE BOTTOM LINE: WHAT KIDDER PEABODY COST GE

General Electric's troubles did not end with Kidder Peabody's sale. "GE is indemnifying us against all the liabilities of Kidder," said Donald Marron, PaineWebber's chairman. "GE is paying for all the down-sizing." Right after this statement was made, experts suggested there was every reason to believe that the bill was going to be quite salty.

General Electric took a charge of around $500 million as a result of Kidder's sale. This brought the total cost of its ill-fated involvement with investment banking to more than $1.5 billion. That's three times the money GE lost in the early 1970s in its foray into computers. Here are the statistics:

- GE paid $602 million for 80% of Kidder in 1986 and subsequently injected another $800 million of capital.
- By early 1994, Kidder had returned a total of $250 million in profits, but since then it had lost $85 million.

When the dust finally settled, the deal with PaineWebber was worth a net $90 million to GE. PaineWebber acquired Kidder's highly regarded retail stock brokering business, which generated around $500 million of revenues a year, as well as Kidder's fund management operation. It also took over parts of the firm's investment banking and trading businesses.

All counted, PaineWebber received an estimated $580 million in net assets from GE. In return, the securities firm issued $670 million of ordinary, convertible, and preferred shares to General Electric, which was supposed to give the industrial group a 25% interest in the resulting company—small potatoes when the size of the investment in Kidder was counted and when one accounts for the fact that General Electric kept all the unsalable parts and undertook to pay compensation to any Kidder staffers laid off by their new bosses. Before 1994 was over, part of these unsalables created $800 million of losses for GE Capital.

With the toxic waste that surfaced at GE Capital, the image-conscious General Electric was seen to have thrown away billions, including the write-off of investments in Kidder, the mortgage-backed financing losses, severance, and possible litigation settlements. The irony of this was that even when GE bought it in 1986 Kidder Peabody had been analyzed and turned down by several potential buyers. During the next eight years the company seems to have been chronically mismanaged. At the time, Six Sigma was not yet invented, and this deprived GE's top management of the pattern of Kidder's internal control.

At the beginning of 1994 Kidder Peabody held $12 billion of mortgage-backed bonds for its own account, a high leverage given its capital base. An obvious question, after the value of mortgagebackeds began to slide in February 1994, was whether Kidder had a realistic valuation of its holdings. Did it mark every security to an accurate bid price? Wall Street analysts thought that Kidder's own prices were unrealistic; they were too high and were not factual. But the broker's officials insisted that valuations were fair and marked-to-market and that positions were hedged wherever possible.

Traders at other brokerage houses were not convinced, so in May 1994 Kidder Peabody commissioned an independent valuation of its positions. This too did not change the general market sentiment. What is known in terms of valuation is that in mid-1994 Kidder had $73 billion in assets supported by just $778 million in equity. At face value this was a leverage of 1-to-94. It took four years for Long-Term Capital Management to match that record, as you will later read.

Where was Kidder's high gearing concentrated? Among the experts to whom I posed this query, few doubted that the fixed-income division accounted for most of the balance sheet explosion. The general opinion has been that:

- The firm was holding almost $94 in bonds, stocks, or other assets for every dollar of equity—a very risky ratio that compared badly with an average of 20:1 for the other main U.S. broker-dealers.

- Even if only total proprietary positions for Kidder's own account were counted, these stood at about $25 billion—still a high and perilous gearing in a market correction.

One lesson from this case that is directly applicable to all firms operating in the new economy is that General Electric never really controlled Kidder Peabody. Like most trading teams, the loyalty of the broker's traders was with the size of their next bonus checks.

- As an independent firm, Kidder had paid them so highly they had rarely been tempted to control their appetite for risk.

- The bonuses were legendary even when in reality there were losses, not profits, as in the case of Jett.

All by itself, the Jett affair was not enough to bring down Kidder Peabody. Even if the broker had to take a huge after-tax charge against first-quarter 1994 earnings, no Kidder customer lost any money. The big loser was General Electric, the proprietor, as attested by the fact that the majority of lawsuits filed were from GE shareholders.

In terms of sheer weight on the balance sheet of GE (the highest capitalized American company at that time), Kidder Peabody barely merited all the publicity it got. While the losses represented more than 10% of GE's equity capital of $26 billion in 1994, the profits were disproportionally low compared to this huge exposure.

GE's operating earnings of $6.6 billion for 1993 were more than 15 times Kidder's stated 1993 profits of $439 million. Yet General Electric did its best to reassure Kidder's clients and employees that it stood firmly behind its brokerage unit—in a way not unlike what Prudential Insurance did to reassure clients of its Prudential Bache Securities unit when the latter faced turmoil similar to that of PaineWebber we saw earlier in this chapter.

Were there no signals to foretell the downfall? There were, but they were not acted upon. Some Wall Street analysts pointed out that Kidder Peabody held big positions in the unmarketable parts of old mortgage-backed financial products. These were unmarketable because it was impossible to value them accurately. Therefore they were both dead weight and explosive.

The pricing problems of Kidder's inventoried positions were compounded by a sharp contraction in mortgage-backed liquidity. As issuance collapsed, many secondary market spreads widened significantly. In the event of a forced sale, Kidder might have lost over $100 million from the difference between inventory valuations and fire sale prices at which securities could really be sold. Some Wall Streeters also suggested that Kidder's mortgage portfolio was perceived as being unmanageable. Even accounting for the portfolio's impressive past contribution to Kidder's earnings and its turnaround potential, overall the operation was stuck in the red.

Let me add this in conclusion. Boards and CEOs of companies expanding by leaps and bounds in the new economy would do well to heed the advice of an Athenian senator in Shakespeare's *Timon of Athens:* "Nothing emboldens sin so much as mercy." An ever alert questioning management that is able to challenge the obvious and willing to punish wrongdoers, starting with executives at the top, is the best insurance that a company will continue to prosper.

CHAPTER 5

Lessons from the Long-Term Capital Management Meltdown

On Thursday, September 24, 1998, bank regulators in the United States scrambled to contain the financial fallout of the Long-Term Capital Management (LTCM) meltdown. Thursday was the "day after," when some of the world's largest commercial and investment banks (under the patronage of the Federal Reserve Bank of New York) put together a $3.5 billion rescue plan. The money was intended to save the highly geared hedge fund that teetered on the brink of collapse. Long-Term Capital Management was rapidly sinking under the weight of its wrong bets.

As first the rumors and then the news spread, the shares of all sorts of financial institutions fell sharply both in the United States and in Europe. Investors were concerned that in the end, the effort to keep Long-Term Capital Management afloat would not bear fruits.

The fall of what many insiders believed to be the most brilliantly engineered deals by a hedge fund had the potential to precipitate a financial crisis despite the market skills of three Salomon Brothers alumni (John Meriwether, Lawrence Hilibrand, and Eric Rosenfeld) and the rocket science know-how of the two Nobel Prize–winning economists (Dr. Robert Merton and Dr. Myron Scholes).

The people who set up shop as LTCM had a pedigree of sorts. At Salomon Brothers, for example, Lawrence Hilibrand collected a $23 million pay check in 1991 based on commissions. Merton and Scholes had won the 1997 Nobel prize in economics for their model for price options, which they introduced in 1972 together with the late Dr. Fischer Black.[1] While this failure in rocket science in no way means that models have lost their place in finance, it does carry two messages:

- Like people, models fail. Therefore one has to be aware of their limits.
- Lust and greed are much stronger than modeling, and they are deeply embedded in human nature.

In retrospect, losses mounted very fast on nearly $200 billion of the bets LTCM had done in financial markets around the world because the hedge fund was overgeared. To save the day, the Fed pressured commercial and investment banks to bail out LTCM because of concern about a financial market meltdown. The U.S. regulators would take no chances.

Neither was the Federal Reserve the only authority doing damage control. Britain's Financial Services Authority and the Swiss Banking Commission asked banks in their jurisdictions to provide details of their exposure to Long-Term Capital Management and other hedge funds. A lasting lesson was being learned on how fast gearing can get out of control.

FREE FALL OF THE BOND MARKET AND PAIRS TRADING

Long-Term Capital Management formally began trading in February 1994, the year that saw one of the biggest bond market routs. Many bondholders were desperate to sell at any price. As one of the few buyers, LTCM with its contrarian strategy found ample disparities between price and value, and the hedge fund returned 19.9% after fees for 1994.

In the first year of the new hedge fund's operations, the partners also noticed that 29-year U.S. Treasury bonds seemed cheap in relation to 30-year Treasuries. The hypothesis they made characterized many LTCM future trades: Values of the two bonds, the partners

---

[1]In 1994, Dr. Fischer Black won the Swiss Academies of Sciences Chorafas Award in finance.

figured, would converge over time. So they bought $2 billion of the 29-year Treasuries and sold short $2 billion of 30-year bonds, with this result:

- The bet worked and six months later they took a $25 million profit.
- Because of leveraging, they had only invested $12 million of capital used to execute the trade; therefore, the $25 million was manna from Heaven.

With this and similar strategies that exploited market anomalies, the new hedge fund's returns hit 42.8% in 1995 and 40.8% in 1996, always after fees. That outpaced the average performance of 16% to 17% by other hedge funds.

But leveraged success stories also proved to be LTCM's undoing. Soon its traders were no longer the only big players in bond arbitrage. Fast-growing competition squeezed the margins. So LTCM quietly began investing in more risky business—for instance, pairs trading, or convergence trading (which is discussed in Chapter 8).

In practical terms, convergence trading is dealing in two related stocks. This is known as a pairs trade. Essentially it is an arbitrage between two equities, often in the same industry, that tends to move closely together though sometimes has the nasty habit of diverging. Here is an example.

Shell Transport owns 40% of Royal Dutch/Shell Group, and Royal Dutch Petroleum owns 60% of Royal Dutch/Shell Group. Both Shell Transport and Royal Dutch get their income from dividends from Royal Dutch/Shell Group, but historically Shell had sold at an 18% discount to Royal Dutch. When the discount rose above the 18% level, LTCM bet that Shell was cheap compared to Royal Dutch. Therefore, it bought shares of Shell Transport and simultaneously sold shares of Royal Dutch.

In the background of this bet was the assumption that if oil stocks moved up, Shell would rise more than Royal Dutch. Alternatively, if oil stocks moved down, Shell would fall less than Royal Dutch, because it already sold at a discount. Instead, the stocks diverged even further leading to huge losses for LTCM.

Pairs trading can be very risky because the hypothesis behind it is really a speculation. On one try, LTCM lost some $100 million on a bet on the proposed takeover of MCI Communications by British

Telecom. But the hedge fund was lucky: eventually, it made the money back when MCI was bought by WorldCom.

Convergence trading can also be done in bonds. One of those practiced by LTCM exploited the gap between the returns on high-risk debt, such as Venezuelan government bonds and U.S. Treasury bills. Here was investor psychology at play:

- **A widening gap results from divergence in bond deals signaling that investors are getting scared.**
- **A narrowing gap, therefore convergence, shows that calm is returning to the financial markets.**

For example, as recently as October 1997, the J.P. Morgan emerging market bond index showed that an investor who bought an "emerging country" bond was demanding a return on an average of 330 basis points (3.3 percentage points) more than the return on a comparable U.S. government security. But in August 1998, Russia's default scared investors and the yield spread bulged to an enormous 1,705 basis points (17.05 percentage points) on September 10. The gap later shrunk to "only" 1,045 basis points, but banks, hedge funds, and treasurers that played pairs trading on Russian debt got burned.

LTCM also bought commercial mortgage-backed securities and shorted Treasury bonds, betting on a narrowing of the spreads between them. Contrary to its forecasts, the spreads more than doubled. Then in mid-October 1998, after the LTCM debacle, the spreads did narrow but only slightly.

Another convergence trading gamble that failed took place with European bonds versus U.S. Treasuries. The "experts" at LTCM favored the Europeans and shorted the Americans. But within a week after the Russian default, U.S. Treasuries were skyrocketing, throwing their relationship to other securities out of bed. The investors' panic caused the European bond market to fall apart. One after another, LTCM's biggest bets were blowing up, and no one could do anything about it.

Bonds were not the only worry. As the Dow Jones took a dive, in a few hours on August 21, 1998, the hedge fund had lost $150 million in a wager on the prices of two telecommunications stocks involved in a takeover. Then, a single bet tied to the U.S. bond market lost $100 million. Another $100 million evaporated in a similar trade in Britain.

Still another gamble that went sour for the superleveraged hedge fund was a bet on the convergence of short-term interest rates in Europe in advance of the January 1, 1999, introduction of the euro. Contrary to what the LTCM wizards prognosticated, Italian and German three-month Treasury rates (which had been slowly converging) diverged dramatically at the end of August 1998. Then, in mid-November 1998 (nearly two months after the LTCM debacle) they returned to the differential of midsummer 1998. That came too late for gamblers at the hedge fund.

SHORTING VOLATILITY: LTCM'S GAMBLE IN THE EQUITIES MARKET

LTCM was overleveraged not only in bonds, but also in equities. Because of its huge equities exposure, particularly in shorting volatility, the investment banks among its shareholders feared that if the hedge fund had to liquidate its large equity positions, there would be an earthquake in the stock market.

As David H. Komansky, the CEO of Merrill Lynch, suggested, "That whole potential scenario of unwinding their equity portfolio under a forced environment could have had extremely negative consequences on the [overall] market."[2] This is true of every fire sale of large propositions and there is no argument that leveraged investments also leverage the negative results.

"We were most concerned about the equity book," said Jon S. Corzine (then chairman of Goldman, Sachs), referring to LTCM's equity holdings. Because his firm stood to take a hit from market turmoil if the Long-Term Capital Management fund had gone bust, Goldman, Sachs now wants to see that finally hedge funds get regulated.

During a November 16, 1998, speech at a business meeting, Corzine endorsed "greater transparency and official reporting, if not regulatory requirements, for hedge funds." And as a Goldman, Sachs executive suggested in an interview, "If [a hedge fund] has borrowed $1 trillion, we should know about it. We're regulated. Why aren't they?"[3]

---

[2]*BusinessWeek*, November 9, 1998.
[3]*BusinessWeek*, November 30, 1998.

Many Wall Street experts were startled at the enormous size of many of LTCM's equity positions. Practically all counterparties seem to have known about the fixed-income gambles, but in all likelihood they had no idea about the extent of geared equity exposures. Although each firm that traded with LTCM knew about its own equity transactions, it was not aware of the extent of LTCM's trading with others or the amount of bets. As revealed with the bailout, LTCM was deeply involved in four types of equity deals: overall market volatility, pairs trading, total return swaps, and risk arbitrage.

The hedge fund's arbitrage position in merger stocks, which made up the risk arbitrage channel of operations, was some $6.5 billion. LTCM's bets in individual takeover stocks were said to be 5 to 10 times as large as those of other high flyers in Wall Street's risk arbitrage positions. Just as scary proved the hedge fund's total-return swaps. Rather than buying stocks and selling stocks short, LTCM aggressively used the total-return swaps strategy which had a dual aftermath: it geared up its own positions, and it shifted much of the risk from LTCM to its trading partners.

Total-return swaps permit one to capitalize on the discrepancy between the prices of two companies that have announced a merger but feature some anomaly in their stock pricing. This is another geared example of convergence trading. The case of Citicorp and Travelers is a case in point.

Considering the merger terms, Citicorp was underpriced relative to Travelers. Therefore, rather than buying Citicorp, LTCM bought a total-return swap from a bank which agreed to pay LTCM the total return on Citicorp stock, including stock appreciation and dividend. This allowed LTCM to own the stock without putting up a penny in margin. However, if Citicorp equity declined, LTCM had to pay the bank the decline in price.

To hedge itself with this deal, the counterparty that sold the swap had to buy Citicorp stock as a guaranty against a rise in stock price. In the case that Citicorp stock fell in price, this counterparty would ask LTCM for its money, but because the hedge fund was overexposed and the market turned against its bets, LTCM was fast running out of capital. Therefore, its counterparty was left with positions that were hard to make a buck or even to unwind.

LTCM also had a huge exposure in more traditional equity trading, but it did so in novel ways. Its bet was that swings in the stock market (which were quite wide) would revert to a more stable pattern. There was money to be made from that transition. Theoretically (but only theoretically), the principle is this:

- **The more volatile a stock, the more expensive the puts and calls connected to it.**
- **And the more volatile the overall stock market, the higher the prices of puts and calls on stock indexes.**

LTCM privately sold a large number of options in the debt and equity markets, gambling that it would buy them back cheaper and make a fat profit. The hypothesis made by its partners was that option prices would fall because market volatility would decrease. This too proved to be the wrong bet.

It is indeed difficult to understand why people who profess to be experts in the financial markets and are paid big money for their assumed know-how could not see that the word for 1998 was *volatility*. Volatility carries with it a significant amount of price risk, particularly in stocks. Keep in mind:

- **The market in 1998 was close to maximum P/E ratios.**
- **A richly valued market is highly vulnerable to any bad news.**

In early 1998, LTCM believed that stock market volatility was too high, which meant that puts and calls on the indexes were overpriced. On this belief, the hedge fund shorted volatility by selling puts and calls on stock indexes to Wall Street firms. The bet was that volatility would decline, so that the prices of these options would drop.

Contrary to these expectations, however, volatility zoomed and option prices reached record levels. Therefore, LTCM had to put up more collateral to cover its losses and maintain its put and call positions. This was another drain on its overleveraged resources, and the hedge fund was on its way to go bust.

"SUCKING UP NICKELS FROM ALL OVER THE WORLD"

LTCM's deals in equity arbitrage began in 1995, a year after the hedge fund was started. Its partners believed that their bond expertise was portable to equities and that they could be the masters of the New York Stock Exchange and other stock markets. Besides, they needed equity trading to provide for diversification (though, as shown in Chapter 8, diversification can also fail).

Theoretically (but only theoretically), stock arbitrage is similar to arbitrage in bonds. The trader would go long one bond and short another bond, in the expectation that the spread between the two bonds would converge to its historical relationship. Practically, however, equities have their own rules and their own secrets.

LTCM never bothered to cover its knowledge gap in equities. It did not hire an experienced equity arbitrageur. Rather, one of its partners, Lawrence E. Hilibrand, headed the hedge fund's move into equity arbitrage. At the time, at least one Wall Street analyst had predicted that this would not work. "I am not sure when the crunch will happen," he said in a meeting. "But I have no doubts that it will happen."

The statement about "no doubts" regarded both high leverage and special skills. During his time at Salomon Brothers, Lawrence Hilibrand made his name as a quantitative expert on mortgage-backed securities, but he was not known as an equities arbitrage expert. Yet, LTCM was doing complex deals:

- Going long on a basket of stocks of target companies, and
- Going short on a basket of other companies that were expected to acquire them (as described in the previous section).

Neither was LTCM limiting itself to the big deals. "Myron [Scholes] once told me they are sucking up nickels from all over the world," said Merton Miller, himself a Nobel Prize winner in economics. "But because they are so leveraged, that amounts to a lot of money"[4]—made or lost.

With the market moving the traders' way, for several years risk arbitrage was profitable for LTCM and many other hedge funds

---

[4]*The Wall Street Journal*, November 16, 1998.

whose strategy was fairly similar. But in August 1998 Long-Term Capital Management was hit with massive losses in both its geared fixed-income positions and its geared equity positions.

Clearly, diversification of risk had not decreased LTCM's risk exposure or its losses. As a result of adversity, LTCM was forced to liquidate its bets in risk arbitrage. It had to meet margin calls. And as several leveraged positions crumbled, the ball got rolling all the way to near bankruptcy.

There are parallels between LTCM's leveraged strategy and that which some years earlier had damaged other hedge funds and an assortment of speculators. Because this precedent happened in the bond market, it is surprising that Meriwether, Rosenfeld, and Hilibrand had not learned a lesson from it. People rarely really register the reasons for other people's pain, and even when they do, the memory is short lived.

Ironically, as if it were meant to be a reminder of past experience, the bond crash of 1994 was, in disguise, repeated in the third quarter of 1998, just before and shortly after LTCM's near bankruptcy. Nonperforming loans of emerging market debt added to that crisis by swallowing a massive chunk of the capital of international banks. LTCM made good money in the 1994 bond crisis but became one of the sufferers in that of 1998.

Some financial institutions estimated that losses in the United States, Japan, and Europe in total could potentially cause a $9 trillion contraction in lending—more than the GDP of the United States. While within a time frame of three to five years about half of these bad debts may be covered as banks liquidate the collateral behind them, bankers have no reason to underestimate the losses.

By October 1998, some analysts were saying that there was more than $1 trillion exposure with investors who had leveraged their bets by "only" 1-to-4 or 1-to-5 versus the 1-to-20, 1-to-30, 1-to-40, and 1-to-50 of the pros. Such high gearing made the credit crunch the nearest thing to a global capital crisis. Credit simply disappeared because banks would not intermediate. As an estimated 35% to 40% of the world's bank capital was going up in smoke, there was a massive shrinkage of credit in the global financial system, and this lasted some time.

For years economists would debate hedge funds' role in launching the East Asian crisis of July to November 1997. The credit crunch

starting in Asia in the second half of that year resulted from the
unwillingness or inability of banks to lend. By August 1998, the
Russian crisis hit the recovery timidly starting in the worst-affected
capital markets because of the 1997 events in East Asia, with this
effect on global markets:

- **Western capital markets dried up alarmingly after the Russian
  government defaulted on its debts in August 1998.**

- **But even in the months preceding the Russian crisis, the
  economic situation was precarious. It was a time to retrench
  rather than to expand.**

It is therefore most surprising that the investment experts and
their rocket scientists at LTCM not only kept but also expanded their
highly leveraged positions. With a more rational attitude, they would
have started to close down positions as fast and as much as the market could afford without a fire sale. Had they moved in a prudential
manner when the global alarm signals rang, the LTCM partners
would have avoided both loss of capital and loss of face.

Contrary to LTCM's bravado, as the eye of the storm seemed to
be around the corner, some of the better managed investment banks
and securities houses became averse to taking risks. They wanted to
rebuild balance sheets hurt by losses on lending to hedge funds and
emerging markets. This has resulted in unwillingness to trade, which
in turn made the markets illiquid.

In the aftermath of Russia and LTCM, bid–ask spreads in most
assets have risen sharply. This phenomenon, which had started in
Asia, migrated to Europe and America, and it paralyzed markets.
Indeed, in the aftermath of the 1997 crash of East Asia, the 1998
Russian bankruptcy, and LTCM's meltdown, investment banking is
much less profitable than it used to be.

There are other ironies to keep in mind in connection to these
events. Most commercial banks that rushed into investment banking
chose the wrong time for their conversion and lost a fortune. The
amount of money that went down the drain in risk taking is terrify-
ingly large. Trading in derivatives (particularly options) is a big reason behind big losses, because banks are mainly net sellers of options.
Keep in mind these principles of volatility:

- Profitability depends largely on accuracy in predicting that a market will be less volatile than buyers have assumed.

- If the market is more volatile, the banks will bleed, and many markets have been vastly more volatile than banks and hedge funds expected.

MARKET UNCERTAINTY, ILLIQUIDITY, AND HIGHLY LEVERAGED DEFAULTS

Highly liquid investments with maturities of three months or less and insignificant interest rate risk are usually classified as cash and cash equivalents. They are practically as good as cash in hand, but also they are an anathema to hedge funds because, instead of producing big profits, they are slightly more productive than money hidden in a mattress.

Investments with maturities greater than three months and less than one year are classified as short-term investments. These too do not generate big gains unless they are leveraged—leading to the strategy of LTCM and other hedge funds, which came unstuck.

Investments with maturities greater than one year but less than three years are medium-term, though some banks take as medium term the one-to-five–years time frame. Those of more than five years are classified as long-term investments, and whether they are liquid or illiquid depends on the nature of the instrument, the market in which it trades, and prevailing economic conditions.

A credit crunch can arise for a number of reasons. One is that banks lost so much money in nonperforming loans, derivatives, and other instruments that they are left with no more money to lend. Senior management must watch out for compliance to capital reserve requirements of 8% for international institutions and 4% for local ones; plus the reserves necessary for capital at risk because of trading exposure which is guestimated through value at risk (VAR) updates.

A second basic reason for a credit crunch is that—even if banks have money available—in a morose or highly uncertain market, credit risk is high and banks become risk-averse. Institutions usually do not make loans or at least are not proactive in looking for new clients when they know that they face inordinate counterparty exposure.

A credit crunch also comes into existence as consumers move their money out of savings accounts, time deposits, or the money market and into the capital market. By getting out of current accounts and savings and time deposits, they dry up the low-cost deposits base of financial intermediaries, leaving them with no ready capital to lend.

Savers can get into equities, government bonds, corporate bonds, junk bonds, initial public offerings (IPOs), and secondary offerings. They do so individually or through mutual funds and other vehicles. The money will be invested by fund managers in short-term or long-term investments. In either case, the public's money is denied to the intermediaries that usually provide funding to business and industry.

Companies too may desert the commercial banking sector, hiring an investment bank to help in issuing commercial paper. During most of the 1990s, this approach provided abundant capital at reasonable prices. But the major market correction in August-to-October 1998 had these effects on capital:

- The price of debt capital increased quite substantially,
- While the ability of companies to get new capital through debt issuance dropped.

This has debased the banking system. First, it deprived it of its traditional role of intermediation, and then it flushed into the market danger signals that made bankers run for cover. Excess speculation is at the heart of the second happening. Such speculation led to this effect on the market:

- **The quality spreads in the fixed income market in 1998 tended to stay at the wide side.**
- **At the same time, corporate profits weakened and corporate cash flow deficits widened.**

As if these conditions characterizing the second half of 1998 were not enough, the markets were hit by the likelihood that LTCM would be defaulting. On one hand, corporate liabilities were rising at an annual rate of more than 100% (at midyear 1998), and on the other, the stock market would have crumbled because of a massive unloading of leveraged deals.

If LTCM had defaulted, its counterparties would have been obliged to immediately close out their positions. If these counterparties had been able to do so at existing market prices prior to the default, their losses would have been rather affordable. By contrast, many experts thought that the capital market was ready to implode, because when many firms rush to close out hundreds of billions of dollars in transactions simultaneously, they are singularly unable to liquidate collateral or establish offsetting positions at previously existing prices.

Crises see to it that markets move sharply, and losses would have amounted to a torrent of red ink. Knowledgeable estimates indicated that several billion dollars of losses would have been experienced by the more than 75 counterparties of Long-Term Capital Management. As losses spread to other market participants, this would have led to tremendous uncertainty about how far prices could move downward.

Under these circumstances, there was a likelihood that a number of players in the credit market—and the interest rate market itself—would experience extreme price distress and possibly cease to function for a day or longer. This would have caused a vicious cycle:

- Loss of investor confidence,
- Rush out of private credits,
- A further widening of credit spreads, and
- More liquidations of positions.

Risky business (which had been the darling of financial markets until August 1998) suddenly became a pariah as greed gave way to fear of losing. By late October 1998, bank loans for securities purchases were up to 60% year-on-year, the highest ever. The banks seemed to be doing their share to support market conditions. Although some of this was the LTCM bailout, a lot of debt was still building up in the financial markets.

Are we really out of the woods? Although within seven months, the immediate LTCM crisis was temporarily contained, the problems that triggered it have not been. The months following LTCM's near bankruptcy saw a worldwide flight out of anything perceived as a risky investment into relatively safer major-nation sovereign debt, such as U.S. Treasury bills and bonds. Then the fever subsided but the market remained edgy till mid-1999.

RUNNING FOR COVER AFTER A MAJOR MELTDOWN

The reversal of fortunes and the undoing of LTCM unfolded on August 21, 1998. Calling from the four corners of the globe, the LTCM partners reported to the center that their markets had dried up. There were no buyers and no sellers. It was impossible to deal, let alone manage to get out of large leveraged trading bets.

Central bankers were doing their best to urge good sense to a global market that seemed committed to nonsense. The meltdown experienced by the hedge fund brought forward events not yet seen in the world of global finance. LTCM lost more than 90% of its assets by the time it was bailed out, and the markets were shaken for weeks. Here's the total fallout from LTCM:

- **Short-term, many sophisticated institutional investors were forced to redefine the ways they manage risk.**
- **Longer-term, LTCM triggered calls for tougher regulation of hedge funds and their wheeling and dealing.**

Some financial analysts suggested that a key reason behind LTCM's collapse was its accounting. It used net replacement value (NRV) principles rather than gross replacement value, and netting misled the partners into thinking that they were hedged. Therefore, the logic goes, netting should not be used in financial reporting.

That netting is a dangerous practice—even if a growing number of central banks and regulators (unwisely) now permit it—should be understood by nearly everybody though few admit it publicly. In fact, a much better example than LTCM is the netting done by Germany's Metallgesellschaft, which reached the brink of bankruptcy when its system of short and long futures contracts came unstuck. In my judgment:

- **There is a poor correlation between LTCM and the NRV practice, because there are a thousand other reasons why the hedge fund rushed to financial precipice.**
- **The most potent factor for LTCM's downfall was weak management, which was high on expectations of huge profits but downplayed prudential risk control.**

Although by all evidence its risk management system was lacking, LTCM was not shy in marketing its supposedly market-neutral stand (as shown in Chapter 8). It appealed to a very wealthy clientele who wanted to be able to tell people that their money was being managed by Nobel Prize winners and other winners with the Midas touch.

While supergearing was the order of the day, over four years, with only a couple of exceptions, practically nobody seems to have sensed that the superleveraged vehicle was approaching the precipice. Nor was anybody immune to the sales pitch when offered the opportunity to join. Banks, brokers, and even individual account managers invested millions for themselves and for clients, feeling lucky to have joined the A-Team.

The Nobel and Fed connections were essential. "Meriwether was very good at marketing them," says Roy Smith (a former Goldman, Sachs partner). "Investing in this thing was done on the basis of networking, wanting to do the cool thing and trusting the superstars."[5] This is as good an example of the herd syndrome as one can find.

While a sales pitch is an integral part of any business, for a financial firm excessive attention on marketing blurs the risk management lines and it can negatively affect the attention that must be paid to quality. For all their drummed-up expertise, the LTCM top brass didn't seem to have learned the basic principles of investing:

- **Risk and return are interrelated. Therefore, one must set reasonable objectives for returns, not extreme ones.**

- **Investment capital becomes a perishable commodity if not handled properly, and in investing one must expect the unexpected.**

- **Leverage works both ways. More money has been lost in searching for high yield than at the point of a gun.**

Because of being professionals in the investment business, Meriwether, Hilibrand, Rosenfeld, Mullins, Scholes, Merton, and the others should have appreciated that the management of other people's money is not a sport. It is, instead, an important concentrated

---

[5] *The Wall Street Journal*, November 16, 1998.

effort aimed to achieve predetermined financial goals, and it should balance risk tolerance with the desire to enhance capital gains.

Even allowing for the psychological aftermath of a middle-age crisis, men in their mid- to late 50s should have known that investment management practices are complex and time consuming. They require iron discipline, great patience, consistency in bets, and far-sighted control rather than an unheard-of 50-to-1 gearing. Both the pros and the individual investors should follow simple, time-tested tenets that improve the odds of achieving success and reduce the anxiety naturally associated with uncertain undertakings.

Nowhere are these principles more important than when handling money that is not one's own. In fact, it is beyond comprehension how the "experts" have failed to appreciate that no system works all of the time and that the rules guiding one investment vehicle (bonds) are not applicable to another vehicle (equities). Experience, like history, is a guide. It is not a template.

Playing at the Edge of the Abyss: Learning from LTCM and Other Recent Disasters

The details of a sound risk control policy are described in Part Three. Part Two presents real-life examples of what happens when a rigorous global risk control policy has taken a leave and, with it, management's own accountability. This is the story of Long-Term Capital Management, Tiger Management, and some other institutions.

CHAPTER 6

Managing Exposure to Greater Risk and More Types of Risk

The emergence of a market in financial derivatives during the 1980s was part of a much greater change in the nature of banking and trading. It came with the wave of disintermediation, globalization, new technology, and the wider use of networks replacing brick-and-mortar branches. These changes made banking more impersonal but more dynamic than ever before.

One characteristic of the 1990s was the market's rapid acceptance of derivative financial instruments. Financial derivatives and the new economy correlate. One of the basic patterns of both of them is leverage. The leverage of assets and liabilities has grown exponentially. In its heyday LTCM placed a guestimated $1 trillion in highly geared derivatives bets with only $4.8 billion in capital. But this highly geared net worth dropped to a "mere" $600 million by the time of the bailout in September 1988.[1]

The LTCM story is interesting as a case study in modern finance because the company's fate represents the sequel to the first shots of the new economy; the global economic earthquake that started in mid- to late 1997 with the deep crisis in East Asia (with examples discussed in Chapter 2), and followed up with the August 1998 crash in Russia. East Asia, Russia, and LTCM are milestones in the course of the new economy. They are the forerunners of events that will most likely unfold during the next 10, 20, or 30 years.

---

[1]*EIR*, January 21, 2000.

An interesting characteristic that East Asia, Russia, and LTCM have in common is that they represent the meltdown of mountains of liabilities. With globalization, the issuance of international debt, investments in multinational equity, the ability to tap the capital markets for commercial paper, and intensified over-the-counter (OTC) trades, the stage has been set for rapid developments in finance and banking by leveraging debt. Innovation was promoted by the migration into banking of research and development (R&D) activity, as institutions employed rocket scientists and went well beyond the well-established concept of more classical analytics.

R&D in banking largely concentrated on derivative financial instruments. Derivatives became the common denominator of innovative financial products and with them came a switch away from established exchanges. Bilateral agreements, however, brought with them a greater exposure in credit risk as well as the need to rate counterparties—a job effectively done both by credit institutions and by independent rating agencies.

By the early 1990s, the OTC market, particularly in interest rate swaps and currencies, was growing at a rate far in excess of exchange-traded instruments. This led to a morphing of financial risk and the introduction of new exposures beyond those of unexpected changes in prices or rates. Some of these new exposures were viewed as components of market risk, but counterparty default started taking center stage. Credit risk is, to a substantial medium, an integral part of counterparty risk.

Other risks to which senior management's attention has been brought include:

- Liquidity risk, resulting from a large and stressful or unexpected negative cash flow over a short period of time,

- Settlement risk, particularly associated with Herstatt-type exposure,

- Operational risk, which ranges from management skills to trading errors, fraud, and substandard technology, and

- Legal and regulatory risks, which significantly increase with cross border trades.

Herstatt-type risk is a good example of a class of exposure associated to globalization of financial service. In its fundamentals, it is the risk that while one of the counterparties has performed in accordance to its contract, the other party defaults before having executed its part of the same deal. To a large measure, Herstatt risk is legal risk that can happen with obligations binding counterparties in the same country. But it becomes much more complex in transborder deals, because different countries have different legislation regarding the aftermath of bankruptcy. Under continental European (Napoleonic) law, for example, the cut-off time is midnight; but under British law it is 12 noon. This difference can be significant in terms of the defaulting party's assets.

With globalization, banking strategy has been changing. From fundamentally domestic institutions many banks progressively became international, actively establishing extensive networks all over the globe as well as growing by acquisitions abroad. New markets have opportunities, but they also expose the institution to conditions its management is ill prepared to handle. One of them is the synergy between local and global volatility.

"The great emphasis on volatility in corporate finance we regard as nonsense," suggests Warren Buffett, one of the best known investors of the late 20th century. He adds, "As long as we are not risking the whole company on one throw of the dice, we don't mind volatility in results."[2] In fact, volatility should even be welcome because it provides excellent business opportunities, if and when you know how to manage your exposure. In the bottom line, whether you talk of market risk, credit risk, or any other risk, this is what risk management is all about.

RETHINKING YOUR EXPOSURE TO CREDIT RISK AND MARKET RISK

An entity is exposed to credit-related losses in the event of nonperformance by counterparties. Therefore, it is absolutely necessary to monitor creditworthiness of counterparties and default likelihood. The credit exposure resulting from all types of financial transactions is the fair value of contracts with a recognized positive fair value. By contrast, a negative fair value indicates market risk.

---

[2]Special issue of *Outstanding Investor Digest* on stockholders meeting of Berkshire Hathaway, September 24, 1998, volume XIII, numbers 3 and 4.

An entity is exposed to market risk arising from changes in interest rates, currency exchange rates, equity prices, and equity indices as well as other commodities. For instance, a company with products and services marketed in, say, 80 countries and with manufacturing sites in 10 countries is exposed to risks arising from changes in foreign exchange rates. To face these risks, companies do hedging but often fail to realize that hedging involves new types of exposure, sometimes with more unknowns than they were facing before the hedge.

In managing their foreign exchange risk, companies enter into various currency contracts. Principally, these are forward exchange contracts and purchased options. Companies manage interest rate risk primarily through the use of interest rate swaps and cap-and-floor agreements. The latter aim to achieve a cost-effective mix of fixed- and variable-rate indebtedness.

Entities that do not use instruments containing leveraged features may aim to change the tenor of existing indebtedness from fixed- to variable-rate debt or from variable- to fixed-rate debt, as the market warrants. They seek to limit the effects of rising interest rates on their variable-rate debt through the use of interest rate caps. Companies entering into this type of transaction often fail to appreciate the synergy between pricing an instrument and assumed risk.

Any financial product at any time is worth whatever the market thinks it is worth at that particular time. The price is set by market players, but not the true value. Here's the difference in these three terms:

- *Price* is what you pay,
- *Value* is what you get, and
- *Cost* is what you have incurred.

Risk is a big chunk of the cost, but few people see it that way until all hell breaks loose and they or their company loses a fortune. Then they are like a rat in a trap who no longer wants the cheese but the only thing left to do is to eat it.

Jack Ringwalt (former CEO of National Indemnity, an Omaha insurance company) used to state his philosophy in simple terms: "There is no such thing as a bad risk. There are only bad rates." (Ringwalt knew what he was saying. His specialty was unusual-risk auto insurance.)

Whether its top management understands it or not, practically every financial institution today—particularly ones with global operations and/or derivatives exposure—is taking unusual risks. What's more, this happens in the double sense of the word *unusual:* these are commitments involving extreme events (e.g., as Ringwalt targeted with his insurance,) and unusual risks in the sense that senior management is still unaware of them and their aftermath.

This is synonymous to wheeling and dealing in uncharted waters, with the result that management does not really know the dangers the institution faces. Add to this the near impossibility of doing one's own pricing, because the global market, rather than the company's own management, decides on prices—to protect the bottom line, management has to cut costs.

Dr. John Maynard Keynes is the first on record who, in the mid-1930s, brought attention on how crowds impact market prices. The stock market, the derivatives market, and any other market is essentially just a crowd of people, consisting of anyone buying, selling, or even only analyzing prices and risk factors at any one moment. Therefore, keep in mind these key points:

- **This crowd (which comprises the global market) resets prices every minute, and its decision is not negotiable or subject to appeal.**
- **This crowd action, reaction, or inaction make up the moment's market volatility and often volatility in the longer term.**

The often quoted John Maynard Keynes was also a fast learner. He once silenced a challenger by saying, "When I am wrong, I change my mind—what do you do?" But most senior managements are not of that calibre to change their mind when they are proven wrong; their deals are too dangerous to the firm or they turn sour practically overnight. Neither do they appreciate that no matter which is the product or instrument, their risk management strategy should be driven by these principles:

- **Return on investment (ROI) should be a prime objective.**
- **ROI should also guide the hand of all risk management efforts.**

By and large, the concept of return on investment is absent among traders and rocket scientists. They are concerned only with one thing: selling products to counterparties. Yet there is a basic theorem in the junction of trading and ROI. Managers and professionals should not only care about how many new contracts are signed and how much is sold in derivatives products. Nor should they be interested in an isolated number reflecting risk and return: instead, managers should monitor the following:

- The profit as a percentage of capital the entity puts at risk in its daily business, and
- The standards put in place to ensure that all trades abide by ROI and prudential rules.

Some of these standards might be contradictory—for instance, zero counterparty risk and high return on investment. As an example of misguided ROI, Figure 6.1 presents return on investment by "Indocam Strategie 5-7" over a five-year time frame. This is a French mutual fund investing in bonds. Promoted and managed by Credit Agricole, it invests only in French government securities, and has been rated AAA by Standard & Poor's.

Figure 6.1
A Five-Year Evolution of Performance by Indocam Strategie 5-7

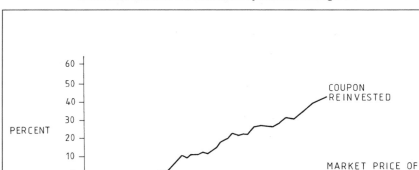

Figure 6.1 shows that the capital is secure, but the return is trivial: in fact, the fund's market price has the nasty habit of moving steadily south. The only benefit to the holder comes from reinvested coupons and even this reaches only 40% over a five-year time frame, in spite of compounding. This happens over a time frame where a two-digit ROI per year is not unusual.

Risk managers must be absolutely unwilling to relax their standards when performing all of the following functions:

- Developing instruments.
- Selling them to counterparties.
- Measuring performance in trading, giving loans, and doing investments.
- Computing risk exposure.

But to follow standards, risk managers must first know what they want to do and have set standards to guide their activities. By and large, trading errors are the result of people forgetting what they really want to achieve.

Finally, bankers, treasurers, traders, and investors often fail to appreciate that a series of market decisions does add up to a personality trait. If these decisions tend to be ill studied or reckless, then the person(s) who made them is (are) also reckless.

The best way to tune the accuracy of our decisions is to do postmortems. For example, Johnson & Johnson (J&J) has a policy of postmortems made two years after a big acquisition. This process involves senior management and takes the form of a rigorous audit. Here are just two benefits of evaluating previous deals and their concomitant risks:

- The postmortem control restates original projections and the primary reasons for the deal.
- It identifies the people who made the arguments and compares these arguments to how the deal worked out.

J&J's policy is highly effective. Its execution requires that hours are spent examining stupid blunders including quantification and qualification of projected effects, opportunity costs, risks and benefits in a return-on-investment sense, and assumed exposure. In a banking environment, postmortem control should be applied with counterparties as well as with all financial instruments in which your bank deals.

The Failure of LTCM Will Not Mean the End of Superleveraging

Senior management must be on the lookout for failures and potential failures seven days a week, 24 hours per day. Capitalizing on what has been learned with the superleveraging of assets, light-weight hypotheses, and rather incomplete models of LTCM vintage, regulators increasingly require banks to:

- Rethink their existing risk management systems and internal controls, and

- Disclose more about their exposure to hedge funds as both investors and lenders.

In all likelihood, during the coming years regulators will be slower in permitting financial institutions to do nontransparent use of their internal risk-management models in calculating how much capital they need to put aside. In one stroke, which came with LTCM's debacle, the days of great attention to models and of precommitment seem to be past.

It is well most likely that some of currently prevailing hypotheses may be quite inaccurate. In controlling their exposure, most banks assume that diversification across a wide range of markets and instruments reduces their risk. But as recent events show it is possible that different markets move in the same direction at once, amplifying the risks being taken rather than leveling them out.

Other changes too are in the wind. Because few rocket scientists have a banking background, regulators now worry that technology and the growth of global institutions that rely on risk models may increase the chance of further financial storms. Therefore, they would like to see a larger amount of capital held by financial firms to protect themselves against extreme conditions such as events that trigger a vicious liquidity-draining circle.

The 1997–98 crises in East Asia, Russia, and LTCM also strengthened those whose governments should be limiting guarantees to institutions that make only tightly circumscribed investments. These are known as narrow banks. This proposition poses the question of toughening capital requirements for institutions that are *diversified* and at the same time implicitly backed by taxpayers' money. The leading thought is that such institutions should not be allowed to indulge in superleveraging.

Faced with such changes in regulatory thinking necessary to avoid precipitating a systemic crisis, tier-1 institutions are developing an early warning system. "If you are worried about something in your business, the best thing to do is to correct it, and get back to your work as usual," said a senior British banker. "One of the worst things you can do is to get greedy, and go deeper and deeper into the situation worrying you searching for inordinate profits." Here are some general recommendations:

- **Financial institutions should be ready to make bold moves when others are fearful.**
- **But they should also be most careful regarding what happens next when others take an inordinate exposure.**

Dennis Healey, former chancellor of the exchequer, once stated the first law of holes: "When you are in one, stop digging." If John Merriwether, his Nobel Prize winners, and other pals had followed that advice, they would not have brought LTCM to the edge of the abyss, creating in the process the nearest thing to global system risk in the 1990s.

While greed is the motor behind superleveraging, an inordinate amount of exposure requires more than knowledge on how to design exotic instruments. Risk control is part and parcel of financial product design. When rigorous risk specifications are missing, supervisors are left with no other option than to tighten the reigns on leveraging.

There is no better way to dramatize the direct effects of leveraging than by bringing to the reader's attention the fact that in the late 1990s stock markets became a sideshow. Figure 6.2 shows the effects of this leverage by comparing the growth of U.S.-held derivative instruments to the growth of U.S. gross domestic product during the 1990s.

Figure 6.2
Gross Domestic Product versus Notional Principal in Derivatives in the U.S., 1990–99

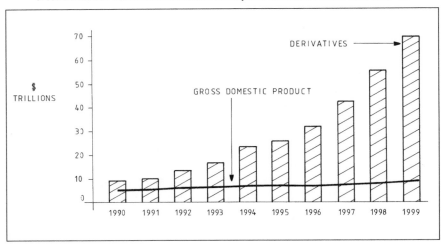

If notional amounts are considered, then in 1990 there were $9.6 trillion of derivatives in the United States, compared to a GDP of $5.8 trillion, or $1.66 in derivatives for every $1 of GDP. But consider these statistics, which characterized late 1998:

- The level of derivatives exposure had increased 474% to $55 trillion, while GDP in the United States had grown just 48%, to $8.5 trillion.

- This means that as 1998 came to a close there were $6.4 in derivatives for every $1 of GDP—always in notional principal amounts.

A different way of making this statement is that on December 31, 1998, in terms of GDP every man, woman, and child in the United States was leveraged 640% independently of whether he or she knew it, let alone agreed to it. There is no limit to how much the banking system can expand the money supply, had said former Federal Reserve chairman Dr. Marriner Eccles.

Notional principal amounts are not the true measure of exposure. This is obtained by demodulating the notional amount by a factor of 20 in case of credit risk—under conditions of normal inspection. Hence comparing true exposure to GDP, there was at the end of 1998 $0.32 of credit risk for every $1 in GDP. That's a high figure.

This ratio of 32 cents to the dollar becomes much higher if we pay attention to the fact that in America the real economy composed of manufacturing and agriculture represents much less than 32% of GDP. Figure 6.3 shows 50 years of U.S. employment trends for manufacturing and service industry employees. Consider this broad overview:

- **Today there is more money at risk with derivatives than is gained through real economy activities.**

- **That ratio is getting worse by the day, as the virtual economy expands at the expense of the real economy.**

Figure 6.3
50 Years of Manufacturing versus Service Industry Employment in the U.S., 1950–2000

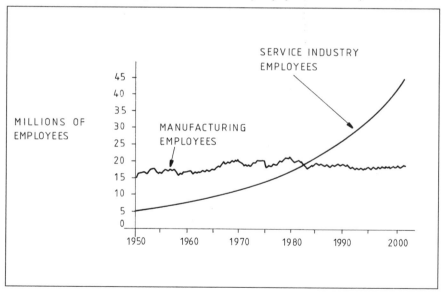

Finally, whether simple or sophisticated, financial products have to be sold and this often involves peculiar practices. During 1967 congressional hearings, Dr. Paul Samuelson testified that even a third of a century ago, 50,000 mutual fund salespeople, roughly 1 for every 70 investors, were combing the United States. Samuelson added that most were fully incompetent but kept pushing the products to consumers; what sustained them was the mutual funds industry's abusively high fees.

While salespeople are in the field marketing a growing array of financial products, bankers and rocket scientists are digging into databases and tearing apart data feeds in search for anomalies. "I have always found the word *anomaly* interesting," says Warren Buffett. "What it means is something the academicians can't explain, and rather than re-examine their theories they simply discard any evidence of that sort."

In classical science, when an analytical mind finds information contradicting existing theories, he or she feels the obligation to look at it rigorously. That is what Dr. Julian Huxley called, "a beautiful theory destroyed by a little nasty fact." The problem with the majority of people, however, is that their minds are conditioned to reject contradictory evidence or simply to express disbelief.

DEVELOPING A RIGOROUS RISK MANAGEMENT METHODOLOGY

Financial institutions with experience in establishing and following a rigorous risk management methodology appreciate that it operates on three levels:

1. It concentrates on precision in the method as well as in the definition of analytical tools that should be used.

2. It employs data mining and models to measure exposure and flash what might have existed but no longer does.

3. It uses a counterfactual technique on the premise that we cannot understand past events without understanding what did not happen but might have taken place if certain things had changed. With this, it experiments through what-if scenarios on the most likely aftermath of these "certain things."

Taken together, these three levels of reference show that to control exposure, risk managers must not only be concerned with cycles, fluctuations, patterns, changes, and repetitions of risk events, but must also challenge the obvious. They should ask questions that could only be answered over the long run. In the short run, they must focus on trader habits and observe top management rules for exposure.

The key is understanding the risk appetite of your bank and appreciating the aftermath of current actions. Much more than being a test of knowledge (and far from being an exercise in memorization), risk management is about understanding. LTCM's top brass, in the last analysis, took risks it did not understand. The best risk managers are those who have a flexible body of ideas and are able to marshal those ideas. Bear in mind these general principles:

- **Reading statistics and standard reports is too passive and far from being a rewarding exercise.**

- **Instead, risk managers need to engage in on-the-spot analysis, active revision of hypotheses, and stress testing.**

He or she must also keep close to the trading floor. During the Third Symposium on Risk Management, Financial Services Authority executive gave the example of two British banks.[3] One had 30 people doing risk management, but they were located 30 miles away from London where the headquarters was and where trading took place. The other had only five people to manage risk, but they were working on the trading floor close to the action. This second bank controlled its exposure much better than its competitor, which operated at a 30-mile distance.

The use of high technology is recommended because the human mind cannot easily integrate the huge volume of trading data as events take place and distill in real-time what is needed to effectively control exposure. The role of models, expert systems, and agents is to act as risk managers' assistants who inform their manager in a split second about anything out of tolerances as well as about all unwanted trends.

Motivated by the LTCM meltdown, in an effort to avoid its repetition in their own houses, top-tier banks calculate credit exposure on derivative transactions by using simulation, experimentation, and worst-case scenarios. However, in my research, I found that only a few top executives appreciate a worst-case scenario message.

---

[3]Geneva, Switzerland, March 22–24, 1999.

A worst case is essentially a hypothesis of unexpected happenings of remote-likelihood realistic events. We may be right, but we may also be wrong in thinking this worst case will take place—but we wish to know what would happen to our bank if it does. "The singular feature of the great crash [of 1929]," Dr. John Kenneth Galbraith once suggested, "was that the worst continued to worsen."

Compared to the more common models at the bottom of the food chain, a worst-case analysis is quite informative in terms of the possible aftermath of assumed exposure and its amplification because of greater than expected market volatility and/or counterparty risk. After LTCM, many knowledgeable bankers have disagreed with the approach taken by VAR (value at risk) and CreditMetrics of looking at a risk profile for a one-year fixed time horizon. Instead, they calculate risk by assessing the following:

- The risk distribution across time—for instance, until maturity of the instruments held in their portfolio, and
- The possibility of extreme events not accounted for by current models.

These strategies are a positive result of the LTCM meltdown. Other developments, however, are negative. About one third of the institutions that have developed their own VAR model incorporated hypotheses of diversification of risk across all their areas of operations as if, after it happens once, the diversification of risk becomes a permanent feature of business life.

Knowledgeable bankers know that this is untrue. The fact that such assumptions are made reveals a miscomprehension in exposure modeling because risk should be readily and easily assessed across all business lines, instruments, areas of operation, and counterparties—without netting and diversification assumptions.

The problem with these diversification assumptions, as well as with netting, is that these processes are typically too optimistic and therefore a long way from reality even if netting is now permitted by many regulators. Another problem the supervisors face with risk estimates made by different institutions under their authority has to do with the fact that they use different versions of VAR. Therefore, the results are not comparable from one bank to the other.

There is no general agreement on the number of distinct methodologies used to calculate value at risk. Parametric approaches and historical information are used by the majority, Monte Carlo simulation is employed by the more technologically advanced banks, while others employ "improved versions" such as parametric delta gamma.

A sound risk management methodology needs models, but not just any models. More disturbing is the false belief that VAR can solve practically all risk-connected problems. Also, a large number of bankers think that VAR captures both general and specific market risk as well as market risk and counterparty risk. These assumptions are false. Furthermore, more than 90% of banks making this statement have not yet integrated market risk and credit risk, nor do they have plans to do so in the near future.

Only a few tier-1 financial institutions appreciate that credit risk and market risk have to be combined, and therefore they have to get busy developing and using integrative methods. Also, only the few banks with successful experience in modeling understand that VAR alone is far from a sufficient measure of their exposure.

Because the general mindset is not accustomed to challenge the obvious, few institutions are ready to discuss the question of whether VAR should be replaced with a better model. In the general case, this query draws an ambiguous response. Only people and banks that have tested VAR's shortcomings are now saying that at the bottom line "VAR is just another measure, and it is based too much on historical data."

Some of the tougher VAR critics suggest it does not typically provide information on the size of the potential excess loss, because it does not account for extreme events. They also make the point that most likely the greatest VAR weakness is that it is frequently implemented by people and institutions that do not understand the implications of a poor risk-mapping methodology.

To correct one of the more glaring VAR weaknesses, clear-eyed financial analysts are now accounting for nonlinear risks. Slowly but surely nonlinear approximations are gaining favor in becoming one of the value-added features of modeling.

STRATEGIC ADVANTAGES IN A TECHNOLOGY-INTENSIVE FINANCIAL ENVIRONMENT

Depending on the supporting technology, including datamining, real-time computation, and interactive visualization, banks are or are not able to capitalize on intraday trading, exercise intraday control of exposure, reset limits that have gone out of tune with market variables, and detect on an instantaneous basis the violation of internal rules and directives by branches, desks, and traders. Yet, short of this ability, in a market more global, more innovative, more rewarding but also more risky than ever, top management is not in charge.

Experimentation and simulation provide a significant advantage to institutions that know how to capitalize on tools available to them. But not every tool will do, and only the steady upgrade of our concepts can offer true strategic advantages in a technology-intensive financial environment.

One reason that finance and economics are littered with broken forecasts is that, as market conditions change, old models prove to be unreliable. For instance, stocks used to respond predictably to a set of variables with which analysts were familiar for years: interest rates, inflation, price/earnings, and growth of corporate profits. Up to a point, these criteria remain elements of study and analysis. But the increasingly technology-driven economy has introduced new important variables.

Rapidly evolving technology-intensive economic and financial conditions greatly impact both corporate profits and investor behavior in a way not reflected by traditional guideposts. Analysts who tend to rely on static economic models developed decades ago miss the market pulse.

This statement is valid both for microeconomic analysis and for macroeconomics. One issue puzzling experts is the U.S. economy's resilience. In mid- to late 1997 and in mid-1998 when the meltdown in emerging markets spread and took down U.S. equities, analysts and business publications quickly concluded that, as *Fortune* put it, "The Crash of '98" has arrived. But the market proved them wrong.

Because the time-honored criteria used to judge an economy's resilience are no more holding water, some analysts have been changing the criteria guiding their strategic moves. In 1997, Fidelity Investments abandoned its practice of not buying companies it saw as overpriced. Instead, it decided to pay for companies with strong, sustainable profit growth.

Other money managers are looking at the best companies in any industry and are basically buying them at any price. This very choosy attitude accounts for the fact that the average stock at the New York

Stock Exchange and among midcaps fell 23% between March 1998 and March 1999—something old models do not explain, let alone foretell.

This does not mean that new models are infallible. What bankers and rocket scientists should learn from engineering and physics is that the risk of model failure is always present. In every evaluation, particularly one made with some degree of approximation, there are bound to be positions that are firmly priced (whether in gains or losses) and others whose value is questionable.

The reason for questionable or soft data may be the assumptions that were made, simplifications going hand-in-hand with modeling, or else obsolete, incomplete, or altogether missing data. Considering these questionable outcomes as defects, we can plot results in a c-chart of percent defective making it possible to visualize how well a model we have developed or chosen fits the pricing and risk characteristics of our portfolio.

After going through the wonders of VAR and other modeling artifacts, and after appreciating both their contributions and their shortcomings, the board and senior management should look for tools that provide sustainable strategic advantages rather than running the institution by headlines. In a highly competitive environment, banks able to depend on the information they use are ahead of the curve, leaving their competitors in the dust.

CHAPTER 7

Managing Risk in Highly Leveraged Institutions

There used to be a difference between hedge funds and managed futures funds. Hedge funds (whose historical development is briefly described in Chapter 8) use leverage in an attempt to beat the returns they would have made through a classical investment strategy. Managed futures funds, in contrast, use derivatives to speculate. Their deals particularly center on futures traded in exchanges on margin. Futures and options can be used to create financial gearing. They allow investors to gain market exposure to the underlying instrument with minimal investment of capital.

Futures make it possible to buy and sell securities that will not actually be priced until some future date, and do so on margin. At the same time, lenders, which are increasingly commercial banks, enter into transactions with highly leveraged institutions (HLI), enabling them to speculate.

This new trend has seen to it that since the mid-1990s the old dichotomy between types of alternative investment vehicles has become blurred. Practically all types of hedge funds today are trading in leveraged securities and are borrowing against assets from credit institutions. And in many investment banks (and at times commercial banks) there is hidden a hedge fund operator.

An example of instruments used for gearing are structured notes (discussed in more detail later in this chapter), which offer coupon formulas that are leveraged and move inversely to the direction of interest rates. Inverse floaters have a profile that maps the return pattern of a highly leveraged position in a fixed-rate bond, altering the classical concept of debt trading.

Credit institutions are regulated, but hedge funds and other HLI are not. Mutual funds too are regulated. The Securities and Exchange Commission (SEC) monitors the investment practices of registered open-end and closed-end mutual funds. It also makes them subject to certain constraints on leverage designed to protect investors by restricting high-risk gearing; here are two examples of such constraints:

- **American mutual funds are required to limit leverage to 50% assets preleverage, or 33% of assets postleverage.**

- **Mutual funds are also required to fully collateralize investments in futures with high-quality securities, thereby minimizing risk.**

A problem faced by regulators, however, is that the ongoing innovation in financial instruments has created a range of new exotic derivatives that have outpaced the existing regulatory framework. Mutual funds use these exotics for economic leverage reasons, knowing that such investments currently fall outside SEC limitations on gearing. With this background, let's look at leveraged and highly leveraged institutions as well as the risk management system they require.

RISKS INVOLVED IN GEARING UP

"We never wanted to leverage up," says Warren Buffett. "That's not our game. So we've never wanted to borrow a lot of money . . . We've got all of our money in Berkshire, along with virtually all our friends' and our relatives' money. Therefore, we never felt that we wanted to leverage up this company like it was just one of a portfolio of 100 stocks."[1] But other investments and financial institutions have exactly the opposite opinion.

As Chapter 1 explained, gearing (or leveraging) is the uncanny ability to have impact beyond one's normal reach characterized by resources under one's control. Behind this notion of a virtual amplification of assets is the hope of gaining outstanding profits. With gearing, however, comes a hefty amount of change in market behavior and morals as well as in financial responsibility.

---

[1] *Outstanding Investor Digest,* New York, NY, September 24, 1998.

A great deal of gearing in the financial market is the result of a search by investment managers for the silver bullet supposedly found in alternative investment strategies. "Alternative" is a misnomer because what such strategies are supposed to offer is a much higher return than otherwise available. This is typically done through leverage.

What bankers, treasurers, investors, and asset managers are seeking from leverage is means to make the money that they have go a long way. As explained in the introduction to this book, one strategy to do so is by effectively borrowing big amounts to speculate in the hope of improving investment returns. Another way is trading on margin. In both cases, if the bets go badly they will destroy the assets on which the whole pyramid rests.

By and large, the market knows "Who is Who" in leverage, but this does not deter dealing with HLIs. The concern for serious investors, including institutional investors, is that they are given little chance to assess the total level of leverage employed by a hedge fund or other HLI. This became quite clear during the LTCM debacle— for example, consider these alarming facts about LTCM:

- **LTCM reportedly had derivatives exposure of up to $1.4 trillion against a capital base of $4 billion.**
- **The problem was that not one of the banks that lent money to LTCM, or its direct investors, knew what the total exposure was.**

Theoretically (but only theoretically), the first people to know how much borrowing a fund has are the lenders, since leverage is difficult without them acting as the source of borrowing by HLI. Practically, this is not true of the hedge fund's lenders. To make matters more complex, money-center banks are eager not only to lend but also to trade in derivatives with the HLI.

This dual exposure magnifies the level of dependency one institution has on the other by an unprecedented amount of double gearing. Because of the risks involved in this game, the International Organization of Securities Commissions (IOSCO) set up a task force to examine highly leveraged institutions and their mode of work. Its mission is to look at a variety of issues including:

- Risk management,
- Internal controls,

- Settlement systems, and
- Public disclosure.

Some countries are now studying how to limit leverage and huge international money flows through taxation. In February 1999, the Danish parliament debated a proposal by the Socialist People's Party (a populist conservative party) that the government, through international organizations, investigate the possibility of implementing the "Tobin tax" on all speculative financial business. (Yale University Professor James Tobin has proposed to tax speculative profits in large currency transactions.)

Not everything is negative about leverage, as long as it does not come near to tearing apart the global financial system. In its fundamentals, leveraging is indivisible from innovations in the capital markets expanding the range of investments available to traders and account managers. Derivatives have increasingly become an important component of portfolios—and this has both pluses and minuses, for example:

- **Derivatives are used to hedge a portfolio's exposure to market risks as well as to structure unique risk-and-return profiles.**
- **But, at the same time, derivatives introduce more market risk and credit risk connected to all sorts of investments.**

For instance, short positions in futures contracts serve as a hedge against rising interest rates and are used to mitigate total portfolio risk. Yet, even such simple derivative instruments create economic leverage. Other products that offer higher yields than are otherwise available do so at the expense of greater total return volatility.

Securities lending too is an example of gearing. Repurchase agreements have been a source of incremental income for institutional investors as the lender charges a financing rate. Borrowers do not object to paying that rate because they use the assets they temporarily own for gearing. Theoretically, the lender achieves a low-risk source of income, and this looks like a good deal because of the repo transaction. But in practice, unacceptable risks may be incurred if the proceeds are reinvested in collateral or mismatched to the term of the lending agreement.

This makes it most important to determine whether lenders of securities are adequately compensated for the incremental credit risk, market risk, legal risk, and operational risk attendant to securities lending. The answer is not at all self-evident because the control of exposure requires skills in short supply, while increased competition has resulted in diminishing returns. Assumed exposure is not accompanied by a commensurate reward.

One of the ironies with gearing is that few bankers, treasurers, and investors are willing and able to understand that if they want a big upside, they should accept that there could be an even bigger downside. One of the more unsettling aspects of such downside is the number of unknowns embedded in the more complex financial instruments and in the newest markets, not just emerging markets.

The Internet stocks and brokers are an example of the newest domestic markets. In mid-April 1999, at its high water mark, Charles Schwab was trading at 170 times earnings and 42 times book value. By comparison, shares of Morgan Stanley Dean Witter (whose market value of $65 billion makes it the only pure brokerage firm with a value bigger than Schwab's) was trading at less than 18 times earnings and five times book value. The leading Internet stock brokerages have been attractive because investors thought that the potential return on every dollar they invest was far higher than what they earned elsewhere. Moreover, they do not have brick-and-mortar investments and brokers sitting around in branches. And they are trading on the strength of technological capital and the leverage this makes possible.

Investors have reacted as if Internet stocks are spinning gold through a new alchemy. Charles Schwab's market value has been more than double the $26 billion that would most likely have been assigned to Goldman, Sachs if it had gone public. This is a different kind of leverage done by willing buyers and willing sellers, and anyone in this crowd who is buying or selling should be able to follow a decent risk management strategy.

IMPROVING REGULATION AND OUTSIDE OVERSEEING OF HIGHLY LEVERAGED INSTITUTIONS

By and large, at least up to this time, when it comes to market risk taken with leveraged financial instruments, investors have been willing to act without their lawyers. There are, of course, exceptions to this statement, such as the court action against Bankers Trust by Procter & Gamble, Gibson's Greetings, and others; and the House of Lords ruling in favor of Hammersmith and Fulham. But so far legal risk has typically been contained.

Containment of legal risk is a result of the fact that supervisory authorities have taken care of unintended consequences from credit risk and market risk. There is plenty of both, whether we talk of over-the-counter trades or of established exchanges. Figure 7.1 gives a glimpse of publicly disclosed derivatives losses in the years 1987–99. Derivatives have become a highly leveraged market with HLIs at the core of the bubble.

In fact, this statement on leveraging is valid not only for derivatives but for other investments as well. Figure 7.2 shows a similar story to that of Figure 7.1, but this time in connection to stocks. It took the Dow Jones Industrial Average 66 years to get from 100 to 1,000, but only another 15 years to reach 10,000 in early trading on March 1999 and then, less than 30 days later, to hit 11,000 in intraday trading. The trend lines in Figure 7.1 and 7.2 have practically the same shape, but there is a major difference between them.

- At least up to this point, the rapid growth of Dow Jones (Figure 7.2) represents *gains* for investors.

- By contrast, what the reader sees in the derivatives trend (Figure 7.1) are *losses* from the miscalculation of risks taken with geared financial instruments.

By and large behind the ogive curve in Figure 7.1 are financial institutions with HLIs in the frontline. Both institutional and private investors are the motors propelling the steep rise in market valuation shown in Figure 7.2. How are the regulators reacting to the financial industry's big swing in the globalized economy? Here are at least two recommendations:

- **The Basle Committee on Banking Supervision and several national regulatory authorities favor an indirect control of hedge funds.**

- **They concentrate on encouraging banks to improve risk management practices in connection to loans they give to HLI.**

Figure 7.1
Publicly Disclosed Derivatives Losses, 1987–99

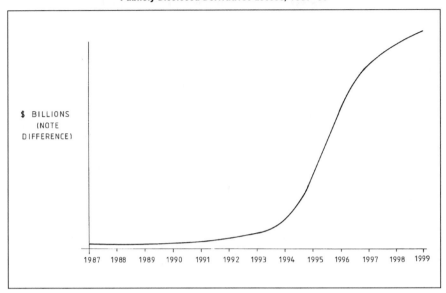

Figure 7.2
The Rapid Rise of the Dow Jones Industrial Average, 1960–99

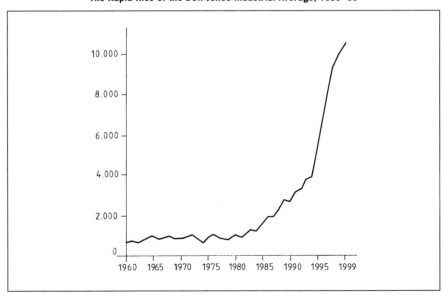

Not everybody, however, is in accord with this policy. On March 18, 1999, addressing the Futures Industry Association's annual International Futures Industry Conference in Boca Raton, Florida, outgoing Commodity Futures Trading Commission chairman Brooksley Born issued a strong warning on the dangers facing the global derivatives markets and likely aftermaths. "The LTCM episode demonstrates the unknown risks that the OTC derivatives market may pose to the U.S. economy and to financial stability around the world," Born warned. "It also illustrates the lack of transparency, excessive leverage, and insufficient prudential controls in this market, as well as the need for greater co-ordination and co-operation among domestic and international regulators. We must urgently address whether there are unacceptable regulatory gaps relating to trading by hedge funds and other large OTC derivatives market participants."

Current guidelines by the Basle Committee include the need for clear policies and procedures on an entity's risk appetite and a more rigorous credit standards-setting process as well as adequate information to make sound judgments of counterparty credit quality and due diligence. Among the requirements currently under discussion with a view to new regulation are:

- Developing more fundamental measures of potential future exposure, including collateralized derivatives exposures, and

- Handling such measures in conjunction with meaningful overall limits for counterparties, which are managed dynamically.

Underpinning such concepts is the requirement for stress-testing counterparty credit risk under a variety of scenarios that take into account liquidity and volatility prevailing in the market. Attention should also be paid to collateral arrangements, covenants, and termination provisions.

Other basic requirements include the assessment of counterparty credit quality and timely monitoring of counterparty transactions as well as credit exposure. The new risk management concept currently evolving is to try to do away with negative incentives set by regulators (e.g., those embedded in fixed ratios) that do not encourage banks to take proper account of counterparty risk and leverage.

A preliminary document following this examination of business relationships involving highly leveraged institutions contains an outline of possible direct or indirect approaches by supervisors. The

Basle Committee is rather in favor of a solution seeking at first to encourage an improvement in banks' risk management practices as counterparties to hedge funds.

The prevailing opinion seems to be that more direct regulation of HLIs may be necessary should indirect measures and an enhanced market transparency prove to be insufficient. A rumored depository of information on HLI, covering gross positions as well as net, would allow regulators to police prime brokerages. According to the Basle Committee, credit institutions must focus their attention on the following areas:

- Establishing clear policies and procedures that define a bank's risk appetite and drive the credit standard-setting process,
- Obtaining timely and adequate information to make sound judgments of counterparty credit quality and associated risk, and
- Performing due diligence and developing rigorous measures of both present and potential future exposure.

Another focal point is that of using advanced methods and tools to help set and monitor meaningful overall limits for counterparties. Adequate stress testing of counterparty credit risk under a variety of scenarios that take into account liquidity is also suggested. This would go beyond the credit risk models currently used.

Further emphasis is placed on closely linking nonprice terms to assessments of counterparty credit quality—including collateral arrangements, covenants, and termination provisions. Equally important is timely monitoring of counterparty transactions and credit exposure. This factor largely depends on the institution's technology—which, as noted, is not adequate enough.

In connection to enhanced transparency, the Basle Committee sets out two guidelines: a general review of adequacy of public disclosures provided by global players, and the concept of a credit register for bank loans to be extended to hedge funds, while providing adequate assurance of confidentiality of information.

The advent of a credit register would see to it that not only entities but also instruments are scrutinized. This is necessary because of the polyvalence of new financial products. Since the late 1990s we have seen an increase in credit-linked notes in which the investor takes the credit risk of reference securities. Such instruments often consist of government bond or corporate bond issues from an emerging market, and are normally owned by the counterparty.

The credit risk associated with these instruments is expressed through payment defaults on the reference securities. In some instances, the risk of payment default can be extended to any or all debt obligations of the reference entity. Eventually, the credit register will contain a great deal of information with relevance to bankers, treasurers, and investors. (See also in *Managing Credit Risk* the credit register kept by the Bundesbank and the knowledge engineering constructs the central bank uses to improve the accuracy of its contents.)[2]

RISK SECURITIZATION AND SUPERCATASTROPHES

One of the trends of the late 1990s was leveraging with structured financial instruments. An example is a highly leveraged structured product launched in 1998 when a Cayman Islands special-purpose vehicle (SPV) issued AAA-rated euro medium-term notes and commercial paper. The objective was leveraging equity capital raised from different institutional investments. The proceeds were invested in a portfolio of investment-grade assets managed on a daily basis through hedging.

This instrument was primarily medium- to long-term asset-backed debt. The issuers were financial institutions, corporations, and sovereigns. The cost of the instrument's debt was low because of good rating. The underwriter received a continuing fee for its role as investment manager, while investors expected to receive a LIBOR-plus return from the credit spread between the company's assets and the cost of its debt.

This is an example of risk securitization; it is a form of reinsurance because it involves the issuance to the capital market of products based on risks from industrial companies, banks, and insurance firms. Such products are addressed to institutional investors and high–net-worth individuals operating in the global capital market.

The method(s) of risk securitization may be complex, but its framework could be described simply. In return for payments that represent an interest rate higher than the one prevailing in the market, investors purchase a sort of insurance-linked bond issued by a credit institution, special-purpose vehicle, insurance company, or guarantor acting as a trustee. In general, these are securities with conditional

---

[2]D. N. Chorafas, "Analyzing, Rating, and Pricing the Probability of Default" in *Managing Credit Risk*, Vol. 1 (London: Euromoney, 2000).

or unconditional entitlement to repayment and the rate of interest and/or repayment of capital dependents on catastrophe risks.

Such risks are embedded in the instrument in question, which is the object of risk securitization. The issuer does the servicing of the securities either directly or through the trustee. The buyer takes credit risk as well as market risk.

This is the general reference line. What changes with new financial vehicles intended to cover a supercatastrophe is that the capital represented by the securities being issued will be used to cover the financial loss(es) defined by the description of catastrophe event if this indeed takes place.

The principle is that insurers and bankers assume risks of their clients and of their own firm. They always have to do so when they deal with risks. For instance, by means of credit, a bank allows its clients to operate. Credit is generally extended on the basis of profit and loss projections that, when the credit is offered, are uncertain. The bank also assumes risks when it sells options and futures.

For their part, institutional and other investors are potentially interested in investing in credit risks as a means of diversifying their portfolio. Therefore, it is not far fetched to believe that the capital markets will try to compete with insurers and reinsurers in assuming risks by investing in them—in a manner analogous to the Cayman Islands example, in connection to structured instruments.

One may of course argue that capital markets have not yet achieved a significant breakthrough in securitization of risks, let alone catastrophe risks. This, however, does not mean these instruments have no potential. On the contrary, there are various reasons why a market breakthrough might occur in the not-too-distant future.

There is a major difference between the way highly leveraged institutions operate today and what can be done through risk securitization for supercatastrophes. The by now classical way in which hedge funds operate is akin to people who think they found a fifth gear able to override economic fundamentals and excite investor psychology by promising higher-than-ever returns.

By contrast, the securitization of catastrophe risk premium is an extension of the work insurers do. Insurers assume risks on the *liabilities* side. In contrast, the capital markets primarily assume risks on the *assets* side though they are not averse to dealing with liabilities. Therefore, they may well be interested in assuming risks on the liabilities of the balance sheet.

This shift in emphasis placed by capital markets—from the assets to the liabilities side—fits well with the importance played by volatility and its impact on risk. This statement is made in a dual sense: because both credit risk and market risk lead to the notion of vulnerability, which has become a key issue in a dynamic financial system. Volatility is part of the larger aspect of the concept of vulnerability and its real-life impact. Moreover, limits to vulnerability are a constraint that could be addressed through securitization of risk.

Another reason why in coming years risk securitization might become a keyword for investors is that it makes it feasible to integrate the concept of extreme events by means, for instance, of extreme event securitization. In case no transferable catastrophe claims arise during the term of an insurance-linked bond, investors receive the following benefits:

- Full repayment of their capital since there will be no claims, and
- The maximum agreed rate of interest, less the fees of the trustee.

By contrast, if there are transferable catastrophe claims, the issuer is first reimbursed from the general fund of investors' capital. The investors only receive part of their capital if the claim is less than the general fund. Notice that this is neither market risk nor credit risk. Instead, it is risk related to natural and man-made catastrophes. (Keep this in mind when we talk of models for risk management.)

HANDLING EXTREME EVENTS THROUGH RISK SECURITIZATION

One of my professors at UCLA taught his students that the best way to analyze a situation full of unknowns (extreme events fit that description) is to move conceptually at a meta-level. This permits one to examine what is not yet common knowledge and to pursue an analytical approach in connection to what one doesn't already know.

This is why I chose the securitization of risk as an introductory theme to models for the control of exposure. Concomitant to this statement is the fact that a credit institution will be so much more successful in addressing the capital markets for reinsurance in connection to extreme events if it follows a policy that analyzes market developments at a high-up level.

Chapter 1 explained this issue and its importance, but Figure 7.3 presents a reminder. Briefly, the credit risks your bank faces are divided into three major classes: expected, unexpected, and catastrophic. Correspondingly, the financial cost is most likely to be:

- Small or average for *expected losses* that take place during the normal course of business,

- Big to very big for *unexpected losses* whose likelihood is lower, and

- Extreme in connection to *catastrophic events* that are very rare but do happen.

Typically, the existing credit risk models address the issue of expected losses, under certain hypotheses. By contrast, the method that I developed (and explain in *Managing Credit Risk*) can successfully address the risks in the second and third bullets. It can also be used for stress testing.

Figure 7.3
A Chi-Square Distribution Shows the Three Major Classes of Credit Exposure and Their Frequencies

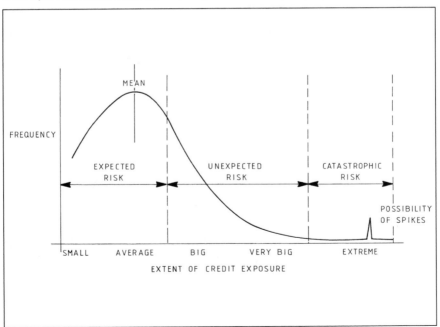

A bank can best benefit from its knowledge about this distribution of possible losses connected to its business if it has a system that can help absorb severe shocks. The securitization of risks connected to extreme events is part of this system. The financial institution able to benefit from this approach in the best possible manner must have in place a notion of accountability for each member of its board and senior management, because otherwise the system I am describing might become another sort of high leverage. Keep in mind these guidelines:

- **Accountability for managing risk should embrace objectives, policies, missions, and attitudes—in short, the whole business culture.**
- **Transparency as to accountability is crucial to the entity's wish to appeal to the capital markets to cover extreme events.**

The notions conveyed by these two issues are vital whichever of the avenues described in Figure 7.4 top management wishes to follow. Basically, the alternatives are between a direct approach for risk protection through global capital markets, and an indirect one. Up to a point, the indirect approach may use internal resources (such as own equity and reserves or hedging through derivatives). An external resource of the indirect approach would be, for example, established reinsurance channels.

Whichever strategy is chosen, senior management must remember that the potential size of supercatastrophe risks (i.e., of LTCM and similar size) may well exceed the capacity of one single channel—but, at least under current conditions, it is unlikely to reach the limits of the global capital market. Therefore, the option of more than one reinsurance strategy should also be examined.

In terms of interfacing between the entities demanding protection from big risks and the capital market, some experts discuss the possibility that a special-purpose company is licensed as a reinsurer and guarantor of catastrophe-linked bonds. Such interface could also be suitably employed to carry out the transfer of big risks to the capital market, acting in this capacity as a clearer, with the following effect:

- Investors would assume an entity's ongoing big risk(s) against regular interest payments.
- Risk transfer would depend on the occurrence or nonoccurrence of claims connected to insured extreme events.

Figure 7.4
Using the Capital Markets As a Risk Transfer Mechanism

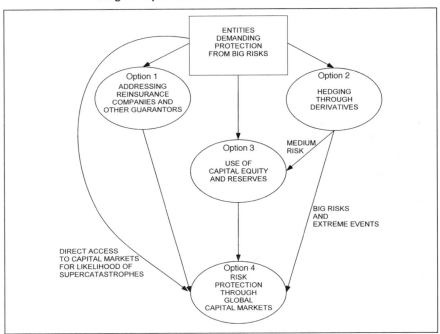

In the background of this process lies the fact that, like the new current practice of reinsurance by tapping the capital markets, extraordinary events in loans and investments can be used to transfer risk. The target is risks associated with extreme events with which the banking industry is not well acquainted so it does not know how to control them. Typically, these will be disaster risks.

For the purpose of placing catastrophe bonds, institutions could benefit from their public profile. Legislation and regulation are, however, necessary to limit possible Ponzi schemes some operators may put in motion once a catastrophe risk market starts developing. Indeed, the proposed solution for catastrophe reinsurance may well have the following disadvantages:

- Lack of understanding by most investors in the capital market of catastrophe securitization, and

- Fear that it might lead to a very lax risk control environment because checks and balances are not in place.

The appropriate legislation, adopted by at least all of the Group of Ten countries, enhanced through a proactive cross-border regulatory authority, can take care of these disadvantages. It can as well be the agent for ushering financial institutions into the new economy, making them knowledgeable advisors to their clients. By sharing counterparty risk with the capital market, banks recast themselves as ingenious asset managers and information technology experts—activities that are fee generators.

Investment banks and commercial banks are obliged to make this transition because it has already taken place on the end of their most important clients. Companies that traditionally depended on credit institutions for loans and financial engineering support are now running the show because these former client companies are well capitalized and far less regulated, with a strong view of financial risk.

Such firms are major players in the financing and investment game. Assisted by investment banks, they are issuing their own bonds, making markets in swaps, and running a full set of services competitive with banks. The mid–2000 announcement by Bank of America that it will sell part of its loans portfolio and concentrate on fees is, for any practical purpose, a reflection of this trend.

REINSURANCE-LINKED CLAIMS FOR CATASTROPHE RISKS

There are plenty of reasons why guarantors can play a key role in building market confidence in connection to catastrophe reinsurance schemes, such as those described in this chapter. Investors will look more positively toward the new instrument if securitized supercatastrophe risk has been underwritten by specialists with knowledge of:

- What may be involved in extreme events in credit risk, and
- How to do worst-case scenarios to analyze risk and return.

The process that I have described is basically a derivatives product because supercatastrophes are underliers. Both the nature and extent of securitized bond risk are derivatives, and they can differ as to form and extent from the underliers' risks. From this simple fact may result a whole new family of financial products.

The reinsurance risk being transferred under supercatastrophe bonds should be of a transparent, unambiguous, and demonstrably defined nature. In principle, this risk should be diversifiable. Investors must be able to evaluate the exposure to which they subscribe as well as determine the pricing of the supercatastrophe bonds and their ongoing fair value. This can be effectively done through information that permits risk and reward evaluations.

Most crucial to the success of a primary market will be the existence of a secondary market where supercatastrophe bonds can be traded. Other things being equal, these bonds will be more attractive to investors if they can be bought and sold during their term comparably to how American options are traded rather than European-type options.

All this is written in the understanding that the market for supercatastrophe bonds addressing extreme events in financial risk is not yet developed. Even for the securitization of more classical insurance contracts, the volumes of business to date have not been significant, but practically all markets have a slow, prudent start.

Some analysts believe that a key reason for a slow start in connection to supercatastrophe securitization in the insurance industry lies in the relatively small number of investors who are at present prepared to purchase insurance-linked bonds. Neither has there been enough information in their regard or a rigorous sales campaign.

Figure 7.5 presents in a nutshell how the suggested system could work. It is evident that information deficiencies have to be corrected. Mastery of the dynamics of the system as well as of supercatastrophe insurance technicalities could be instrumental in developing this kind of market. The links to be built up should extend over the whole portfolio of insured risk(s) from extreme events such as the meltdown of Long-Term Capital Management or another big hedge fund.

Extreme risk securitization solutions may be able to offer integrated coverage including multiple lines of business involving both credit risk and market risk. Precedence could play a key role. In the insurance business, for example, exists the concept of alternative risk transfer (ATR) whose coverage tends to be more cost-effective than traditional insurance or reinsurance.

With ATR, terms and conditions generally reflect the client's individual loss experience. Therefore, they tend to provide a certain degree of insulation from the more classical business cycles of the insurance market. At the same time, ATR solutions are personalized rather than resting on collective risk sharing—as is the case with other insurance and reinsurance schemes.

Another characteristic of the evolution in the insurance/reinsurance market (which should be of interest to financial institutions confronted with extreme events in credit risk) is that to gain competitive advantage, insurers are systematically looking for opportunities to save on transaction costs. The process of risk intermediation is streamlined by means of disintermediation:

- Both companies and their clients profit from a leaner value chain in commercial business.
- At the same time, financial risks are moving closer to tailor-making the client's exposure.

Figure 7.5
Reinsurance-Linked Claims for Catastrophe Risks Confronting a Financial Entity

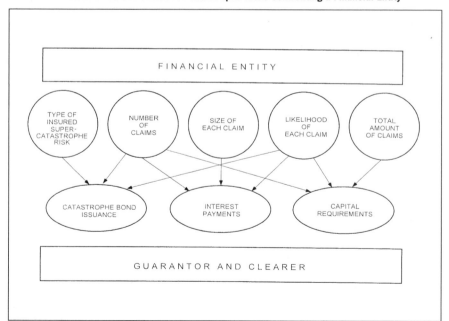

The Internet has been suggested as a catalyst to the securitization of risk along the described line, at least in connection to expected risks. Part of the reason is the excitement about brokerages that do business online and the broader market enthusiasm for companies linked to the Internet. Unlike their peers in many of the Internet-related industries, several of the online brokers are already profitable. In addition, their valuations are exponentially larger than those of brokerages still depending on brick and mortar (as discussed earlier in this chapter).

A more potent reason is that the Internet can reach vast market strata at low transaction cost. Because this might turn risk securitization in a modern version of Lloyds names, however, clear regulatory rules are necessary before the general public's appetites open to credit risk securitization though a popular medium like the Internet. The Securities and Exchange Commission should have full authority to deal with this market before it assumes dimensions that become difficult to control.

New challenges require imaginative solutions, and these generally involve nontraditional rules and supervisory chores, because they have to do with nontraditional risk transfers and risk financing techniques. Supercatastrophe reinsurance for credit institutions falls in this category. A similar statement is valid for all instruments that can be hard hit by outliers to the "normal" trend of business and associated exposure. Outliers, for instance, may consist of:

- Unpredictable high-frequency losses,
- One-tantum high-severity events, and
- Losses that may not be reliably predicted over a period of several years.

Both high-frequency losses and low-frequency/high-severity exposures threaten a company's very existence. Therefore, they require a form of risk transfer services priced specifically according to the nature of exposure. But risk securitization should in no way become carte blanche for frivolous risk taking, as it happened in the case of Long-Term Capital Management.

Provided that this solution is approached in the most serious manner, ingenious design features can see to it that extreme event reinsurance could even cover risks that are traditionally considered uninsurable. By securitizing different, not perfectly correlated exposures—and exposure that can be proven as not being correlated—even political risks may be handled. The key lies in rigorous analytics and an undisputed documentation.

CONCLUSION

The objective of a new departure to risk management through securitization is to enhance value by avoiding large hits to earnings. This might be accomplished by transferring risks to capital markets. Gigantic risks could be addressed by the capital market because of its enormous financial capacity and its steady search for better return. But the market players would not move into action until a reliable system of risk control assures them that the underwriters are in charge of their business and they are dependable in what they are doing. Keep this in mind when we talk about hedge funds and LTCM, in Chapter 8.

CHAPTER 8

The Art of Risk Management with Hedge Funds

Although most people associate hedge funds with George Soros, Julian Robertson, and some other high fliers, their origin is more mundane. The first hedge fund was formed in 1949 by Alfred Winslow Jones and, at least theoretically, hedging was its primary goal. The name *hedge fund* dates from this beginning. Half the entity's capital was used to buy long positions, mainly undervalued shares; the other half was used for short-selling equities considered to be undervalued. The theory has been that the long position was more or less hedged by the short position.

Today, the use of the term hedge fund is confusing because it tends to suggest these entities mainly pursue hedging strategies, which is not the case. On the contrary, hedge funds deliberately assume risks in pursuit of self-imposed performance targets. In the five decades following the appearance of highly geared hedge funds, their number increased steadily and considerably, and their goals significantly diverged:

- By 1999, there were more than 5,000 hedge funds worldwide, more than 3,000 of which were managed in the United States.
- Among them, these 5,000 hedge funds managed an estimated $200 billion to $400 billion coming from a variety of investors.

Official figures are not available and the real amount tends to be toward the upper limit of this range, short of a market meltdown. There is no simple definition of how this money is invested by hedge funds because each has its own strategies, managerial culture, and business characteristics. Usually, however, under the hedge fund name are institutions that have certain things in common:

- They are structured as limited partnerships,
- They tend to operate offshore,
- They are largely unregulated, and
- They charge big fees: 20% of profits or more.

Another common characteristic of hedge funds is their excessive use of leverage. In late September 1998, the near bankruptcy of Long-Term Capital Management (LTCM) brought home the perils from high gearing which has become a policy when investing in derivatives— whether interest rates, currencies, equity indices, or other products.

A high exposure is the result of superleveraging along the breadth of a hedge fund's operations. In a report released in October 1999 (a little over a year after Long-Term Capital Management came to its knees), the U.S. General Accounting Office (GAO) concluded that the case of the hedge fund shows that "regulators need to focus greater attention in systemic risk."

The GAO is not alone in this conclusion. Other entities too have by now developed some interesting views of the LTCM affair. For instance, since the $3.5 billion September 1998 bailout engineered by the Fed of New York, Asians have taken a second look at the way the hedge funds/IMF system operates and, according to rumor, concluded that globalization should be discredited as a crooked financiers' scam. This may be one reason behind South Korean government's refusal to sell off bankrupt Daewoo (as described in Chapter 2).

There is still another common ground between hedge funds and the new economy that should be emphasized. This is the fact that because they are currently almost entirely unregulated, hedge funds are being used by trading desks at a bank or broker for speculative purposes in the (vain) hope of hitting the jackpot. There is a synergy between hedge funds and the banking industry. Keep in mind these points:

- **Such massively leveraged bets as LTCMs are usually financed through bank loans.**
- **But at the same time, massive leveraged bets can go bad with a vengeance, tearing the global financial fabric apart.**

Limits must be placed on leverage. But what sort of limits? In the wake of the LTCM disaster, financial experts suggest that regulators need to set trigger points at which banks, funds, and all sorts of companies—private or public—would be forced to disclose their leverage but not necessarily their investment strategies.

Rules to control the amount of gearing should apply to any investment vehicle doing business with financial institutions. This includes all sorts of offshore funds run by banks, as well as independent hedge funds and trading firms. Regulators talk about a close look at the loans banks give to hedge funds, but stop short of sweeping measures.

How the Hedge Funds Business Is Similar to Arbitrage

Hedge funds are not registered. To avoid prudential supervision, they structure themselves so that they do not need to register with supervisory authorities. This makes a very significant difference not only because they escape regulation but also because registered funds have a ceiling of leverage of 300%, which is essentially 3-to-1.

Hedge funds don't have any leverage ceiling. For some years there was a sort of self-discipline in leveraging up to 5-to-1. By the mid-1990s this had been 10-to-1, then 20-to-1, but the lack of a ceiling in leveraging enabled Long-Term Capital Management to reach well beyond the 50-to-1 gearing of its capital. Eventually this led to its downfall. Because they are not regulated, hedge funds take major risks. In brief, they concentrate on making big money, and they are not interested in outperforming an index.

Yet, in spite of their high gearing many hedge funds see themselves not as speculators but as arbitrageurs. They define their work as going after assets whose prices are temporarily out of line with their fundamental values—the so-called anomalies. This definition, however, is mostly smoke and mirrors.

Because solutions connected to problems of superleveraging are so complex, Bill Clinton instituted the President's Working Group on Financial Markets including (among other members) the secretary of Treasury, chairman of the Federal Reserve, and chairman of the Securities and Exchange Commission. The members of this group don't comment on their deliberations, but there apparently is no unanimity on the best course to follow to bring hedge funds excesses under control.

In the answers he gave to the House Banking Committee on September 16, 1998, Dr. Alan Greenspan stated that hedge funds "are strongly regulated by those who lend them money." Robert Rubin, however, countered this argument by stating, "It assumes that the creditors are careful." Rubin (a former CEO of Goldman, Sachs and Wall Street trader) believes that when times are good, even smart people can do very dumb things.

Many cognizant financial analysts are of the same opinion. They say that what hedge funds really do is *expectations arbitrage,* which is defined as risk taking in situations where there is a likelihood that the chances of making a profit exceed the chances of making a loss. This involves both risk taking and betting—usually the big way.

In conducting their business, hedge funds follow many strategies. Some bet on macroeconomic factors and trends, such as the direction of an exchange rate. Others focus on special events, such as bankruptcies or mergers. Many special events offer expectation arbitrage opportunities. Those hedge funds that don't shy away from saying that they speculate add that there is nothing wrong in that. Markets need speculators. By taking one side of a trade that others do not want, speculators improve liquidity.

How much money do hedge funds borrow in order to speculate? About one out of four say that they do not borrow at all, while about half borrow roughly the amount of equity their investors put into them. Wall Street as a whole, however, believes that a more representative figure is a 2-to-1 or 3-to-1 leverage. Among the remaining quarter, the gearing factor goes from 3-to-1 to 30-to-1, with an average somewhat above 10-to-1 at least for the time being. LTCM was probably unique in its very high geared borrowing of more than 50-to-1.

Because hedge funds are secretive about the money they have under management, there exist no reliable statistics on their finance. The best thing available is educated guesses, which suggest that in 1998 money under management by hedge funds was about $340 billion. Consider the impact of this amount of money:

- **Taking this figure at face value and accounting for the more than 10-to-1 average leverage factor, hedge funds have under control real and virtual assets of about $4 trillion.**

- **This is nearly half the gross national product of the United States, and no central bank has enough funds to withstand an onslaught of such big money.**

Therefore, given the lack of regulation and supervision, hedge funds could easily tear apart the world's financial fabric. The extent of damage depends on their gearing and their strategy of taking ever greater risks. Many hedge funds follow this strategy in betting:

- **When the bet is relatively safe, the profit to be made is small— unless one bets big, increasing by so much the second- and third- wave effects.**
- **That is why the large hedge funds, such as Quantum and LTCM, depend more on derivatives to leverage their bets than do the smaller and quieter hedge funds.**

Although some regulators tend to assure that even the most lever- aged hedge funds would not have a devastating effect on the global economy, market circumstances may decide otherwise. For instance, the fall in the western stock markets in August 1998 and the Russian meltdown produced hefty losses for everybody who was highly lever- aged. George Soros was said to have lost $4 billion out of $21.5 billion under management. Half this money went down the drain in Russia, out of a crisis Soros himself helped to produce. The worst day (which took care of the other half of the money he lost) was August 31, 1998, when the Dow Jones Index fell by 512 points.

Yet, in spite of losing nearly 20% of its capital, Soros Fund Management showed a 7.45% gain for 1998 because of large gains in other transactions. Other big losers in 1998 among the hedge funds have been Leon Cooperman, Marty Zweig, Jo DiMenna, and Julian Robertson. The latter lost a rumored $800 million. As a percentage of its capital, the biggest of all losers was John Meriwether and his Long-Term Capital Management. At the end of August 1998, Meriwether's hedge fund had lost $2.1 billion (42% of its assets).

How LTCM Benefited from the Hype of "Market-Neutral" Hedge Funds

One of the issues that seems to preoccupy the financial community is that limiting leverage might cut into the derivatives business. If that's the case, so much the better. LTCM's near cataclysm proves that the risks from overblown gearing do not justify the rewards it can provide to a few "winners." The financial market is too important to be placed at risk by irresponsible excesses.

The near bankruptcy of LTCM in September 1998 highlights the risks inherent in hedge funds and their trades, which become increasingly complex. Hedge funds have come a long way from their origins when they bought securities they found to be undervalued and sold short other securities deemed overvalued. For the first two decades of this industry sector, the game plan was to try to be immune to movements in the market but to benefit from pricing inefficiencies.

However, as the market for old instruments became very competitive and the margins shrank, hedge funds broadened their field of activity to include unregulated investment pools of all types. In so doing, they used leverage through bank loans and derivative financial instruments. The Nobel Prize winners and other rocket scientists working for LTCM particularly labored to identify pricing discrepancies (or anomalies) between bonds from different countries and between corporate and government bonds.

Long-Term Capital Management also borrowed very heavily to gear up its bets, and found parties willing to pour in big money. In the end, LTCM proved to be more money-hungry than other hedge funds. It was necessary to employ so much debt because the trades did not target the securities themselves but the spread between them. This spread was the object of speculation, and it had these results:

- **As the spread moves, the value of an underlying portfolio may change only fractionally.**
- **But because of high gearing, the value of the fund's capital may swing wildly, hopefully to the positive side.**

A large part of the risk is that the market may move the other way than the prognosticators suggested and to such an extent that, to stay in business, the fund needs a massive capital injection in a hurry. LTCM is a good example. Short of this, the bleeding may be so massive that the only way out is bankruptcy.

A great deal of this game of superleveraging is played on the strength of the so-called greater fool theory, under which an investor can safely buy even the riskiest piece of paper under the assumption that it can always be sold to some bigger fool. In the world of the greater fool,

- Companies with poor credit ratings sell billions of dollars worth of junk bonds and they find takers,
- Unwisely, banks make billions of dollars of loans to companies and individuals who are deemed poor credit risks, and
- Hedge funds take wild bets with other people's money while, like LTCM, most of them believe they are too big to fail.

The irony is that these wild bets are presented to investors as being "market-neutral" strategies. Indeed, one of the many misconceptions found in new financial theories is the so-called "X-neutral": delta-neutral, gamma-neutral, market-neutral. If you believe these claims, you will believe anything and you fully deserve your losses.

Market-neutral strategies were Long-Term Capital Management's field of special interest and expertise—and we have seen the results. In fact, LTCM had even branded its bets, giving them identities, to distinguish them from everything else out there. One of LTCM's specialties was to exploit tiny differences between the price of a newly issued, or *on-the-run*, 30-year U.S. Treasury bond and a similar 30-year Treasury issued previously (known as *off-the-run*).

Investors use off-the-run Treasury issues to take advantage of their higher yields. But because there is little economic reason for these bonds to have different yields, speculators are buying off-the-run Treasuries and selling their on-the-run counterparts short. This sounds like the work of a genius. There are two problems however:

- The potential profits are no more than a few basis points, and
- To make money in this way, speculators must multiply their bets by borrowing.

Knowledgeable analysts suggest that in LTCM's case, such positions were leveraged up to 40-to-1, while at the same time the hedge fund was superleveraged (albeit at a lower ratio) on its bet that yields on European mortgage-backed securities would converge with those on American Treasuries. This was a much riskier speculation.

Theoretically, LTCM aimed to be about as risky as the U.S. stock-markets as a whole, but in reality it was far more leveraged than other so-called market-neutral hedge funds. When the market was friendly, this had shown in performance. Less leveraged outfits earned an average of 14% a year in the mid-1990s, compared with LTCM's average of 40% a year in the 1994–97 time frame. But in 1998 came the debacle.

After the $3.6 billion bailout of Long-Term Capital Management, Federal Reserve Chairman Alan Greenspan testified to Congress that it is questionable whether global hedge funds should be regulated by the United States alone. Instead, he said, regulators should impose controls on bank lending to the funds.

Following this testimony, central bankers and regulators of the G-10 have been generally endorsing Greenspan's recommendation. The Fed itself is issuing new rules for hedge fund lending. If control through bank lending does not give expected results, will regulation of hedge funds themselves be next? To my judgment, much depends on the reason why this solution proves to be inadequate as well as on the chances of systemic risk.

On January 28, 1999, a panel of the Basle Committee on Banking Supervision warned that some hedge fund activities may threaten the world financial system. The world's foremost reserve institutions want banks to closely monitor loans to hedge funds and become harder-nosed about the collateral hedge funds offer. Collateral can plunge in value when markets fear that huge portfolio liquidations are imminent; that's a secondary effect of a big hedge fund's bankruptcy.

The way to bet is that hedge funds would resist supervision by any means they could muster. One problem G-10 regulators face is that many hedge funds are domiciled in loosely controlled offshore financial centers. Tighter regulation could face big political obstacles since the offshores' local politicians do appreciate all sorts of favors extended to them by hedge funds.

CAN FINANCIAL INSTITUTIONS CONTROL RISK THROUGH DIVERSIFICATION? NOT REALLY

The justification for diversification is the precaution of not putting all of one's eggs in one single basket. However, many moves done for diversification's sake have failed utterly because they paid only lip service to the basic concepts—particularly when diversification concerns credit risk. Long-Term Capital Management provides an example.

Concentrations of credit risk exist when changes in economic, industry, geographic, or other factors affect groups of counterparties whose aggregate credit exposure is material in relation to a bank's or other entity's total credit exposure. Another reason for concentration of credit risk is that institutions tend to deal with a few names in lending, trading, or both. After all, there is a limited number of AAA and AA+ companies, and megamergers further shrink that number (Chapter 11 discusses the effect of megamergers on managing risk).

Diversification of credit risk is no one-tantum decision. Ongoing business may change even the most carefully laid plans. Although an institution's portfolio of financial instruments may be diversified along counterparty, industry, product, and geographic lines, the stream of ongoing transactions characterized by market changes may turn this diversification on its head.

Both concentration and diversification are based on management's best estimates reflected in valuation assumptions. For instance, exposure toward specific counterparties, as well as the carrying value of short-term financial instruments, receivables, and payables arising in the ordinary course of business. Typically, here's what happens in connection to credit risk:

- Line management conducts the day-to-day credit process in accordance with core policies.
- These are guided by the overall risk appetite and portfolio targets set by senior management.
- But market changes can upset preestablished policies and turn sour previously "secure" commitments.

Line managers are generally required to identify problem credits or problem programs, monitor process quality, and correct deficiencies as needed through remedial action. At headquarters, the credit policy office or committee conducts independent periodic examinations of both portfolio quality and credit processes at individual business channels. In normal times, this can be expected to work fairly well, but this is not true when confronted by major market changes.

Precisely because business conditions are not steady, credit standards and credit programs should be reviewed annually, or even more frequently when necessary. Approvals are made on the basis of projected outstandings as well as maturity and performance of a given product and of a given customer relationship. In case of panic, if an institution is not geared, it can sit on its assets and liabilities, and wait until the market calms. But overgearing is a different matter; debtors won't wait (as LTCM and so many other firms have found out).

This is as true of market risk as it is of credit risk. In its heyday, LTCM had spread its bets among many markets around the world. But the balancing act was precarious and this strategy did not protect it from the chain reaction that hit global markets in August 1998. As a result, a month later LTCM found itself against the wall. If anything, the complexity and diversity of its holdings made the last-minute rescue effort very difficult. In the aftermath, investors are justified when they wonder whether a diverse portfolio offers real protection from future financial storms.

Although few people would challenge the concept of diversification in its fundamentals, a growing number of financial analysts are now rediscovering the old adage that "all that glitters is not gold." First and foremost, few experts have bothered to study in a fundamental manner the synergy between different instruments, different counterparties, and different markets.

Therefore, we lack a factual ground regarding correlations and covariance. Beyond that, postmortem many analysts suggest that the evidence from LTCM and other firms prove these lessons:

- **Most diversification hypotheses are lightly made.**
- **The risk control metrics and measures are lacking.**
- **And there is a significant paradigm shift in the markets, for which the diversifiers typically fail to account.**

Chapter 5 made reference to this event. As markets around the world moved at the same time in the same direction, LTCM's supposed diversification crumbled. This is part of the risk convergence traders take because they identify securities whose prices have deviated slightly from their historical relationships to one another, and they then place bets that those prices will return to their more classical patterns, as a perceived anomaly takes care of itself. Because of superleveraging, when this does not happen the exposure grows very fast.

There are several fallacies with the bets, including the lack of the all-important financial staying power that is necessary until the convergence takes place. Leveraging makes a mockery of financial staying power, and it obliges the speculator to shorten his investment horizon—which is precisely the opposite of what convergence trading needs.

Apart from the convergence example, Long-Term Capital Management had bet millions on the convergence of bonds issued by Brazil, Mexico, and other Latin American governments as well as Brady bonds issued by the same nations but secured by the United States. In a nervous market, those convergence bets became losers, as issues backed by the U.S. Treasury had more appeal for investors.

By mid-September 1998 the only things converging on LTCM's partners were their losses, which were so diverse that they made it difficult for the hedge fund's creditors and for the regulators to respond. The troubles were affecting so many far-flung markets that there were no parties willing to stick their neck out and rescue those who had failed.

This brings us back to the doubtful argument regarding diversification. In theory, LTCM had reduced its risks by scattering its investments among many markets and types. But in practice, anxiety began to spread through most markets after Thailand's currency collapsed in the summer of 1997. Prices fell and businesses failed all along the Pacific Rim. In response, by early 1998, investors worldwide began seeking a haven in U.S. Treasury markets.

Then came the Russian default in August 1998, which magnified the exposure of who was leveraged. More than any other event in recent years, the Russian default led to a flight to safety with unexpected consequences for Treasury bonds:

- The 30-year bonds climbed in price, but the nearly identical 29-year bonds did not share in the rally.
- This divergence hurt LTCM because it had bet heavily that the bonds' prices would move closer together.

Long-Term Capital Management's experience, said Dr. Henry Kaufman, the known economist, showed that international diversification worked in bull markets but failed in bear markets. "We now live in a much more homogeneous financial world," he added. "We all talk to each other, share the same information, and have the same biases."[1]

---

[1] *Herald Tribune,* December 8, 1998.

As a result, Dr. Kaufman suggested that world markets now tend to move in lockstep. Alert analysts have also detected broad structural changes in the financial marketplace, including wider use of derivatives, the increasingly global nature of investment, and immaturity of some emerging markets as well as specialized markets. And there goes diversification.

Starting on a New Foot: The LTCM Marketing Offensive

If the events that led to the meltdown of the Rolls Royce of hedge funds were to be presented in chronological order, it would have been more appropriate to start this chapter with the present section. Quite often, however, it is intellectually more rewarding to look at the aftermath and then flash back to the beginning.

Well prior to LTCM's existence, John Meriwether targeted people with academic excellence. The search for talent and big names was the continuation of a policy at Salomon Brothers where he invited scholars to present papers, while he mingled with PhDs, promising them high earnings on Wall Street compared to the relatively low wages of academia. This made it easy to recruit some of the best thinkers.

At Salomon, Meriwether brought in Dr. Robert Merton as a consultant and then persuaded Dr. Myron Scholes to join Salomon. Both university professors, they became his partners when he set up LTCM. Among others who came on board was David Mullins, Jr., a former Harvard professor who also served as the Fed's vice chairman.

With the big names on display it was not difficult to attract other academics. At one point, LTCM counted 25 PhDs on its payroll, earning the laurel of being, most likely, the best academic finance department in the world: rocket science, high tech, and leveraged finance all in one package.

Neither was the boss of LTCM marketing shy. In 1993, John Meriwether and Eric Rosenfeld traveled to Omaha, Nebraska, to persuade Warren Buffett to invest with them. Even his moral support would be worth a great deal in raising more money. But Buffett refused—though in September 1998, after the debacle, he momentarily changed heart.

Well-known investors and big names in academia were part and parcel of a spirited marketing campaign that canvassed the whole world for clients. The LTCM partners made the most of their days at Salomon Brothers and their ability to search the global bond market for opportunities.

To improve its marketing punch, the hedge fund hired sales-people from Merrill Lynch as sales agents. It also featured the aca-demics in the road shows along with other dignitaries whose name added to the sales pitch. For instance, during his sales presentations David Mullins, Jr. explained that because he once was the Fed's vice chairman, he knew the way Fed members acted and could "figure out" what they would decide.[2] That's more powerful prognostication than mathematical models provided.

But there was also arrogance in these sales campaigns. On November 16, 1998, *The Wall Street Journal* published an interesting story about Myron Scholes and other LTCM top brass who met with senior executives at Conseco Capital Management, the investing arm of the big insurer. The fund, Scholes said, would leverage its capital to take advantage of pricing "anomalies" in global markets.

"You're not adding any value. I don't think there are that many pure anomalies that can occur," observed Andrew Chow, Conseco's vice president in charge of derivatives. Scholes is said to have gazed at Chow and then derided him for believing he knew "all the answers," adding, "As long as there continue to be people like you, we'll make money."

Arrogance left aside, the timing of the sales pitch was good. In 1994 the globalization of investments was still starting. It is also said that Merrill Lynch schooled the hedge fund partners in the language of investors to make the pitch more compelling. There came such slogans as the one that described LTCM investments as "market-neu-tral" or uncorrelated to stock, bond, or currency markets.

How much confidence the LTCM partners had in their coming bets is exemplified by the restrictions that they implied. Whereas most hedge funds permit investors to withdraw annually (in some cases quar-terly), LTCM insisted that its investors not be allowed to withdraw money for at least three years. LTCM also set a required $10 million min-imum, one of the biggest in the industry, and there were very high fees:

---

[2] *The Wall Street Journal,* November 16, 1998.

- Investors were subject to an annual management charge of 2% of assets, plus 25% of profits.
- This contrasted to the 1% and 20%, respectively, for most other hedge funds.

These large capital requirements, high fees, and restrictions concerning the freedom of opt-out action by investors were coupled with assurances by the LTCM top brass that theirs was a very low-risk strategy. This "high profits but low risk" marketing pitch was successful and scores signed up.

Indeed, there was at the end a competition in parking big money at LTCM. Those left out regretted missing the golden opportunity. Those in got on board not only their companies' wealth but also their own—and in some cases that of their kids and their parents. In the end, they regretted those decisions, as did LTCM's own partners.

When the salvage operation was finally confirmed at the 12th hour, the time came for the 16 partners of Long-Term Capital Management to count their stakes in the hedge fund. Not long before the crash, in paper profits, the partners' stakes were valued at $1.6 billion. At the conclusion of the agreement to limit to 10% the equity of the old parties, the partners' stakes had dwindled to just $30 million.

Four of the partners were also on the hook for personal loans totaling some $43 million. They and their lawyer pleaded that the consortium use some of the bailout money to help partners pay off their loans. But Jon S. Corzine (then CEO of Goldman, Sachs) and others held firm. They maintained, "Our money isn't there to bail out the individual shareholders."[3]

FINANCIAL INSTITUTIONS HAVE UNDERWRITTEN THE LTCM ADVENTURE

The LTCM partners were not the only parties to feel sorry. The PaineWebber Group invested $100 million of its capital while its chairman, Donald Marron, added $10 million of his own cash. Merrill Lynch did much better. It raised more than $1.5 billion of the fund's assets and put $15 million of its own capital in the portfolio—

---

[3] *The Wall Street Journal,* November 16, 1998.

even more if one counts the contribution of the broker's pension fund and of its chairman.

Educational institutions too got in the get-rich-fast track. St. John's University in Jamaica, New York, invested $10 million after members of its investment and finance committee told St. John's president, the Rev. Donald Harrington, and its board that John Meriwether was brilliant. The University of Pittsburgh invested $5 million of its endowment in LTCM.

In Europe, Dresdner Bank signed up. Edmund Safra got in through a joint venture between his bank, Republic National Bank of New York, and Safra Republic Holdings. In France, Credit Agricole, the popular-agricultural federation of banks—and its investors—got burned. Why agricultural banks would go for supergearing is something that falls into my knowledge gap.

The French SICAV (Societé d' Investissement a Capital Variable) are a sort of popular mutual fund to which the government has granted some fiscal advantages. The SICAVs are not supposed to be speculative. Yet, Credit Agricole, on behalf of its SICAV, invested French francs 200 million ($37 million) in the ill-fated Long-Term Capital Management adventure. Following LTCM's meltdown this money shrank to about FFR 20 million ($3.7 million). Investors in the SICAV exposed to this burnout have paid for the speculation by the fund managers and for their negligence.

Other SICAVs sponsored by French banks lost money in LTCM. However, the exact amounts are unknown because the SICAVs of Credit Agricole are the only ones transparent in terms of their investments. Yet, all mutual funds should be transparent in the ways they use or invest other peoples' money.

Bank Julius Baer was one of several private Swiss banks to throw money down the LTCM road. Julius Baer also invested through Creinvest. But the big fish caught by LTCM in Switzerland has been UBS (see Chapter 9). This was the old Union Bank of Switzerland which merged in late 1997 with Swiss Bank Corp. to form the new UBS.

As the run in throwing money to the LTCM superstar gained momentum, European investors worked hard through middlemen in London and Zurich, doing their best to be part of the show. They paid a premium to buy existing equity in LTCM from people and companies seeking to cash out early. These were the smart guys who took their money and ran. The rush of new investors showed how effective LTCM must have been in its marketing and how swarms of new entrants were scrambling to get a piece of the action.

A big catch among European financial institutions was a central bank—The Bank of Italy or, more precisely the Ufficio Italiano Cambi (UIC) which it controls. The mission of UIC is to monitor foreign currency exchanges of Italian banks. LTCM must have been proud of itself since it caught as an investor one of the regulators.

The Ufficio Italiano Cambi participated in the LTCM highly leveraged derivatives adventures with at least $250 million of the Italian central bank's official reserves. As with all LTCM gamblers, the stakes started with $100 million; then UIC lent another $150 million to the hedge fund. The irony of this gamble is that had UIC caught one of the Italian commercial banks playing this game, it would have crucified it. But when the regulators become the gamblers, there is nobody around to administer the torture.

The two main players who took UIC to the cleaners are said to have been Mario Draghi (general manager of the Treasury Ministry) and Alberto Giovanni (an exdirector of the Bank of Italy, who at the time of the blood bath was a consultant to the European Union on the euro). Pierantonio Ciampicali, director of the UIC, confirmed in public statements that his office had acted as a strategic partner with LTCM since 1994. The UIC board that approved the operation in 1994 included Antonio Fazio, governor of the Bank of Italy.

This was a relationship bordering on conflict of interest, as LTCM had accumulated positions on the convergence of European interest rates and the Bank of Italy was making crucial decisions regarding this convergence. As reported by the Italian daily *Corriere della Sera*, on October 11, 1998, LTCM was also heavily involved in arbitrages on Italian state bonds. In that period the interest rate of the state bond was 1% higher than the rate to be paid for operations on the lira on the European markets. The difference was primarily due to a special tax imposed on foreign investors in Italy—one of the anomalies mentioned earlier in this chapter. LTCM had found a system to make a profit on the difference, buying lira on the European markets and using an Italian strawman to operate in Italy.[4]

To make the operation particularly profitable, a fortunate coincidence occurred, as reported by *Institutional Investor.* The Italian gov-

---

[4]*EIR,* October 30, 1998.

ernment decided to abolish the special tax, producing a big profit for those in possession of state bonds, LTCM included. It was the Italian Treasury Ministry that decided to end the tax.

- If market "anomalies" don't take care of themselves, and get out of the way on their own will,
- Then, there is always the possibility of using political connections—and the reward can translate into a windfall in profits.

After the LTCM meltdown, some financial analysts said that the markets for financial derivatives and many other relatively new kinds of investments, which have been hailed as the ultimate way of financing, are in the process of degrading into pyramids of the famous Ponzi style of business transactions. As *The Observer* noted on November 15, 1998, the calls for budgetary restraint from the governor of the Bank of Italy lack a certain credibility after his investment of some of Italy's reserves in the Long-Term Capital Management hedge fund.

Not only investment and commercial banks and the hedge funds, but also reserve banks have to be able to persuade the public that what they do is serious stuff based on decisions which have been properly researched and are well thought out. No investment has ever been a one-way elevator going up and up. Indeed, the hardest thing with investments is knowing when to let go.

CHAPTER 9

The Bottom Line in Credit Risk: LTCM and the United Bank of Switzerland

Risk management, the way we know it, was established in response to the growing importance of controlling exposure within what was at the time rather traditional financial lines. As Lev Borodovsky aptly points out in his foreword, this classical concept is challenged by the new economy. The risks originating from products that now dominate the financial landscape are not the same as those to which we have been accustomed. Examples of more demanding instruments are:

- New derivative financial instruments
- Private equity investments
- Large-scale Internet commerce projects

As a result, the more traditional value at risk modeling is falling by the wayside. The new crucial issues demand to figure out our exposure to hedge funds, auditing those models on which we still depend, questioning the securitization of debt and its pricing, putting volatility estimates under stress testing, understanding the impact of an emerging country's default, being ready for a major firm defaulting on its obligations, and appreciating how a commitment based on derivatives may bring a torrent of red ink. This is what this chapter is all about.

The 1997 Annual Report by the United Bank of Switzerland stated that, at the end of 1996, the contracted notional principal amount in derivative financial instruments was SF 2.647 billion ($1.709 billion). This amount was higher by 15% compared to the corresponding derivatives exposure in 1995, or 29% including exchange rate factors.

The positive gross replacement value of the institution's derivatives portfolio came to SF 55.4 billion ($37.4 billion), while the negative gross replacement value was higher at SF 58.4 billion ($39.6 billion). The difference of $2.2 billion represented recognized but not yet realized losses in derivatives contracts—an increase over the 1996 figures the credit institution could ill afford.

To better appreciate the impact of these figures, keep in mind that banks take as effective credit exposure the net replacement value—i.e., the amount owed to other institutions and trading partners under derivatives contracts, and being owed by them—after allowing for all legally acceptable netting arrangements with counterparties. The netting of receivables and payables with the same counterparty assumes that an agreement to this effect has been signed.

The dollar billions or trillions of derivatives exposure are not necessarily representing an equal amount of financial risk. If in a forward rate agreement the notional principal amount is $100 million and risk is estimated at, say, 4 percent, then at the time of such estimate the exposure embedded in such notional principal, for this specific contract, stands at $4 million. This can be obtained by dividing or *demodulating* the notional principal by 25—which amounts to calculating a *credit equivalent* risk position.

By using the proper algorithms and methodology, what was presented through this very simple example is applicable to all derivative contracts inventoried in our bank's portfolio. The exact value of the divisor varies with the composition of our bank's inventory of derivative financial instruments. However, experience with demodulation of notional principal amounts suggests that in calm markets a divisor between 25 and 30 would do, while in nervous markets the divisor becomes 20 or less. Hence, demodulation by 30 is very favorable to the risk profile of the bank.

- Even if a demodulator of 30 was used for credit equivalent computation, then for $1.79 trillion of outstanding derivatives contracts the risk would have been $53.6 billion.
- The reason why the reported exposure is well below this figure of $53 billion, or higher if a smaller demodulator is used, is that banks practice netting which is approved by regulators, but carries its own risks.

For example, the UBS 1997 Annual Report says, "We are able to net 31 percent of the positive replacement values of all derivatives in 1996 against the negative replacement values due to the existence of contracts outstanding with the same counterparty." As a consequence, despite the sharp rise in gross replacement values, positive net replacement values remained practically constant.

Netting reduces the real exposure of banks. Besides this, institutions are increasingly using simulation to estimate the potential change in net exposure to derivatives contracts, employing statistical estimates of expected movements in market prices. These scenarios, however, fail to consider complex relationships—such as the one between UBS and LTCM—as well as extreme events. Therefore, what has happened in the UBS/LTCM case is most instructive and worth a close look.

In trying to understand the fundamentals of what went wrong in the UBS/LTCM case, it is appropriate to ask two questions. First, why would UBS enter into such a mess? The answer is the herd syndrome (to which many banks fall victim) as well as lust and greed, which showed up with the worst possible timing.

The second question is why the hedge fund's partners and managers would purchase call options on their fund instead of just borrowing the money. The answer is that the options underwritten by UBS gave three times the leverage of a conventional equity stake and there was, as added value, a 50% reduction in taxes which magnified the windfall. With options, the internal revenue authorities can be taken for a ride, because the tax law does not cover this type of windfall.

UBS HAD A COMPLEX RELATIONSHIP WITH LTCM

In 1993, when they were laboring for setting up shop for what later became the Long-Term Capital Management legend, John Meriwether and Eric Rosenfeld traveled to Zurich to meet with senior executives at the Union Bank of Switzerland, the old UBS. Would UBS create a unit where Meriwether and his former colleagues from Salomon Brothers could trade? Or would the bank finance a fund set up by Meriwether? At that time, the risks looked extensive, so the UBS executives were not interested. UBS's credit group recommended that the request be declined because the hedge fund had such a limited track record, and it was borrowing so heavily elsewhere anyway. Later on, the bank invested in a big and curious way in LTCM.

Still in Zurich, John Meriwether got a break at Bank Julius Baer, where Raymond Baer is said to have answered that if the former Salomon Brothers trader started a hedge fund, he could count the bank in. Julius Baer also contributed capital through Creinvest, a publicly traded fund of funds. This way, UBS entered through a back door, because it is a major shareholder in Julius Baer. But more was to come as Long-Term Capital Management gained fame and momentum and so many financiers around the globe suddenly became eager to jump on the bandwagon.

But LTCM top brass must have made some inroads at a level of personal contacts, and at the time of the initial contacts as well as appearances certain senior UBS executives kept pressing the bank's credit group for an approval of the credit requests. Finally, top management made available the financing.

At first, the experience was rewarding, as 1996 was a year of big profits for LTCM. As a latecomer, however, UBS did not get a big piece of the action right away. The hedge fund was already performing quite well and did not see a reason to add new equity investors to its blue ribbon list. This situation changed in the summer and fall of 1997 as Dr. Myron Scholes is said to have come up with an artefact that made all parties happy. Prior to examining Scholes's new opportunity, however, it is proper to recall that this was the worst possible time for UBS to take a new big risk.

- In October 1997 it was revealed that UBS had lost about $600 million through ill-conceived options in Japanese banking stocks at the Tokyo Stock Exchange (which is discussed later in this chapter).

- Senior UBS management would have (or at least should have) known of the ongoing disaster in Japanese banking industry investments, but it did not stop that deal.

- Having a hot potato in its hands, UBS management should have thought at least twice prior to entering into another overleveraged options deal in the United States.

The new great business opportunity Scholes suggested to the beleaguered bank was that of issuing still more options, this time tuned to LTCM's fortunes. The plan called for UBS to buy more than

$1 billion of stock in the hedge fund while the LTCM partners would pay UBS some $266 million for a seven-year option to acquire from the bank $800 million of stock in their own company at a fixed price.[1]

In theory, but only in theory, the transaction was ingenious because it killed two birds with one well-placed stone. UBS got a piece of the LTCM action while, at the same time, the options deal reduced the partners' personal tax liabilities. If the LTCM partners had simply borrowed money to buy larger stakes, a portion of their investment returns and fees would have been taxable as ordinary income at 39.6%. But with the new deal, they did not own outright the additional fund equity. Here's how the new deal differed from the 1993 offer:

- The option to buy the shares at a fixed price in seven years was a different algorithm altogether than those income patterns IRS is after.

- The long-term gains on those shares eventually would be taxable at 20%, half the money demanded by the more classical alternative.

At the time UBS issued the options, the stakes these represented in LTCM equity were worth about $800 million. If the hedge fund prospered and the value of the underlying shares of the options rose to, say, $4 billion (which seemed plausible), then the LTCM partners and managers could sell the options and profit from the difference between the $800 million original value and the $4 billion that they would now be worth. This was a cool $3.2 billion profit to be taxed at 20%. For the privilege, LTCM partners and managers paid UBS $266 million.

At UBS, the LTCM stakes were considered such a prize that various divisions claimed part of it for their own P&L. As a result, the bank's trading desk began soliciting bids for the position it held in LTCM, which was supposed to be a much better deal than owning a rich gold mine. The bank's Treasury department (headed by the president-to-be of UBS) won out, and for the privilege of taking hold of the LTCM equity position, it paid a 5% premium in internal management accounting terms. But the euphoria of having won that prize did not last. Before too long, this position turned to ashes.

---

[1] *The Wall Street Journal*, November 16, 1998.

The 1996 blunder, which exploded in 1998 with the fall of LTCM, cost the new UBS (resulting from the merger of the old UBS and Swiss Bank Corporation) $900 million plus the extra $300 million it was obliged to pour into LTCM for the salvage. Four of the bank's top executives had to quit, including chairman Matthis Cabiallavetta (who previously headed the Treasury department that had "won" the LTCM competition), chief credit officer Pierre De Weck, director of trading Werner Bonadurer, and chief risk management officer Felix Fischer.

UBS's Risk Management Methodology Failed

In the aftermath, UBS publicly acknowledged shortcomings in risk management. Until then, risk management was an operation that could do nothing wrong, though in its investigation regarding the big 1997 losses in Japan the Swiss Federal Banking Commission criticized the weakness in risk management (described later in this chapter). Nor could senior executives at UBS or LTCM say they did not know how leveraged and how risky this second big options deal was.

Did UBS roll the dice? The most likely response is that it had so much faith in the magic of LTCM that it not only went ahead with the options but also invested its fee in the hedge fund, putting a total of over $1 billion at risk. Top management must have decided that if it did not join the LTCM high-stakes revolution, it would be run over by it.

There is a lesson to be learned from this debacle. Banks are not as careful about credit risk as textbook cases tend to suggest. Good credit is a valuable and rather scarce commodity. A strategy of obligors is to always try to borrow money at the lowest possible cost with the least number of covenants attached to it. Bear in mind these basic principles:

- **Credit risk is the oldest form of exposure in financial markets, and there is a rule book of do's and don't's in most credit institutions.**
- **But many of these same credit institutions bend their own principles and conditions, leaving themselves exposed to the probability of default by the obligor.**

Sometimes good fortune sees to it that this works out, with no harm to the bank, but in other cases it does not. On some occasions, the banking industry has grown its way out of its problems created by adopting generally unsound funding and lending practices as well as half-baked hedges. But in many cases, reckless lending costs the bank dearly.

This example of the rotten LTCM–UBS connection also documents how incomplete and near-sighted hedges can be. When UBS bought more than $1 billion in LTCM stock, it hedged itself for the $800 million in options it had written plus its proprietary trading. Essentially, the bank hedged itself for *market* risk, not for *credit* risk, in case its counterparty went bust.

This is a dramatic example of how senior bankers can blunder several times on the same deal. If nothing else, experience should have taught them that an unsafe credit can explode at the most inopportune moment at a cost of billions. Bubble blowing is especially likely if there is leverage, which sees to it that the bank goes short on credit.

Shorting credit is the strategy UBS has unwisely followed in connection to LTCM. The responsibility of the institution's top management does not end there. The bank failed to protect itself against a decline in the value of LTCM. This absentmindedness violated one of the top rules of risk management: downside protection. Even with a bet that looks like a multibillion-dollar "sure thing," a reliable safety net must always be in place.

THE FAILURE OF VAR AND OTHER RISK MANAGEMENT MODELS

The new UBS needed capital and in July 1998 it sold one of its pearls, the Banca della Svizzera Italiana, to the Italian insurer Generali for SF 2 billion ($1.5 billion). The intake was about equal to the money thrown into the LTCM pit. But there was also the other unfortunate affair to clear in terms of responsibilities, the huge losses with the options on Japanese bank equity, taken on the fallacious hypothesis that by the mid-1990s the financial sector in Japan was on its way to recovery.

In July 1998, the Swiss Banking Commission cleared Matthis Cabiallavetta, Werner Bonadurer, and Felix Fischer of their role in the Japanese banks' options blood bath. However, it criticized the bank's risk management policies and procedures. The new UBS lost no time in pointing out that these shortcomings have "now been eliminated," and risk management was in control.

Contrary to these assurances, the mismanagement of risk seems to have been so advanced that (according to financial press reports) well after the merger, the only hard information that UBS received from the hedge fund was an announcement about "the inner worth," a kind of stock value. To make matters worse, this too-little/too-late information only came once per month. The LTCM data was already obsolete when received, but by the time risk reports reached senior management, it was completely out of date and unreliable. It is therefore most surprising that UBS calculated its consolidated value at risk based on this highly unreliable number.

Value at risk is the most likely maximal loss that the bank could suffer in the worst case based on all of its commitments at a given level of confidence. Because this level is less than 100, VAR is in reality the minimum recognized loss. According to Basle Committee requirements, this computation is made at the 99% level of confidence. Simply stated, this means that normally:

- **The worst case of losses computed through VAR should be exceeded only in the 1% of all cases.**

- **But the 1% that are not included may hide huge losses because of extreme events.**

Value at risk is computed according to the 1996 Market Risk Amendment and it is intended for regulatory reporting, as well as for senior management information so that corrective action can be taken in time. In itself, the VAR algorithm is rather simple, but the quality of output directly depends on the quality of input data. From examples such as the UBS–LTCM case, the real worth of VAR information has been zero.

Two things should be pointed out in connection with the failure of VAR modeling at UBS. First, this is not a one-bank phenomenon. It is widespread among financial institutions, so it diminishes VAR's value in a general sense. Second, value at risk is not the only model that is mishandled by banks. It is one of many. Take, for instance, interest rate transaction. This will be often shown as:

- Over-the-counter divided into forward rate agreements, interest rate swaps, interest rate option written, and interest rate options bought, and

- Exchange-traded products. These are typically interest rate futures and interest rate options.

This way of presentation raises two questions. First, what type of gross replacement cost will be used? The answer has been that a gross replacement value will be derived from a model, including certain add-ons connected to the 10-day horizon and time buckets. For OTC trades, the result of this computation goes against a credit limit.

So far so good, but there is the second query regarding the coordination between market risk and credit risk. This question is much more important because, in doing a given transaction, the counterparty might not only contract, say, IRS but also take a loan or issue bonds. Taking loans from the banks it was dealing with in geared derivatives had been LTCM's strategy—thus the ripples running through each of its counterparties—and the global financial industry—because of geared positions and the synergy between loans and trades.

The careful reader will also appreciate the significant synergy between organizational challenges and mathematical models. Both affect risk management solutions. Similarly, there is a great synergy between the models and the data these models use, but don't forget that models able to address such complex situations as that of UBS/LTCM are still in their infancy.

Felix Fischer, the former chief risk management officer of UBS, was sanguine when he stated to Zurich's *CASH* newspaper at a press conference, "The model only shows which maximal loss in the next 10 days will not be surpassed with 99% confidence level. If however the remaining risk of 1% takes place, the system does not tell you how big the maximal loss will be."[2]

---

[2]October 2, 1998.

To make a complete and unambiguous statement, Fischer should have added that misinformation is especially likely when garbage data is fed into the model. Then the VAR algorithm is worse than useless; it is misleading: garbage in, garbage out. Furthermore, even if the data was correct, current models are not made to handle extreme values. I have often insisted on this matter. VAR would tell nothing about the Japanese options fiasco and LTCM's bottomless pit.

The way it has been reported in the financial press, Felix Fischer's statement regarding LTCM's uncontrollable intrinsic value raises a serious question about the way both the regulators and the commercial and investment banks commit themselves to VAR in the context of senior management decisions and supervisory activities. It also suggests that the procedures associated with regulatory reporting may be flawed.

Let me repeat these statements in a different form to make sure they are well understood, because today reliance to VAR is blind-folded, which few people appreciate. The risk remaining beyond the 99% level is always present. In the UBS case, its name was LTCM. However, the way the bank handled this risk is very questionable. The risk managers included the LTCM monthly data into their daily calculations of value at risk consolidated at Group level.

"We always used in our model the last available inner worth of LTCM," said Felix Fischer to *CASH*. Then he added, "We complemented it with artificial data which we calculated." But he also said this unreliable "latest available" LTCM information came only once per month—while VAR must be computed daily. Yet it is utterly silly to feed into daily calculations monthly data—even if this data is the most reliable in the world—unless one wants to lie to himself and to others.

Daily calculations should benefit only from *daily* data—even better from intraday information—to be most actual. They should, of course, also represent true intrinsic value and true risk factors. Monthly data that, over and above its timing, is obsolete by the time it's received is worse than poison. If, as stated in the *CASH* interview, "artificial data" (whatever this is supposed to mean) is fed into the model, then the sure result are high levels of unreliability and of irresponsibility.

All this is the stuff that makes up an adventurous and nondependable financial reporting system, at best. Other characterizations are also possible. And since one misfortune does not come alone, in the consolidated value at risk different nontransparent exposures seem to have been mixed up with transparent ones. Therefore, the 99% level of confidence meant absolutely nothing.

I am flabbergasted about how unreliably banks are being managed and how lightly senior management takes the issue of risk control. I'm not only speaking of the new UBS, even if I chose it as a case study because of the LTCM affair. It is a general statement concerning the way most institutions handle risk. No wonder there are so many huge losses these days.

For more flavor, let's add that in late August 1998 (six weeks prior to the *CASH* interview), Marcel Ospel, chief executive of the United Bank of Switzerland, had told reporters how much the new UBS had decreased its risk appetite. But life has surprises. When the near bankruptcy of LTCM hit, this particular exposure cost the shareholders about 50% of the worth of their equity.

Neither could UBS and the other major shareholders of Long-Term Capital Management close this painful chapter once and for all. Each investor in LTCM had to pump in new money. UBS did so to the tune of $300 million, raising to $1.625 billion the money down the drain, and few people think the story will really end there.

THE YEAR 2000 SEQUEL TO THE 1998 LOSSES: ELLINGTON CAPITAL MANAGEMENT AND UBS

The complexity of the instruments that characterize the new economy, the unknowns these involve, and the sudden scarcity of people in charge when leveraged bets turn on their head create a snowball effect that can haunt the company's management for years. A good example is the Year 2000 case of Michael Vranos and his Ellington Capital Management (ECM) against the United Bank of Switzerland.

In a suit filed in state court in New York in mid-2000, Ellington Capital Management alleges that the U.S. securities unit of UBS wrongly used a margin call to force it to liquidate a chunk of its bond portfolio. According to this suit, the costs to this hedge fund and its investors have been high.

- Ellington Capital Management alleges that the unwarranted cost has been more than $85 million, and asks UBS Warburg for damages.

- If true, this case would further demonstrate that major lenders and hedge funds are vulnerable to each other because of the sort of deals they do.

The events the courts would have to sort out date back to the late 1990's bond debacle when markets around the world went into a frenzy because of the near implosion of Long-Term Capital Management. ECM alleges that on the morning of October 13, 1998, an official from Warburg Dillon Reed, as the UBS unit was then known, called Michael Vranos demanding repayment of loans by the close of business that day.

The timing was unsettling because liquidity had dried up. At that very moment some of the world's biggest lenders were scrambling to sever ties with hedge funds and get out of exotic derivatives that were highly volatile. Maybe UBS was more keen than other banks to call back its loans money because it had lost so much through its relationship with Long-Term Capital Management, or maybe there were other less known reasons.

- Analysts on Wall Street suggest that after LTCM the board of UBS promised shareholders a more conservative approach.
- That, ECM alleges, meant cutting off hedge funds, which UBS aggressively courted during the mid-1990s.

To add some spice to this story, a recently published article in *The Wall Street Journal* (July 20, 2000), added some picturesque details. When he got the margin call on Ellington's trading floor in Old Greenwich, Connecticut, Michael Vranos was livid: "Well, f— you." "Though I don't recall whether I uttered those two words specifically," Vranos said following the court action, "in the heat of the moment it's possible that I did. I'm very passionate about advancing the best interest of my investors."

F-word or no f-word, it seems that late in the evening of October 13, 1998, UBS sent a faxed memo, demanding that $17.4 million be repaid "by the close of business that day." Nothing usually happens overnight unless heaven breaks loose, and therefore the next day ECM was informed that it had defaulted on the loans.

According to the Ellington Capital Management suit, one of its officials called Warburg Dillon Reed and demanded to know what market values it had placed on ECM securities when determining the margin call, also cautioning not to sell the securities in a fire-sale manner. Subsequently, three Ellington Capital Management funds seem to have wired $8.3 million to Warburg Dillon Reed, but by then the latter had started liquidating ECM's accounts by selling the funds' repurchase agreements and other holdings. This was done "in a commercially unreasonable manner and at prices below fair market value," according to the suit which notes that for 1998 ECM funds posted a loss of 16.75%, compared with an average loss of 7.69% industry-wide. This was mostly due to activity in one month, October 1998, when the problems with lenders began and the Ellington portfolios plunged 24%.

The same ECM suit also alleges that there has been larger market damage because Warburg Dillon Reed's fire sale lowered the benchmarks for similar securities, deflating prices throughout the industry. Officials at UBS and its securities unit were allegedly "in a state of panic" and sold hundreds of millions of dollars of ECM's securities at a big loss (according to the suit). This seems to have made it more difficult for Ellington Capital Management to get financing. As a result, says ECM:

- Exacerbated by a tepid market for the mortgage bonds in which Ellington specialized, the company's assets have fallen 27% to $800 million from $1.1 billion in 1998, and

- Where Ellington once routinely borrowed as much as $5 to $6 for every dollar invested, in the aftermath of these losses it could borrow only $2.

In my opinion, this is a questionable argument, because the 2-to-1 leverage seems to be in line with many hedge funds today. As such, it says much about how the confidence of even the most risk-taking investors has been shaken by the 1997 to 2000 financial turmoil of the new economy—which started in East Asia, continued in Russia, got a high water mark with LTCM, and still keeps the market nervous.

LESSONS LEARNED FROM THE AUDIT OF 1997 ON UBS LOSSES, BY THE SWISS FEDERAL BANKING COMMISSION

The Japanese banks options gambles in 1997 and the LTCM blowup in 1998 have been a sort of negative dowry of the old UBS to the new UBS. These poisoned gifts have badly shaken the new UBS. Both were lighthearted involvements, a desperate flight ahead into uncharted waters and high risks. At the time of the first big blunder (the Japanese options), the old UBS was paralyzed by Martin Ebner's attempted takeover and other problems—while it suffered from a chronic profit weakness.

Prudence would have suggested going slowly and watching every step. To the contrary, to be able to show a turnaround in profits, the board and senior management pressed on the accelerator. They bet on high-finance mathematics, while lacking the necessary background for doing so and without having in place a real-time intraday risk control system. But is it not true that in LTCM too a good deal of the blame goes to the two high flyers in mathematical finance who were instrumental in supergearing, the Nobel prize winners?

In the wake of these events there is a legitimate query heard in Zurich by financial analysts about the new UBS, the institution, and its top management. "Could there be further losses at UBS because of other involvement of the LTCM type that did not yet come to public eye?" Other analysts ask, "Is this the end of LTCM-connected red ink?" A conservative opinion is that as far as already made investments in the hedge fund are concerned, no further losses might be expected because the total involvement seems to have been written off. But it is very likely that as counterparty to LTCM in trading with swaps and other derivative financial instruments, UBS could suffer further major losses in case the hedge fund finally fails.

How far these losses can go is anybody's guess. New surprises may come from the fact that LTCM has been the most highly geared investment fund in history, to the tune of 50:1. With such an astronomical leverage, any institution can crash like a house of cards. Though the New York Fed will most likely see to it that over time this very high gearing is reduced, it is not impossible that the strategy followed by the Boston Fed in connection to the Bank of New England is repeated. When the leveraged Bank of New England became bankrupt, the Boston Fed put a financial sanitary cordon around it, by appointing new top management, liquidating its huge derivatives portfolio, trying to do something with the bad loans, and leaving it running for a while. But after the derivatives deals were brought down to a level that would not create system risk, the Bank of New England was quietly closed down.

It was, of course, not possible to tell what the Swiss Federal Banking Commission would do with the UBS wounds. But while in the past the Banking Commission depended on financial reports by external auditors, in August 1998 it created a new department, Big Banks, which controls directly Credit Swiss and UBS. Like the Fed, this new department has its own bank examiners whom it assigns to supervisory duties.

No doubt the Swiss Federal Banking Commission will also conduct a rigorous audit of the LTCM fiasco. But this is not yet out, and talking about what might be its findings is pure speculation. Instead, it makes sense to discuss the findings of the Banking Commission regarding UBS involvement with the Japanese banks options in 1997. Results of this audit were made public on July 2, 1998:

- **The 1998 investigation by the Swiss Federal Banking Commission revealed losses of SF 625 million ($470 million) sustained during that year.**

- **These losses have been blamed on misconduct by individuals in the bank's Global Equity Derivatives, Fixed Income, and Currencies along with a number of weak points and flaws of risk control.**

Nearly half the $470 million losses came from proprietary trading in Japanese convertible bonds, which are mandatorily converted into shares at the latest when they mature. Convertible bonds have classically been one of the major trades in Japan. Some analysts ascribe to them part of the lavish credit that led to the Tokyo stock market boom in the 1980s.

Convertible bonds are equity proxies, and they have often been used as instruments for leveraging. One reason why the various options held by UBS could no more be adequately hedged was the collapse in Japanese bank share prices. Another reason (according to the Banking Commission's report) was the quality of risk reporting—which has not informed in a timely fashion senior management regarding the exposure.

The Banking Commission also blames the bonus system, which did not contain incentives sufficiently adjusted for the risks the bank was taking. It is appropriate to emphasize that in the banking industry, this is not an exception. It is a universal practice today, a practice that highly distorts the risk/reward ratio of the traders and of the bank:

- **King-size bonuses give major financial incentives to the traders, so they take unwise risks, leaving lots of toxic waste.**
- **Those who in the end pay the bets are the bank, the shareholders, and depositors. Taxpayers also contribute to the cleanup.**

As in the case of £200 million ($332 million) in losses suffered by NatWest Markets in March 1997 (discussed in Chapter 5) as well as the bankruptcy of Barings and other institutions, huge bonuses and commissions have played a key role in mispricing at UBS. In my opinion, however, the number 1 party responsible is top management, which proved to be lenient in risk control. Because operating results determine the level of commissions payable to traders, commissions tend to be exceptionally high and not commensurate with final P&L results.

The Swiss Federal Banking Commission investigation aptly notes that trading income should be ascertained by a unit operating independently of the trading department. This is absolutely correct, but regulators alone cannot make it happen. The whole banking industry must collaborate in changing a commission system that takes it to the cleaners.

Contrary to the critique regarding trader commissions and risk management, the Swiss regulators found that the audit department of UBS had fulfilled its function. In a number of reports to senior management, the audit department had identified perceived exposure and recommended corrective action. But the remedial measures, the report says, "were . . . not always implemented with the necessary vigor."

Another lesson from this multibillion-dollar failure in Japanese convertible bonds is the need for an independent risk control system with sufficient resources in staff and infrastructure. The Federal Banking Commission's report emphasizes value-at-risk metrics. But these are not enough. Other metrics are needed, one being the demodulation of notional principal amounts (discussed at the beginning of this chapter).

The Banking Commission report also referred to the Audit Committee the bank's board of directors created in 1998 as well as the board's Audit Commission, suggesting that reports should be made semiannually to the committee and quarterly to the commission. When financial reports submitted to the top audit authorities are too sparse, they are bound to be ineffectual.

In my opinion, one-page reports, such as the example given in Figure 9.1, should be provided daily to members of the executive board and senior management. They should also be available interactively on an intraday basis when necessary. A similar type of report must be given at least weekly to the members of the board of directors with further detail available interactively. Of course, this will make sense if the members of the board understand value at risk and the other models. For this they must be trained.

Figure 9.1
A Daily Graphic Report for Visualizing Business and Risks

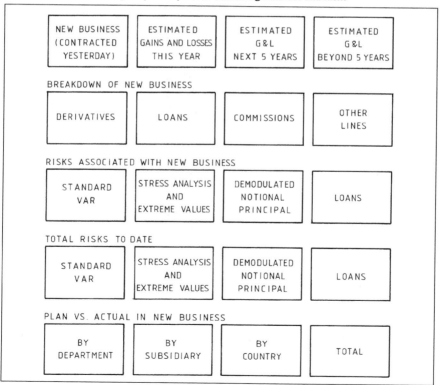

THE SEQUEL TO THE DISASTER CAUSED BY MISMANAGEMENT

There is a sequel to the UBS story with a plain message to both investors and regulators: Once a company comes to its knees, it is very difficult if not outright impossible to redress the market's confidence in that entity, no matter how much one tries. What has happened to the United Bank of Switzerland after the October 1998 debacle confirms this.

First, let's look at the way the bank's chief executive officer presented the disaster at the shareholders meeting of March 1999. The United Bank of Switzerland had to admit that the institution's investment banking unit, Warburg Dillon Read, lost more than $1 billion in 1998 from derivatives trading and a risky stake in troubled Long-Term Capital Management. The disclosure led to a profit warning and forced the resignation of the bank's chairman, Matthis Cabiallavetta. At the same time, under international pressure, UBS had to pony up some $610 million to compensate Holocaust survivors and their heirs for assets the bank had allegedly hidden.[3]

In spite of this hemorrhage, Marcel Ospel, the bank's CEO, expressed confidence that 1999 would be a good year and in the short-term the market reflected that confidence. On March 17, 1999, UBS shares were 44% above their October 1998 lows. But this optimism did not last long because, long-term, shareholders wanted to see solid gains in UBS's strategy of getting synergy out of a global investment bank and more traditional commercial banking.

This did not happen and, after reaching a peak in the beginning of the second quarter of 1999, though never reaching the high watermark of 1998, UBS shares again began to slide as shown in Figure 9.2. Neither did this market sentiment change when, in mid-January 2000, UBS announced a board decision to buy back up to Swiss Francs 4 billion ($2.5 billion) in shares, roughly up to 9.7 million shares.

The fact that the market was uninterested is significant because 9.7 million shares represented 4.5% of the institution's outstanding shares or 5% of shares excluding treasury stock. This amount was more than financial analysts expected and the buyback came sooner than they had envisaged. The only thing that moved UBS shares

---

[3] *BusinessWeek,* March 29, 1999.

slightly north was a rumor that it was a takeover target by Hong Kong and Shanghai Banking Corporation (HSBC).

Figure 9.2
Stock Performance of UBS After the Fall

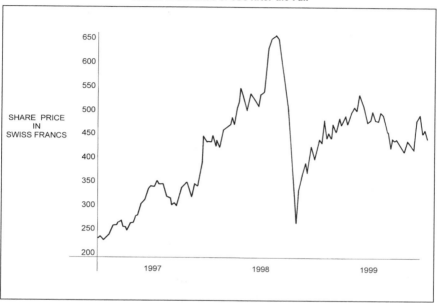

On the surface, the fundamentals looked good. The buyback was expected to improve the bank's tier 1 capital to over 9%. Some analysts even suggested that by the end of 2000 the tier 1 ratio might reach 10.3%. And there was as well the mass effect following the celebrated Swiss Bank Corporation/old UBS merger. But by and large analysts were unimpressed. They pointed out that in the new economy, expertise (not critical mass) is more important. Some said that the American banks' advantage is their ability to tap mature capital markets back home, where they can place billions of dollars worth of new European debt and equity. Others opined that the new UBS had not taken hold of its fortunes. Its information technology was in shambles, relegated to Perot Systems, and no light at the end of the tunnel was visible.

The majority opinion seemed to be that by spinning its wheels in a vacuum after the 1998 debacle, the new UBS may not be in a position to buy better access to the United States than what it already had, which was meager. The concept behind this thesis was expressed by Mark Hoge (an analyst at Credit Suisse First Boston) as far back as March 1999: "Can [Ospel] really go to shareholders and argue that he wants to take $10 billion or more out of profitable operations like asset management or private banking and pour it into a volatile investment bank?"[4]

A year after this comment there was an even more unsettling query: Can operations such as private banking and asset management continue to be profitable if they remain mismanaged for some time more and major clients go elsewhere? In London I heard another criticism that senior management can discard only at great risk. Top management at UBS, said some cognizant people, tried to redress the debacle of late 1998 through moderate approaches and these were doomed to failure. A much more muscular effort was needed, but it was not implemented.

---

[4]Ibid.

CHAPTER 10

The Dangerous Game of Hiding Major Losses Through Derivatives: The Fall of the Tiger Management Fund

Few people—be they novices or professionals—really appreciate the tricks of the trade connected to derivative financial instruments. One trick where derivatives are extensively used is to rapidly generate imaginary profits. Another is in using creative accounting to give the impression that a company is complying with the law, while fictitious profits are shown on the P&L as the real thing.

Similarly, derivatives may be used to hide investment losses, even big ones. Such deals are in the margin between the real and the imaginary, true accounting and creative accounting, and legal practice and illegal practice. Therefore, investment banks that do such tricks are careful to obtain from each client a letter stating that the trade is not a con game and its salespeople have just been helpful intermediaries full of goodwill. In reality, many of these trades are manipulated trade designed to cover up, or at least temporarily hide, a bank's current torrent of red ink.

Take the case of company Kappa (a fictitious name, but a real entity). Its management wanted to know if there was a way it could turn a year in the red into a year in the black by using some sort of derivatives. The goal was to create transactions that showed artificial profits big enough to offset senior losses suffered in previous trades. This would have basically amounted to financial fraud even if it were successfully accomplished, but the whole deal could be structured in a way that a semblance of legality was maintained. At worst, the trick might have been discovered only many years later and debited as an accounting error.

This particular derivatives investor also needed instrument credibility and a safe way of handling the deal. As with so many trades in the margin separating legality and illegality, a basic prerequisite was total secrecy about the act of generating false profits, the way in which this was done, and how it was reported.

Part of the calculation entering into this and other dubious trades is that regulators have a tough time policing creative accounting and associated financial misdeeds. This might well become an impossible task if traders are careful to design and execute complex schemes, which are difficult to comprehend and even harder to untangle. Complexity is in their best interest for several reasons:

- They don't want the counterparty to truly understand the mechanics.
- Neither do they want to get caught by bank supervisors.

This game of hide-and-seek poses lots of questions, starting with the fact that rocket scientists are sophisticated and creative, and they're able to project and implement trading ideas for which the client is willing to pay practically any price. Often the client does so without really knowing the actual worth of the derivative securities or the extent of risk they contain. Complexity also sees to it that regulators don't have the time to analyze all possible scams, particularly when these become daily business.

Let me add another twist to this story. Kappa is an institution that would trade regularly with the likes of LTCM because it appreciates secrecy. With Long-Term Capital Management, some transactions were so secretive that only a handful of people were aware of the new derivatives schemes, and sometimes they were sworn to keep their mouths shut.

This is not an unusual practice. The newer and more complex the instrument, the fewer are people who know about it. Other employees, even those who worked near the initiated people, are in the dark regarding the new financial product's mechanics and its features of great profit and loss potential. In several cases, even the risk managers are not informed of what goes on, so risk control becomes a joke.

PRODUCT INNOVATION AND INORDINATE RISK

Whether in manufacturing, merchandising, or finance, if a company is in the business of making a product that has become indistinguishable from those of its rivals, its goods have turned into a commodity.

Therefore, they will sell chiefly on price. This hits hard the bottom line because pure price competition sees to it that, in several cases, even the costs are not properly covered. The way out of the vicious cycle of price cutting is financial research and development (R&D), which has the following benefits:

- **Through R&D, we can organize the future to compete with the present.**
- **But R&D in general—and specifically in finance—is successful when it is subject to boundary conditions.**

For example, tolerance of risk appetite is a boundary condition that helps to bracket exposure at a level the board and CEO consider adequate for our company's purpose. Limits are boundary conditions. The sort of market to which your bank appeals, or the kind of company it wants to be to its clients, is also a boundary condition.

The omega curve in Figure 10.1 is based on industrial practice, but it is just as valid in finance. If they wish to survive and stay in competition, banks that appeal to the mass market must keep their products' production and distribution costs at rock bottom. With globalization, prices are established by the market, not by the individual company.

Note that the two extremes in Figure 10.1 are mass market and niche market. Branding is the key word in the mass market, as the examples of Citibank and Visa help document. What is happening (as well as what is not happening) to brands has a significance that goes well beyond the makers of commodities such as cigarettes, soft drinks, and soap powders. Consider these basic principles of capitalism that affect success in the market:

- **The winner in the market is the one who makes the best mousetrap at the lowest cost.**
- **Growth statistics significantly influence strategic choices, and growth factors favor off–balance-sheet (OBS) over on–balance-sheet transactions.**

German banks have given the following statistics on business growth in the late 1990s: On–balance-sheet business increased by roughly 1.7% to 1.9% per year; the usual OBS currency and securities futures progressed by 4.9% to 5.8% per year; but the growth rate of more complex derivatives stood at 12.5% to 27.8% per year. Double-digit growth makes senior management salivate.

In other countries too, on average, the growth rate of business in derivative financial instruments is 11 times higher than that of on–balance-sheet business, given the former's leverage and glamor. The derivatives business is booming. Prudence, however, suggests paying attention to credit risk, market risk, operational risk, legal risk, liquidity, and other exposures. As LTCM and Tiger Management (discussed at the end of this chapter) have demonstrated, this is not always the case.

As an example, in mid- to late 1998, improper hedges involving Russian bonds were said to be one of the major roots of the problems at Long-Term Capital Management that caused worldwide tensions and led the Fed to successive reductions of interest rates in the autumn of 1998.

Figure 10.1
The Omega Curve Influences Management's Choice of Product Policy

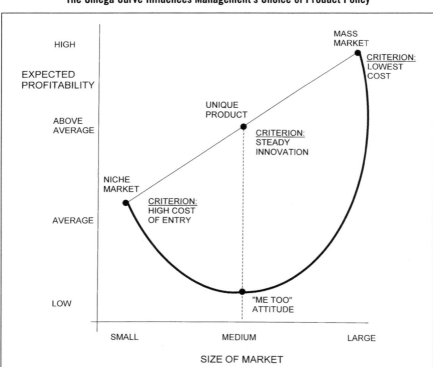

Did this guide the hand of investors to greater prudence? It does not seem so. In early February 2000, the New York Federal Reserve Bank took the unusual step of denying rumors that it was arranging an emergency meeting to discuss losses at a bank or a hedge fund, reminiscent of its 1998 role in rescuing LTCM, whose liquidity crisis threatened global financial stability.

Can great prudence be built into some sort of innovative product design? This does not seem to be in the cards. If lowest cost is the criterion of success, then the mass market in Figure 10.1 presents challenges that are not served through greater prudence. Instead, high cost of entry is the best defense. With derivatives, high cost of entry has two aspects:

- Pirating expert traders and rocket scientists from other banks at exorbitant rates and bonuses, as NatWest Markets did and shot itself in the foot.

- Engaging in significant marketing expenses to gain market share, as Prudential Bache Securities did at great cost and even greater disappointment.

Ironically with derivatives (but not with classical banking product lines), there is some ambiguity in the dividing line between the mass market and the niche market. A niche that is truly lucrative does not last long. One company's success will attract many others into its niche. Only if the entry price is high, they will not jump into it so easily unless they are fool-hearted.

A peculiar duality exists as well between a unique product and "me-tooism." Doing something because somebody else is doing it is the worst strategy ever invented. No matter what the market or the product, "me-too" never succeeds. On the contrary, a unique product strategy makes sense, provided the institution knows how to design an appealing product, develop a good market, and sustain it over the long run.

Research and development is the key to leadership into that market. Product innovation is a never-ending affair. Producers of goods and services that do not particularly know how to manage R&D live in daily terror of their competitor's innovative strategy. All over the world, institutions with an aggressive R&D policy are elbowing aside financial institutions that have been famous for so long that they became reckless in product design, forgot about the market's drives, and let themselves become obsolete.

Innovation is at its best with derivatives. In the arena of classical banking, it has become very hard to make a product that is genuinely different from or better than a competitor's. And it is even harder to stay ahead of the curve. That's enough of a reason why technical expertise in new financial instruments, in modeling, and in information technology is welcome. The trouble is many banks enter derivatives without having the needed expertise in this trade, and without really being able to control risk and, most particularly, their own risk appetite.

Options, futures, forwards, swaps, and other instruments today are widely traded by an increasing universe of financial institutions, industrial companies, and other entities. Customization makes the difference. One reason for the drive toward personalization of financial products (most particularly of off–balance-sheet instruments) is that the appeal of brand name is declining. Another more potent reason are these principles of survival:

- **The bank is obliged to redefine itself, its products, and its markets.**
- **It has to resurrect its fortunes through innovation, and customization helps to innovate.**

New entrants too need to personalize their offers to distinguish themselves from their well-established competitors. In the 1994–96 time frame, Long-Term Capital Management was a new entrant into the derivatives market, even if its partners were old hands from their time at Salomon Brothers. To make its presence felt, LTCM had to overtake the likes of George Soros's Quantum and Julian Robertson's Tiger Management. This it did through customization by betting on high risk.

High stakes was the unique product of LTCM. In a way, emulating the rapid development of new products in manufacturing, LTCM was not locked into the financial equivalent of assembly lines that take months to retool. Its products were innovative and it could draw on a global web of counterparties. But its quality control—and, therefore, risk management—were lacking, leading to its downfall.

In my opinion, LTCM is a prime example of a company where product innovation has been confused with inordinate risks. As the hedge fund was rolling over thin ice, it found protection in its speed.

New formulas, however, were hard to come by and it was ever harder to avoid copycats. There is no copyright in the banking business. Therefore, LTCM chose a greater and greater amount of gearing until in September 1998 its house of cards collapsed.

COSTS, RISKS, AND LEVERAGE AFFECT CAPITAL REQUIREMENTS

I am not privy to the way John Meriwether and his colleagues decided on new instruments and their pricing. However, from what I heard in meetings on Wall Street, the LTCM partners were strong neither in costing nor in risk management. Yet, together with innovation and ingenious pricing, these are the pillars on which rest a successful product and market effort.

Where LTCM was an innovator was in higher and higher gearing, bringing the leverage ratio from a paltry 5:1 to over 50:1. To a significant extent, leverage, risks, and costs correlate. Said Peter Drucker, "We must stop talking of profit as a reward. It is a cost. There are no rewards, only costs of yesterday and of tomorrow." Bear in mind these key points about costs:

- **The costs of yesterday are those we usually consider as expenses.**
- **The costs of tomorrow are the risks we take, which might turn into expenses rather than rewards.**

Globalization has seen to it that firms, even the big and famous, have lost most of their pricing power. In the mass market, the price of a good or service is independent of a single company's will. Competition sees to it that to sell less innovative products, companies tend to cut prices irrespective of the risk they are assuming. In March 1997, this cost NatWest Markets a rumored £300 million pounds ($480 million). It does not take Einstein to understand that it is better not to enter into such deals.

Both volatility and liquidity impact on pricing, and add their weight to what I just said about risks, costs, and leverage. With these factors in mind, able CEOs should reexamine the notion of profit and loss with derivatives, always keeping in perspective that risk management is a lifelong exercise—not a one-tantum affair—and that it cannot be done independently of prevailing business conditions. Keep in mind the extreme results of leveraging:

- **The effects of volatility and liquidity are magnified because of gearing.**
- **Leveraging destroys an institution's financial staying power by spreading its resources thinly over many transactions.**

Under stress conditions, risk grows and grows with leveraging. This is not independent of the fact that turnover in derivatives steadily increases, while modern banking is more or less inconceivable without derivative financial instruments. Up to a point, a modern economy needs derivative instruments, but this is not a reason for getting overexposed. Consider these trends in derivatives:

- **Today, for a growing number of banks, their derivatives business is a multiple of all their other product lines taken together.**
- **The notional principal amount of derivatives is beyond the $3 trillion level for each of the top 20 banks in the world. For the top three in exposure, it is beyond $8 trillion.**

It is not only that these numbers are awfully big, but also that in the minds of many people, including the experts, risk management gets confused with risk taking. If it was not for deregulation, globalization, and technology, Long-Term Capital Management could not have taken its risks or used so much gearing.

Precisely because of such huge leverage, the capital requirements established by the 1998 Capital Accord are no longer sufficient to provide a risk cushion for worst-case scenarios. They must be supplemented by dynamically computed risk factors, which are themselves sustained through a clear-cut structure of organizational responsibility. This is essentially what the 1999 New Capital Adequacy Framework by the Basle Committee on Banking Supervision wants to do, though it still leaves hedge funds off the hook of prudential regulation.

The block diagram in Figure 10.2 presents the concepts underpinning the New Capital Adequacy Framework. The concept on which this presentation rests leads to a revamped global financial architecture. The Basle Committee does not enter into profitability projections. Neither does it set limits to gearing. Rather, it seeks to ensure that a credit institution's capital position is consistent with its overall risk profile and its top management strategy.

Figure 10.2
Loans, Grading, Securitization, Verification of Prices,
and Counterparties for Reliable Risk Management

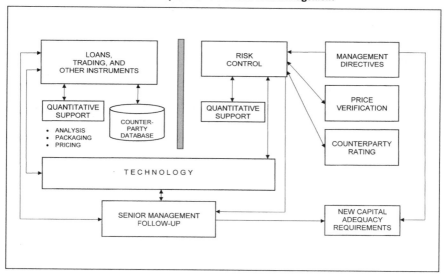

This approach is intended to permit, even encourage, early supervisory intervention. The basic thinking is that supervisors should at their discretion require banks to hold capital in excess of minimum regulatory ratios if their exposure warrants it. Concomitant to this is the drive to convince commercial banks' senior management that they need to take the following actions:

- Develop a rigorous system of internal controls and a realistic capital assessment process, and
- Set targets for capital commensurate with the bank's particular risk profile and business environment.

The expectation is that this internal process would be subject to supervisory review and intervention, where and when such action proves to be appropriate. The Basle supervisors want to see that a bank should publicly disclose qualitative and quantitative information about its exposure. Transparency regarding the risk profile inherent in on–balance-sheet and off–balance-sheet activities is seen as part of market discipline.

Although the new financial architecture is not yet in place (even its guidelines are still being debated), practically everybody appreciates that the grand design established at Bretton Woods as World War II came to an end has been overrun by global financial realities. Establishing the rules of a new financial architecture, however, means making tough decisions. As the 21st century rolls in, there are three issues independent expert opinion considers to be critical to a new financial grand design:

- Whether the Basle Committee, the IMF, or somebody else should take on the role of coordinating private-sector responses to a global financial crisis.

- Whether greater public resources should be made available through the IMF to manage financial panics and, if so, how much money may be enough.

- Whether curbs on capital flows are necessary or are seriously bad and dangerous to global economic health—and what system should regulate them.

None of these three key questions has yet been answered by G-7 governments and the G-10 regulators. Exactly because so much is at stake in a globalized, deregulated economy driven by technology, it is necessary that governments, central banks, and the top management of institutions understand the risks involved with new financial instruments and steadily improve market transparency by ensuring that internal controls and accounting practices keep up with reliable financial reporting requirements.

This reference to rigorous accounting practices and control procedures must be qualified. In some countries, Germany being an example, changes in accounting systems are especially needed because the nation's banks did not participate in the revolution of accounting standards in England and America, though now some of these countries are playing a catch-up game.

Whether seen as part of a new global financial architecture or in the much more limited sense of an institution's own risk management methodology, costs, risks, and leverage definitely have an impact on profitability projections and on capital requirements to face adversity. This is the 21st-century vision, on Wall Street and in the City.

To a large measure, the inordinate risk being taken by credit institutions and investment banks worldwide comes from the fact that business is concentrated in a small number of players. This poses the problem of major systemic risk if one dominant player falters—as happened with Long-Term Capital Management and most likely with Tiger Management.

Of course, optimists say that the good news is that the failure of LTCM, Barings, and other institutions—with their inordinate exposure—can serve as test cases to show if the market can absorb the shock, as lessons to others to avoid excesses, and as needed experiments on how the new economy works. The bad news is that a snowball effect is not excluded. Neither are people really learning from the pain of those who have been imprudent and mismanaged their wealth.

The near bankruptcy of LTCM was different than the failure of Barings in the sense that the venerable British bank managed to wipe out its own funds, while the 50-to-1 leverage of the so-called Rolls-Royce of hedge funds could have brought with it into the abyss the whole global financial system. This has obliged the regulator to broker a salvage that should not have otherwise taken place because—like the 12th-hour country rescues by IMF—it constitutes a moral hazard.

CAN PRUDENT RISK MANAGEMENT BE TAUGHT?

The message is that market participants must always be active in a process of rigorous risk control. This message is lost in many institutions. LTCM is by no means the only example. Organizations are made of people, and many people are imprudent. This is one more reason why rigorous risk management has become a strategic factor as well as why it is necessary to steadily train the people working for your institution both on new business opportunities and on risks connected to new and old opportunities.

One major cost in the 21st century is lifelong learning. In today's knowledge society in which we live, the manual worker is not competitive in his costs with manual workers in the Third World. Only steady improvements in productivity of the knowledge worker can make it possible for Group of Ten countries to maintain their standard of living despite the competition of low-wage economies.

Very few financial institutions pay due attention to what it takes to sustain a lifelong learning program. Nearly everything can be taught; and almost everything taught will become obsolete a few years down the line. Executive efficiency can, and must, be taught. Risk control can, and must, be taught. Only virtue cannot be taught. Virtue is, after all, not a subject but a self-discipline. And people who have no self-discipline are absolutely unfit for risk management duties.

Most of the crucial policies established by the board, the chief executive, and senior management should reflect this simple principle whose observation is vital to the survival of any company. In the case of LTCM, for example, prudence and virtue in risk control were alien to the hedge fund's top management culture. There are also other questions whose factual and documented answers are instrumental to your bank's well-being. These are discussed in the following sections.

Should there be a rigorous audit of internal control by the authorities?

The answer is absolutely Yes! for commercial banks, investment banks, hedge funds, mutual funds, pension funds, insurance companies, and all other financial institutions. Because regulators see the need for a Yes! answer, things are moving the right way. In the United States, Britain, Germany, Switzerland, and other G-10 countries, new laws and regulations require auditors to audit both formal and informal controls. Indeed, the quality of auditing greatly depends on this type of reporting, which is both qualitative and quantitative. But just addressing the commercial banking sector is not enough. All institutions should be subject to the audit of their internal control system. Just look at the Long-Term Capital Management mess.

How detailed should an institution's risk modeling procedures be?

The answer is that it should be detailed, but accuracy is more important than precision. Both pricing models and risk management models should be very accurate and therefore they should be regularly tested for goodness of fit. They should also be specialized by subject. General models do not help. Algorithms and heuristics have to be customized to the problem under study.

Model accuracy has become more important than ever for two reasons. First, the New Capital Adequacy Framework extends the use of eigenmodels to credit risk. Because counterparty samples are small, accuracy issues are more acute than with market risk models. Second, as derivatives portfolios are increasing in size, there should be total transparency in derivatives by all players in the market—and accurate models can be instrumental in reaching this objective.

How to judge model accuracy has not yet been determined, because it has not been studied in its fundamentals. Though back-testing, as specified by the 1996 Market Risk Amendment, provides a basis for judging a model's results, a great deal more is still necessary—particularly in pretesting through an ad hoc verification.

What should be the relative weight of virtual assets versus real assets—and, by extension, of the virtual economy versus the real economy?

Physical commodities that dominated the old economy are real assets, whether we talk of wheat, soybeans, pork bellies, copper, gold, diamonds, or the family home. These assets have intrinsic value and can be used as a guaranty in exchange for other goods or as a payment for services. Real assets tend to be limited in supply and on a snapshot basis they may generate no income stream, but in reality they do have an intrinsic value, which, while it fluctuates, is usually kept within certain bounds.

The new economy's gear is financial, or virtual, assets. These differ from real assets in that they are logical—or, if you prefer, notional—not physical. Their value comes from the fact that they generate an income stream on the underlying physical asset. Because financial assets are a derivative of physical assets or of other virtual assets, they affect the market in several ways:

- **The value of financial investments can be more severely influenced by market forces than that of commodities.**

- **Hence, the old-economy assumptions on which models are often based may turn belly-up.**

Also, given certain economic conditions, the values of commodities and of notional assets can vary in opposite directions. An example is inflation. The value of real assets can be enhanced under inflationary conditions. But currency (a financial asset) is depreciating in an inflationary environment; also interest rates rise and the bond market unravels.

It is not surprising that such real assets as housing and commodities, which have intrinsic value, perform best in periods of high inflation. Notional assets such as stocks and bonds, whose value is based on today's assessment of a future income stream, are underperforming under inflationary conditions. This brings into perspective one more query critical to modeling the real world, discussed next.

What should be the ratio between virtual liabilities and virtual assets?

The answer to this query defines a prudent level of gearing. In the early 1950s, professors at UCLA's Graduate School of Business Administration taught their students that a company whose acid test (current assets over current liabilities) is less than 2 has little financial staying power. By the mid-1980s, leveraging by hedge funds saw to it this ratio was turned on its head: Virtual liabilities exceeded virtual assets by a factor of 2 or somewhat more.

Eventually, the gearing ratio (and with it the practice of leverage) expanded. The ratio became 5-to-1, and for some highly leveraged institutions by the mid-1990s it reached 10-to-1 and beyond. After LTCM, knowledgeable bankers on Wall Street and in the City said they could live with 10-to-1, even 15-to-1, but not with more than 50-to-1. Indeed, it was left to LTCM—to whom prudent risk management was a totally alien culture—to bring the gearing of virtual assets beyond the level of 50-to-1.

Note that 50-to-1 is two orders of magnitude bigger than 0.50-to-1, which means an acid test equal to 2. Dr. Willis Ware, professor of computer design in UCLA's Department of Engineering, taught his students in the 1950s that every time something changes by a factor of 10 the whole approach to decisions should change. Think about the affect on the market of a change of two orders of magnitude:

- A major flaw in LTCM's management (as well as that of most hedge funds and many other institutions) is that decisions are made the same old, inefficient way, while assumed risks are 100 times higher than they should have been.

- The fact that prudent risk control has taken a leave (and, with it, virtue) emboldens the assumption of more and more exposure on false premises, unfounded expectations, and astronomical levels of exposure.

This comprehensive reference helps to identify where lies the greater deal of risk associated with derivative financial instruments, as well as of losses that should be expected. The degree of imprudent management rapidly increases when leverage is king and risk control is put in the time closet—because of not appreciating that anything less than perfect execution of damage containment is likely to send market players tumbling.

Abraham Lincoln used to say to his associate: "Well, Billy, let's hear what there is in the books."[1] The answer to the demanding queries posed by the new economy are not to be found in books because for many of them there is no precedence. As I have already mentioned, Lincoln also said, "Men are greedy to publish the successes of their efforts but reluctant to publish their blunders." Ethical values are very important but beyond them only lifelong learning—on the job and in the classroom—can provide some assurance that we are not going to fall from one blunder into another.

TIGER MANAGEMENT JOINS THE LOSERS' CLUB

Once LTCM overleveraged itself by a factor of 50-to-1 or more and got away with it, it was a foregone conclusion that others would follow the same path; they would even try to improve the score. LTCM crashed in September 1998. Then in June 1999 the global financial system was again brought to the brink of a meltdown. This was repeated in April 2000 with the crash of the NASDAQ.

The mid-1999 event teaches a lesson. According to Wall Street sources, on Friday, June 11, the $13 billion Tiger Management hedge fund was the subject of emergency talks at the New York Federal Reserve because it came near the edge of insolvency. Recall that, at the time, Julian Robertson's Tiger was the world's second-largest hedge fund, after George Soros's Quantum Group. It was not exactly a corner drugstore that went bankrupt.

Though published information was scarce, Wall Street's grapevine carried the news that Tiger superleveraged itself through borrowed money 50-to-1. Cognizant financial analysts have been saying that given its capital (which was 330% more than that of LTCM),

---

[1]Emil Ludwig, *Lincoln* (New York: Grosset & Dunlap, 1930).

this would imply a total market exposure at $650 billion. As the rumors spread, the news had these effects on the markets:

- The aftershock was immediately felt, and the Treasury bond market underwent a minicollapse.

- As a result, interest rates on 30-year bonds were pushed up to 6.14%.

The stock market too became nervous, but the bond market reacted more. Some insiders claimed that if rates had gone above 6.25%, Monday, June 14, would have been another Black Monday— meaning a collapse of global stock markets similar to the one on October 19, 1987—a 14–standard-deviations event. This prediction proved to be premature, but came nearer to realization in April 2000.

Even if there was no market collapse in mid-1999, by the end of 1999, there were grounds to suggest the aforementioned rumors had a reason. Tiger Management ended the year as a poor performer and Julian Robertson, Jr., its chairman and CEO, saw his once successful hedge fund group fall 22% in that year.[2] Furthermore, analysts who looked at gearing as the new wonder admitted that leverage has helped as well as hurt macro funds, which speculate in a wide range of global currency and stock markets. In 1999, it was hurting. Macro funds were up a mere 2.5% that year, with Tiger among the two worst performers. The other players that hurt themselves were short-selling hedge funds, down 7% in 1999. They too used substantial leverage.

It is not at all surprising that well-informed Wall Street analysts got the Tiger news earlier than the rest of the lot. By mid-1999, after carefully scrutinizing the actions of the New York Federal Reserve, Bank of Japan, and European Central Bank, they suggested that something big had happened during the June 12–13-weekend G-7 government meeting in Frankfurt. Allegedly, the rich countries had covertly agreed to a way to avoid systemic risk.

Knowledgeable analysts in the City commented that central bankers of the G-7 let it be known through their market and media contacts that reports on the Tiger crisis were not to be publicized. However, on June 23, *Der Goldmarkt,* a German newsletter, leaked news of the bizarre behavior of the Japanese yen and the major cur-

---

[2]*BusinessWeek,* December 27, 1999.

rency intervention by G-7 central banks during June 1999. It was further suggested that this was part of an attempt to prevent a hedge fund liquidation that would have melted down the fragile global system. At the eye of the storm was speculation on the Japanese yen and its ultracheap credit market, but the gamble had turned sour.

Evidence did not take long to appear. On June 15, three days after the Frankfurt G-7 talks, the Bank of Japan made an extraordinary intervention, selling yen and buying U.S. dollars and euros. Thereby, it weakened the yen. In one day, the bank of Japan sold the equivalent of $10 billion in yen for dollars and $3 billion in yen for euros.

Officially this was done because the bank of Japan wanted to support Japanese exports with a low yen. This argument, however, was ill studied because just three weeks earlier the Bank of Japan had been alarmed about a too-weak yen while, at the same time, Japanese export surpluses were still huge. There was therefore no need to force the yen lower through direct intervention.

By the end of June it was learned that for the whole month the bank of Japan had intervened to the tune of $22 billion in foreign exchange. Some analysts commented that this was part of a coordinated G-7 attempt to bail out Tiger Management and other hedge funds overexposed to the yen crisis because of their miscalculations and imprudence.

The official line released by the Japanese for this huge level of intervention and the beliefs expressed by analysts on Wall Street and the City diverge. Cognizant people suggested a different explanation than the official line. The reason for the huge Bank of Japan intervention that began June 15 was to allow hedge funds to cover their wrong bets—precisely, their short yen positions. Had the Bank of Japan not intervened, there might have been a significant rise in the yen-to-dollar exchange rate. In such a case the open positions of the hedge funds could only have been closed with huge losses, and such losses would have forced them to massively sell U.S. stocks and bonds.

The benevolent action by central bankers, a sort of covert rescue, somewhat calmed the markets but did not end Tiger Management's ordeal. On August 7, 1999, the London *Independent* reported that the explosive increase of bond yield spreads in the previous days was related to the difficulties of an unidentified big hedge fund. This created new fears regarding a repetition of the 1998 crisis of Long-Term Capital Management.

There were unconfirmed reports that Goldman, Sachs and Chase Manhattan had blocked their credit lines to the Tiger fund. Goldman, Sachs itself was said to have registered losses of £200 million ($322 billion) on European options transactions. According to market rumors picked up by the *Independent*, one big American or Swiss bank was in an emergency situation as a result of speculative losses.

Three days later, on August 10, the Zurich stock market was shocked with rumors that the two biggest Swiss banks (UBS and Credit Suisse) had suffered billions of dollars in speculative losses. It was said that these transactions took place on the unregulated off- shore of the Cayman Islands. Despite denials, the rumors persisted, and the stocks of both banks plunged.

A day later, on August 11, it became known that George Soros had replaced his besieged Quantum Fund chief strategist Stanley Druckenmiller with Duncan Hennes, a former executive at Bankers Trust. Market rumors also had it that in the first seven months of 1999, Quantum Fund had sustained losses of $700 million, largely due to wrong bets that the euro would rise and the U.S. Internet stocks would collapse in the spring of 1999. Here's what actually happened:

- The euro collapsed relative to the dollar during the target time period and beyond.
- Internet stocks maintained their steady rise through April, before being cut in half by August.

On Wall Street, experts suggested that the value of the entire portfolio managed by Soros has dropped in the 12-month period of mid-August 1998 to mid-August 1999 from $22 billion to $13.2 billion—a 40% decrease in contrast to the huge profits of earlier years. In fact, the woes of both the Internet stocks and the bond market were attributed to hedge funds bets and those of other institutional investors, which burdened the global marketplace with their wrong guesses—and their greed.

Having gone short on Internet stocks for the first half of 1999, in July of that year George Soros took a 180-degree turn and embraced technology equity. While for six long months his fund had faced losses, by gearing on Internet stocks he turned that into a 35% gain by December 31, 1999. Then the technology selloff in January

2000 knocked the fund with 12% in losses.[3] In mid-April 2000 some analysts speculated about how much NASDAQ's meltdown had to do with George Soros again going short on technology stocks.

THE CLOSING DOWN OF TIGER MANAGEMENT ON MARCH 30, 2000

Having shot itself in the foot while it was in its mouth, on March 30, 2000, Tiger Management closed itself down. Officially the reason for ceasing to operate was that there were no more truly lucrative business opportunities to be found. Therefore, the formerly aggressive hedge fund—number 2 in the constellation of macrospeculators— ended its operations and returned whatever remained of its capital to its shareholders.

This excuse about a lack of opportunities is, of course, nonsense. To appreciate the true reasons, one has to turn back somewhat and learn a lesson from what happened in the late 1980s and early 1990s with the superleveraged Bank of New England (BNE). Tiger Management and BNE have much in common. The most visible similarity is that both were undone by a combination of overgearing and bad bets.

Did Julian Robertson, Jr., close his Tiger Management investment company on his own initiative, or was this part of a nine-month old deal? What about the huge 1999 losses by speculating on the yen—losses that, according to some estimates, were well in excess of $1.6 billion? And what about the money owed to Tiger but not paid by unwilling-to-perform South Koreans?

What Tiger Management Could Have Learned from the Bank of New England

At its height (in the mid- to late 1980s), the Bank of New England (BNE) was the 10th-largest U.S. bank with assets of $32 billion. Less well known is the fact that this credit institution also had $36 billion in derivatives (in notional principal amount); most people think it was undone mainly because of bad debts in real estate. In the late 1980s,

---

[3]*EuroBusiness,* March 2000.

when New England's real estate bubble burst, this created a gaping hole in BNE finances. As 1989 came to a close, it was clear that BNE was bankrupt, even if it didn't officially declare so until January 1991.

Experts on Wall Street suggested at the time that while auditing BNE's books revealed $2.5 billion in nonperforming loans, even more troublesome was the toxic waste in its derivatives portfolio. The Fed of Boston had to intervene discreetly but firmly; following this a newly appointed chairman declared BNE was off the critical list, but it wasn't.

The problems at the Bank of New England came to public knowledge slowly. In March 1990, the comptroller of the currency and the Federal Reserve issued cease-and-desist orders to the bank; that July BNE admitted in its second-quarter filing with the SEC that it might need government assistance to survive. Some $18 billion already lent to the bank was not enough to stop the hemorrhage.

There is a price attached to every rescue. The end of BNE came on January 4, 1991, when it announced a new $450 million loss, which made it officially insolvent and triggered massive depositors' runs on the bank. Two days later, federal regulators officially closed the credit institution. The ultimate cost to FDIC was said to be about $2.3 billion.

Another BNE statistic is far more significant. At the end of 1989, the losses faced by BNE in its derivatives games were a cool $6 billion, for a notional principal amount of $36 billion or a ratio of 1-to-6. With this large derivatives exposure, systemic risk became a distinct possibility. When the closure came in January 1991, toxic waste had been downsized to a more manageable $1.1 billion. That was a terrific damage containment achievement. Congratulations to the Federal Reserve.

So has this successful exercise been repeated with Tiger Management? I think so. In a nearly nonpublicized way, in collaboration with the Bank of Japan, the Fed managed to somehow fix the dollar–yen exchange rate to let "the Tiger" slip through without tearing down the world's financial fabric. But what if a deal was made at the time that Tiger Management would close itself down softly nine months down the line when its toxic waste was not blowing up the global banking system?

This hypothesis is substantiated by the fact that on March 30, 2000, a spokesman for the hedge fund told Reuters that Tiger would close all six of its funds, including its flagship Jaguar. For his part, Julian Robertson told partners he had already largely liquidated

Tiger's portfolio and was ready to immediately return up to 75% of some $6 billion in investments to stakeholders in cash.

Six billion? This sounds like peanuts compared to what Tiger Management used to be worth. At its peak in mid-1998, Robertson's Tiger and its clan had $23 billion under management. The hedge fund ran six investment pools. But a combination of investment losses and heavy withdrawals seems to have left Tiger a shadow of its former self.

The cost of the Russian debacle was a $600 million loss in the autumn of 1998, followed by a $1.6 billion or higher loss on the yen miscarriage. As one misery does not come alone, following these blunders Tiger Management refocused its activities on beaten down stocks in the old economy: US Airways Group, XTRA, Columbia/HCA, Bowater, Sealed Air Corp, Normandy Mining, United Asset Management, Royal Bank of Scotland, National Westminster Bank, and others. Those stocks too proved disappointing as investments.[4]

As if bad judgment with old economy stocks was not enough, Tiger Management had set out to be a macromarkets player in every sense: In the amount of money it managed and in the way it managed it. On the latter score, Julian Robertson had pushed out to the swamps of currency speculators as if in a race to outdo George Soros. Emerging markets is another treacherous domain where big money can be made but also lost.

With Tiger Management's liquidation, as the first quarter of 2000 ended, about $900 million was to be distributed to investors who had requested redemptions, leaving the company with under $5.2 billion in assets. This is a telling story of financial damages created at the junction of leverage and of being on the wrong side of the balance sheet in a series of big investment bets.

After Tiger's admission of defeat, analysts suggested that rumors of this hedge fund's demise have raced through Wall Street before but this time it seemed to be the real thing. With Robertson's funds down about 13% in the first three months of 2000, after a 19% decline in 1999, the end was inevitable—and it came, so to speak, in the right time, preceding NASDAQ's and NYSE's meltdown in April 2000.

What about Tiger Management's track record? Until 1998, this particular hedge fund had lost money only once, in 1987, the year the

---

[4]*International Herald Tribune,* March 31, 2000.

stock market collapsed. In other years, returns exceeded 25% and in certain cases 40%, giving an average of 27% annual gain since the hedge fund's inception in 1980.

Superficially, this track record looks as if it is positive. The careful reader will however appreciate that it does not tell a lot about the hedge fund's future—particularly considering that in a good year 40% returns were obtained on high leverage. Missing from a crust-of-the cake evaluation is the fact that the bill of leverage had to be paid some years down the line, as the geared-up bubble burst. Thank the Federal Reserve for saving the day once again through soft landing of Tiger Management's remains.

SYSTEMIC RISK AND THE LESSON FROM OTHER PEOPLE'S FAILURES

To appreciate the depth of the highly geared gamble by Tiger Management and other hedge funds on the yen, recall that in February 1999 the Bank of Japan brought interest rates effectively to zero. A couple of months later, in April–May 1999, led by the $13 billion Tiger Management, hedge funds decided to use new ultracheap yen borrowings to speculate in U.S. and European markets. With this was invented the so-called *yen carry trade*.

Some analysts suggest that the notion underpinning the yen carry trade is not a 1999 intervention but dates back to August 1995, when the Bank of Japan drastically slashed interest rates to 0.5%. At that time, in cooperation with the U.S. Treasury and Federal Reserve, the Japanese government forced the yen sharply lower to prevent the following events:

- A meltdown of some of the best names among Japanese banks, and
- A further downturn in the Japanese economy that the country could ill afford.

With these moves, however, the stage was set for highly leveraged hedge funds such as Tiger to indulge in what they saw as a one-way bet—a different name for the carry trade—but in reality what was (incorrectly) thought to be the billions-of-dollars "sure thing." This curious clockwork goes like this: The funds borrow a huge amount of yen from Japanese banks and use the cheap yen to buy dollars with the borrowed funds. While the yen loans cost a little more than 0.5%, the dollars are used to make leveraged bets on U.S. and other stocks and bonds, which often pay handsomely. As long as the technology sector of the U.S. stockmarket was king, *handsomely* meant up to 100% or more on Internet stocks. As long as the yen showed no sign of becoming strong again, the billions of dollars in Japanese yen credits of the hedge funds could always be repaid at a huge profit. It looked like a tails-I-win/heads-you-lose situation.

The downturn with this speculative hypothesis has always been that nobody really knows how the market will go. This was the game that blew up in LTCM's face in September 1998 and in Tiger's face in October 1998, losing the fund a rumored $2 billion in one night. That's also the game that led to the bond market debacle in 1994 as the Fed raised interest rates and unraveled similar dollar bets. But people never learn from their misfortunes and those of others.

After the LTCM meltdown, in October 1998 Tiger and other hedge funds got out of their yen loans, bleeding in the process and licking their wounds. However, as subsequent events demonstrate, they learned nothing from that experience. They again jumped on the bandwagon of the cheap yen when in February 1999 the Bank of Japan effectively pushed interest rates to zero to try to jump-start, once again, the country's depressed economy.

By spring 1999, Tiger and other hedge funds were gambling on the yen–dollar again with all its ensuing potential systemic risk. By May, the Japan Center for International Finance reported that the yen carry trade held by overseas hedge funds had risen to a respectable $8 billion. These loans made sense if, and only if, the yen did not rise against the dollar. In the gamblers' judgment, Japan's bleak economic outlook made a weak yen seem certain.

But the hedge funds got it wrong once again. On June 10, 1999, the Japanese government's Economic Planning Agency released exceptionally good GDP data for the first quarter, showing that the economy grew at an 8% annual pace. Immediately, a rush of ordinary mutual fund and pension fund investments pushed the yen sharply higher June 10–11.

While the G-7 governments and the regulators tried to keep the hedge fund woes secret, those initiated ran for their money. On June 11,

1999, a Reuters wire put out that Tiger Fund was hit with $3 billion in redemptions and it had become illiquid. The wire referred to an emergency meeting of the New York Federal Reserve to handle this situation:

- **On June 11, 1999, the U.S. Treasury bond market went into a tailspin, pushing interest rates on 30-year bonds to 6.14%.**
- **The Tiger Fund, it was suggested, found itself obliged to liquidate U.S. and European bonds to raise cash and try to close yen positions.**

Wall Street analysts did not fail to notice that by June 30, 1999, the Federal Open Market Committee (FOMC) met and announced measures for calming the market. There was a ¼% rate rise, but with it the FOMC returned to a "neutral" position in respect to further rate hikes. On that news, the U.S. stock markets soared to record highs.

Analysts also noted that there was a precedent to the June 1999 form of forced selling of U.S. and European bonds to cover yen exposures of Tiger Fund and other gambles. This precedent was the consequence of dramatic and violent market shocks between Japan and the United States in September–October 1998. At that time, Long-Term Capital Management's crisis forced funds to liquidate positions in Japanese yen at a loss. At least some central bankers have admitted the extreme condition of the global markets:

- **At that time the world financial system was brought to the brink of an out-of-control snowball, with disastrous consequences for everybody.**
- **The trouble has been that the current structure of global financial supervision does not have the legal tools that might enable the avoidance of systemic risk in the new economy.**

There were also other indices pointing to mounting systemic risk. On July 16, 1999, a Tiger Management spokesman said in a notice to the London Stock Exchange that the firm had halved its 6% stake in the Royal Bank of Scotland down to 2.99%. Nine months earlier, in October 1998, at the height of the hedge fund crisis after LTCM's insolvency, the imminence of such a reduction was denied by the Royal Bank of Scotland.

Years from now, when more detailed information on LTCM, Tiger Management, and the other hedge funds' travails becomes available, scholars will debate the pros and cons of covert intervention. They will also argue "what if" on July 20, 1999, the Bank of Japan had not intervened to depress the yen, while the Federal Reserve also sold yen in New York acting as agent for the Bank of Japan. Let's recall that in the aftermath the dollar temporarily reached a high of 119.66 yen, but then fell back to 107.

"What if" on July 21, 1999, a major hedge fund (said to be Tiger) was forced to liquidate a large holding of U.K. gilts? In London it was then said that in all likelihood Julian Robertson and his busybodies had made the wrong bets not only in Japan but also in England in their gilts positions. As a result, the banks that had lent to Tiger asked the fund to come up with the cash. This forced Tiger to sell assets.

The Bank of England did not fail to notice the alarming trend of resumed bank lending to hedge funds. The central bank's June 1999 *Financial Stability Review* warned, "Market anecdotes have suggested that financial institutions may have been rebuilding their positions this year . . . that lenders to highly leveraged institutions (i.e., hedge funds) may have begun to relax their terms again, by waiving initial margin requirements, despite the obvious lessons of last year's events."

Time and again, speculators have given the world and its central bankers notice that they don't care to learn from their own mistakes and those of their pals. They simply raise the bets higher and higher, exploiting everybody's fear that if the global financial system crashes, we will all pay for it most dearly. The moral hazard of a 12th-hour salvage contributes to this fear. It is therefore high time to apply some very severe penalties and to rethink the whole system of risk management and internal control.

Part Three answers this call. The risk management policy of any company is the daughter of its trading, loans, and investments policy—which comes to exercise control over its mother's excesses. The constructive discussion presented in the chapters that follow should be seen in this light.

PART THREE

Risk Management Responsibilities in the New Economy

Parts One and Two offered case studies of LTCM, Tiger Management, and other imprudently run, highly leveraged institutions (as well as industrial companies such as Daewoo). Part Three restructures the whole issue of risk management and its associated personal accountability at the vertex of the organizational pyramid.

CHAPTER 11

Senior Management Accountability in the New Economy

We are living in a period of great change. Scientific advances and technological improvements are merging with new economic and financial forces. The aftermath of this process is felt around the planet, within a perspective of growing complexity and of interdependence of crucial factors, many of which are not yet well appreciated.

Companies need to establish mechanisms to report in real-time both expected events and events that do not happen—events and nonevents concerning rewards or penalties as well as inadequacies and breakdowns in controls. At a minimum, companies should follow these basic principles:

- **Senior management and supervisors must always be informed about risks on the most timely basis.**
- **They must have at their fingertips relevant information as well as the means for risk control.**

In the new economy, managerial and supervisory action is not only material but also psychological; indeed, the latter often overshadows the former. Links between lenders—banks, mutual funds, hedge funds, and currency agents—to the recipients of cash flows anywhere around the globe have proved to be so sensitive to real-time information that panic can quickly spread from one country to another around the world.

Real-time reporting on the adequacy of risk management is necessary to maintain an effective financial environment. A basic principle is that efficient reporting procedures can be sustained only if the organization has a good information system that permits accurate, reliable, timely, and detailed data flows to be sent and retrieved. Top management's ability to gather and interpret necessary financial and operational information relating to the control environment is critical.

However, control information, though necessary, is not enough. Another crucial ingredient of a valid system is a flexible but well-documented management plan against which comparisons and evaluations can be made. More precisely, a planning system is needed that permits managers to establish alternatives, compare them to one another, evaluate risk and return associated with each of them, reset goals, and open new vistas in connection to what is "next" and the way it will influence the company's standing. President Eisenhower echoed these words when he said, "The plan is nothing. Planning is everything."

To be able to plan and therefore sustain your accountability in the new economy, you must make projections. Prognostication is one of management's basic responsibilities. Gunnar Andersen, of the National Bank of Iceland, recently wrote, "Given the rapid changes, driven by technology, not least the Internet, what are the Citibanks, Deutsche's, and HSBC's of today going to look like in 2003? In 2005?" Nobody really knows the answer, but one can make an educated guess.

My guess is that Citigroup and HSBC will be among the survivor big banks by 2005. I am not yet sure about the status of Deutsche Bank, which is still digesting Bankers Trust (renamed Taunus) but also suffering from the merger fiasco with Dresdner Bank.[1] Survivor big banks would target Business-to-Business (B2B), Business-to-Consumer (B2C), Consumer-to-Business (C2B), and Consumer-to-Consumer (C2C) on the Internet. If they don't, they are out of luck.

Don't forget that in recent years the dimensions of management and of mismanagement have changed. In the new economy, collaborative technologies made possible by the Internet and other communications facilities make old-economy–type intermediation obsolete. They are also likely to accelerate the trend toward more

---

[1]The following statement is epigrammatic of what I write: "Deutsche made a hash of what was a wonderful business at Bankers Trust," says one senior New York investment banker *(BusinessWeek,* March 20, 2000).

organizational deregulation, spurring the proliferation of temporary collaborations among independent business units—with today's partners becoming tomorrow's competitors and vice versa.

All this is a tall call for the board, CEO, and senior management, particularly because there is also another trend: Mergers and acquisitions lead to bigger and bigger industrial and financial empires which are very difficult (if not outright impossible) to manage centrally. Therefore the model on which to bet is that of federated business units with decentralized management but centralized command and control.

THE NEED FOR OPERATIONAL CONTROL IN MONEY-CENTER BANKS

The notion of a money-center bank was developed by Citicorp a quarter-century ago. Unlike a traditional commercial bank, the money-center bank loans money well beyond its intake of client deposits and capital available from shareholders' equity. It operates globally; acts as both retail and wholesale bank in some countries, but only wholesale in others; and buys money from other banks and entities operating in the eurodollar and other markets. The money-center bank—a pillar of the new economy—is sensitive to three factors: credit risk, market risk, and capital requirements.

Down to the fundamentals, a money-center bank becomes a financial broker—more or less independent of its supply of depositors' funds but dependent on the financial markets worldwide and therefore on its credit rating. The change from the role of the intermediary to that of a money broker has an evident impact on capital requirements, particularly after the 1999 New Capital Adequacy Framework. It also brings to the foreground the need for sophisticated market risk control, as outlined by the 1996 Market Risk Amendment.

For credit risk, market risk, and operational risk reasons, money-center banks need the following controls:

- Rigorous internal control, which has to be global.
- Highly qualified personnel who are versatile in risk management and able to capitalize on lessons learned from banking failures.

- Leadership in technology from real-time networks to sophisticated models for the computation of current and potential exposure.

- The need to clearly distinguish between general accounting financial information (which must be precise, factual, and documented and follow the law of the land to the letter) and the internal accounting management information system (IAMIS) to evaluate risk-connected events, which must be accurate, reliable, very timely, and interactive.

This last need just mentioned emphasizes organizational issues as well as the accountability of members of the board. Senior management must always see to it that IAMIS works around the clock. The responsibility for a proactive evaluation of potential exposure must lie way up in the organization: at board level. Otherwise, the results of even the most accurate risk studies will remain an academic exercise.

Money-center banks need a thoroughly studied, high technology–based risk management strategy, because aggressive risk taking, deregulation, globalization, and innovation cause different types of risk to cluster together. Plenty of cases demonstrate that aggressive trading and transnational lending increase systemic risk because central bankers still lack cross-border experience—though a new framework is slowly being put into place to that effect. Without tough internal risk management policies, the fallout from unexpected events leads to:

- Declining profitability,
- Gaping holes in the treasury,
- Disasters due to leverage,
- Increasing loan losses, and
- Deals being kept secret, which suddenly explode in the face of top management.

One reason for declining profitability is split management attention due to running after so many hares at the same time. Another is that retail banking has become the poor cousin of the banking industry, as investment banking and supposed megadeals take the lion's share of top management's attention. As a recent article put it, "Despite spending lavishly on McKinsey & Co. Consultants, Dresdner (Bank) has weak earnings and is losing money in its retail operations."[2]

Taking inordinate risks is still another factor for declining profitability. Although risk is at the core of the banking business, senior management must be quick to appreciate that the good old days of regulatory fences that kept both excesses and predators under lock and key—thereby leading to predictable profit figures—are gone. By contrast, all sort of risks are mushrooming, including:

- Fast accumulating derivatives risks,
- Global portfolio exposure to loans that may go sour,
- Growing investment risks due to emerging industries and emerging markets, and
- Legal risks because cross-border deals come under different, often incompatible legislation.

All four types of risk identify the darker, less transparent side of the new economy. The fact that from time to time an institution finds itself down the precipice is not surprising. It can happen at any time, in any place, to any bank. What is much more difficult to understand is that the whole financial industry of Japan, the second economy of the world, found itself on the rocks. In my opinion, two major background reasons for this failure were high leverage and low-quality internal control.

Formerly tall institutions are falling apart and are being purchased at bargain basement prices. For example, in mid-February 2000, New York's Ripplewood Holdings bought Long-Term Credit Bank (LTCB) of Japan for a mere $1.1 billion. In March 1999, GE Capital paid $6.6 billion to purchase Japan Leasing Corporation. The difference is that LTCB had gone bankrupt while Japan Leasing was in a little better shape.

These examples are telling of what happens because of overexposure. The solution is better management, not 12th-hour mergers.

---

[2]*BusinessWeek*, March 20, 2000.

The next section looks at some of these banking mergers and what effect the merger has on risk management.

HOW MERGERS AND ACQUISITIONS AFFECT RISK AND RISK MANAGEMENT

In late August 1999, three of Japan's largest banks came together to create the world's largest credit institution. Then in mid-October 1999, two other megabanks merged, creating the world's second-largest bank. Then in March 2000, three other big Japanese banks merged— Sanwa Bank, Asahi Bank, and Tokai Bank. But how much is to be expected from these mergers in terms of weeding out of the system the mountain of bad loans and huge losses because of leveraged derivatives deals?

One of the three partners to the August 1999 merger was Industrial Bank of Japan (IBJ), the only remaining Japanese bank making long-term loans to business customers, following the bankruptcy of its competitors Long-Term Credit Bank (LTCB) and Nippon Credit Bank (NCB). The other two partners to the merger were Dai-Ichi Kangyo Bank (DKB) and Fuji Bank, which were among the best-known of Japan's largest city (commercial) banks. But Fuji, like IBJ, has a multiple of its equity in nonperforming loans which will weight heavily on the single entity forged from the three banks, to be known as the Mizhuo Financial Group, with combined assets of 141 trillion yen ($1.26 trillion). This merger affected the banks' portfolio in two significant ways:

- It makes a very large institution indeed, but the amounts of non-performing loans and of sour derivatives in the portfolio are huge too.

- A portfolio loaded with bad debts and many questionable bilateral derivatives contracts of three big banks is a liability, not an asset.

A similar statement is valid about the October 1999 merger of the two other Japanese big credit institutions: Sumitomo Bank and Sakura Bank. Sakura was the result of a 1993 merger of two other large banks, which was difficult because of their different management cultures. This has a precedent. When I visited Sakura in 1994, the computer systems were in chaos because the effort to combine heterogeneous platforms had not given fruits. Besides this, both Sumitomo Bank and Mitsui Bank (one of the two institutions merged into Sakura) belonged to powerful trading empires that have been competitors in all their history.

In Japan, financial analysts were more positive about the big merger of August 1999 than that of October. They said that IBJ would be the primary beneficiary of the alliance, because for over a decade it had been handicapped by rules preventing it from taking deposits from individuals. A similar weakness had played a key role in the demise of its competitors in long-term credit, Long-Term Credit Bank of Japan and Nippon Credit Bank, which were nationalized in 1998 to save them from outright bankruptcy. For their part, Fuji and DKB have been among the largest individual deposit bases in Japan but, as the analysts were quick to point out, they lack powerful international or wholesale securities operations.

These seemingly positive comments cannot hide the facts behind these two megamergers; all five banks were in trouble, though Dai-Ichi was in better financial health than the other four. In 1998 and 1999, all of the aforementioned institutions seem to have lost big money. The fact that by the time of the mergers four of the five banks were not in good condition poured cold water on official statements hailing the mergers by saying that they would "undoubtedly help" the recovery of the nation's economy, and they would speed the elusive restructuring of Japan's troubled banking sector.

The implosion of Japan's stock and property bubble in the early 1990s was the first major earthquake of the new economy—way ahead of the East Asia crisis of 1997. It left the country's big banks buried under trillions of yen in nonperforming loans. Their inability to shed unprofitable assets, curtail derivatives trades, cut costs, and resume regular lending activity has been widely regarded as a primary reason for Japan's failure to shake off its worst recession since World War II. The merger of big banks is not necessarily a good omen. It may be a sign of weakness.

John Walsh of the Group of Thirty expresses this concept masterfully when he says that in a crisis situation even the precise measurement and careful parsing of risks on which sophisticated financial strategies are based can become irrelevant. At the same time the lowering of financial frontiers through globalization sees to it that major financial distress in one country, or even a megacrisis at a single big intermediary, can trigger losses that balloon throughout the system.

THE CHALLENGE OF MANAGING MEGA COMPANIES

Mergers involve, so to speak, a concept carried over from the old economy where something very big is supposed to be more solid. The new economy does not work that way. Indeed there are dangers embedded in bigness (as well as in stereotypes from the old economy) that could bring the bubble to a bursting point. Moreover, when it comes to managing king-size exposures, the existence of bigger-and-bigger entities is counterproductive. Figure 11.1 shows in a nutshell the megamergers in the new economy.

This is not a flat statement against mergers and acquisitions. Successful acquisitions are the result of first-class business strategies. These are typically developed when acquirers understand why and how buying another company is going to help achieve a company's goals. To help yourself determine whether an acquisition is a business opportunity, you must have an analytical framework that reflects your criteria for value. Also necessary is a battery of queries against which you can test your concept:

- Is this the right target?
- What's the economic vision that justifies it?
- Is the market going to like the deal?
- How much dilution in your stock price will there be?
- What does it take in human capital and other resources to make this deal work?

The answers to these queries cannot be universal. They have to be focused case-by-case, though there will be some common ground in each of the four quarter spaces shown in Figure 11.2. The worst strategy in regard to mergers and acquisitions is "me too." We merge to become bigger, cut personnel, and close branches. We make acquisitions because they have become a trend, a favorite corporate policy. "Me-too"-ism is indeed the reason why the majority of such deals fail to earn back their cost of capital. Some have been disasters for shareholders of the acquiring company.

Figure 11.1
Global Mergers and Acquisitions in the New Economy
1997 to 2000
Value in Billions of U.S. Dollars

BUYER	TARGET	VALUE	DATE
Vodafone AirTouch	Mannesmann	$189	February 2000
AOL	Time Warner	184	January 2000
Vodafone	AirTouch Communications	65.9	January 1999
AT&T	MediaOne	63.1	April 1999
NationsBank	BankAmerica	61.6	April 1998
Olivetti	Telecom Italia	56.0	February 1999
British Petroleum	Amoco	54.3	August 1998
Global Crossing	US West	51.1	May 1999
Banque Nationale de Paris	Paribas	39.8	
American Home Products	Monsanto	39.1	June 1998
Chase Manhattan	J.P. Morgan	36.0	September 2000
WorldCom	MCI Communications	34.6	October 1997
Carrefour	Comptoirs Modernes	34.4	August 1998
Norwest	Wells Fargo	34.4	June 1998
Zeneca	Astra	31.8	December 1998
Royal Bank of Scotland	National Westminster Bank	33.0	March 2000
Banc One	First Chicago NBD	29.6	April 1998
Rhone-Poulenc	Hoechst	26.5	May 1999
Bank of New York	Mellon Bank	24.2	April 1998
Berkshire Hathaway	General Re	23.0	June 1998
Swiss Bank	Union Bank of Switzerland	23.0	June 1998
Lucent Technologies	Ascend Communications	21.1	January 1999
Banque Nationale de Paris	Paribas	19.0	March 1999
Zurich Insurance	BAT Industries/Financial	18.4	October 1997
American Int'l Group	SunAmerica	18.2	August 1998
NatWest	Legal & General	17.2	September 1999
Fortis	Generale de Banque	14.0	June 1998
CSFB	Donaldson Lufkin	13.4	August 2000
Norwich Union	CGU	12.0	February 2000

(continued)

Figure 11.1, *continued*

BUYER	TARGET	VALUE	DATE
UBS	PaineWebber	11.8	November 2000
Commercial Union	General Accident	11.7	February 1998
Banco Bilbao Vizcaya	Argentaria Bank	11.4	October 1999
Lloyds TSB	Scottish Widows	11.0	June 1999
HSBC	Credit Commercial de France	10.65	April 2000
Aegon	Transamerica	9.7	February 1999
Credit Suisse	Winterthur	9.5	August 1998
Axa	UAP	9.2	November 1996
Banca Intesa	Banca Commerciale Italiana	9.0	December 1999
Merita Nordbanken	Unidanbank	5.0	March 2000
Dresdner Bank	Waferstein	1.56	September 2000
Industrial Bank of Japan	Dai-Ichi Kangyo/Fuji Bank	N.A.	August 1999
Sumitomo Bank	Sakura Bank	N.A.	October 1999
Sanwa Bank	Asahi Bank/Tokai Bank	N.A.	March 2000

Figure 11.2
Big Mergers in the New Economy Classified into Quarter Spaces,
Each with Strengths and Weaknesses

	INTER-INDUSTRY	INTRA-INDUSTRY
GLOBAL MARKET	ZURICH INSURANCE—BAT FINANCIAL FORTIS—GENERAL BANK	VODAPHONE—MANNESMANN VODAPHONE—AIRTOUCH BP—AMOCO DAIMLER—CHRYSLER RHONE POULENC—HOECHST AEGON—TRANSAMERICA
NATIONAL MARKET	TRAVELER'S—CITICORP NATWEST—LEGAL & GENERAL LLOYDS—SCOTTISH WINDOWS CREDIT SUISSE—WINTERTHUR	EXXON—MOBIL BELL ATLANTIC—GTE NATIONS BANK—BANK AMERICA NORTHWEST—WELLS FARGO SWISS BANK—UBS BNP—PARIBAS AXA—UAP

When in March 2000 Deutsche Bank and Dresdner Bank announced their merger, for 24 hours the market primed the stocks of both institutions. But then the market had reservations. For the next two sessions, each bank's stock dropped about 8% per day. Eventually market analysts and investors and also the top management of these two institutions had second thoughts about the wisdom of an action done in a rush without appropriate study and consultation.

The fact that the Deutsche Bank/Dresdner Bank merger got stuck reflects not only the incompatibility of their investment banking subsidiaries but also the market's reaction to a deal that does not make much sense. Neither were investors positive about the merger of Swiss Bank Corporation and Union Bank of Switzerland into the new UBS. In its short existence since late 1998, the United Bank of Switzerland has been a poorly performing banking group whose market value has gone from bad to worse, particularly after the LTCM fiasco (see Part Two).

There is always a difference between plans at the time acquisitions are made and the subsequent reality. Often, the strategic objective is to gain majority equity interests and secure management control—an objective applied to both existing subsidiaries and acquisition targets. The problem is that with substandard organizations still tuned to the old economy and retrograde technology (in spite of huge amounts of money spent on IT), internal communications lines become blurred. Management cannot easily reach all four corners of the empire at once. The integration of heterogeneous technologies (particularly old ones) does not go smoothly. Personality clashes and deep cultural differences often get the upper hand. The euphoria of mergers and associated news coverage hides the fact that:

- **Internal controls are often disconnected after a merger.**
- **And end-to-end risk management can be in shambles.**

What I have just described characterizes more than anything else the merger of equals or near equals. It is quite different with small acquisitions, which can be digested rather fast. Even then, however, the difficulty in integrating diverse entities should never be forgotten. The fact that few megamergers increased shareholder value should be kept in perspective. Greater efficiency is rarely associated with king size, if for no other reason than entropy.

Neither are bad surprises unheard of with mergers. If anything, they are the rule (see Chapter 9's discussion of the merger of SBC and UBS). The argument that larger entities may find it easier to reconfigure their portfolio is less than half-true. Indeed, the divesting of operations and product lines that are unprofitable or lack strategic fit does not need to be done only after a merger. And there is a serious case that mega-acquisitions may lead to a synergy of risks, as has happened with Chemical and Manufacturers Hanover Trust and thereafter with Chemical and Chase Manhattan among other megamergers.

How Strategic Plans and Time Exposure Affect Vulnerability to Risk

Given the reality that many megamergers fail, many managers ask the following questions:

- Why do mergers that looked good on paper fail in real life?
- What does it take to make synergy work for us?
- How can we increase the likelihood that our acquisition will be a long-term success?

Any valid answer to these queries must focus on the often overlooked importance of planning for synergy before an acquisition or merger.

Planning ahead of an event and analyzing its consequences is a strategic consideration that characterizes the best practices of entities known for their ability to digest what they buy. Careful planning and analysis must definitely consider all of the critical issues that affect a given case including not only financial and commercial perspectives but also legal and antitrust issues. Key elements are:

- A sound business strategy,
- A sensible valuation base,
- A negotiation based on facts, and
- Direct responsibility for implementation of the merger.

The factors characterizing this direct responsibility are polyvalent. They regard both internal issues (such as those discussed in the preceding sections), and others that are external or may relate to your type of company. If, for instance, your company is a bank with stock priced 1.5 times book value (as Bank One in April 2000), then you should pay due attention to the fact that you may end up being the acquired rather than the acquiror. Keep in mind these key points:

- **In the new economy, companies usually buy others by capitalizing on their leveraged share value (for example, as AOL did with Time Warner).**

- **Market capitalization is a potent weapon, and banks don't perform especially well these days in shareholder value.**

As shown in Figure 11.3, merchandizing and manufacturing firms tend to dwarf banks and brokerages in the economic food chain, raising doubts about allowing them to merge with each other in a viable manner. For example, as of mid-2000, the top three companies in capitalization in the United States were CISCO, General Electric and Microsoft. Credit institutions come way down the list, even after the megamergers of the past few years. Bankers, however, appreciate that the fulfillment of business aims characterizing the new economy can lead to higher market capitalization. Today the aims are different than those followed in the classical industrial environment; just like industrial aims have not been the same as those that have dominated an agricultural economy.

The common ground of service, industrial, and agricultural economies is that all are moved by fear and greed, because without them the heart of the market will not beat.

The point is that senior management must be aware not just of opportunities but also of vulnerabilities associated with the new economy and its evolution. A modern economy is highly dependent on all sorts of services. These range from infrastructure to finance. Service businesses are also the vector of globalization, from direct foreign investment to trading in goods and financial products.

The vulnerability of your institution is not connected only to risks embedded in inventoried positions in your portfolio; nor is the likelihood that it may be an acquisition target something that happens only once. Other factors to be taken very seriously by the board, the CEO, and the strategic planners are:

- Your positioning in relation to virtual marketplaces that will dominate this decade, and
- Time exposure associated with the instruments that you trade.

The marketplace was once seen as a physical location where sellers and buyers, lenders and borrowers meet—for instance, a pit in an exchange floor or the branch office of a bank. But in the new economy the marketplace may be a virtual space created by software, computers, and communications networks. Over the network(s), brokers bring buyers and sellers together by overcoming information barriers—which essentially means that mastery of information technology is a significant competitive advantage.

Figure 11.3
An Order-of-Magnitude Evaluation of Market Capitalization of Industries, Banks, and Brokers in the New Economy (Market Value in Billions of Dollars)

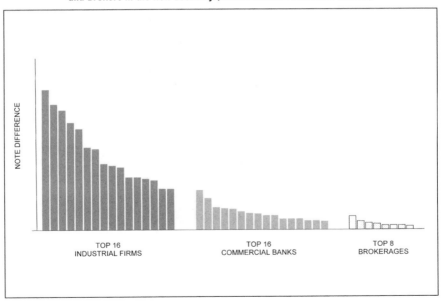

Increasingly advanced information technology solutions must be available to help lending officers, traders, and underwriters as intermediaries between borrowers and lenders, sellers and buyers. Lack of high tech is by itself a major vulnerability. Contrary to brokers who work for a commission, traders take possession of assets and liabilities, at least for a short time. So keep in mind these key points:

> - **The new economy's instruments carry both credit risk and market risk until they are sold to another party, and**
> - **They may as well feature operational risk both before and after the sale is made.**

Operational risk has many aspects. Let me give just one example. A precondition for a transaction done by the trader is that the IOUs are negotiable. If not, the trader would become the investor and would continue to be confronted with credit and market risk. The way to bet is that the more an instrument follows standard agreements (for instance, USDA's) the more it is negotiable. But standard agreements don't cover everything. Exposure can come from pricing, legal issues, and other factors.

The pricing of instruments itself is part of operational risks. Negotiability requires that the trader assess what price the financial paper will command. Specifically, this is the job of market makers. Investors and market makers have different minds, but as Dr. Werner Heisenberg, the physicist, once suggested, "The most beautiful developments have always emerged when two different kinds of thinking met."

Traders hold onto their IOUs for a short time, though this time is longer than that characterizing an arbitrageur. By contrast, commercial banks often hold their IOUs until they mature, thereby increasing some of their risks but diminishing others. The message here is that all agents make money by taking positions in the market—but at different levels of time exposure. Many buy and sell assets and liabilities without having them yet.

- In principle, the risk is lower if the market considers the financial paper to be creditworthy, and if transactions capitalize on significant demand.

- The risk is higher if the IOUs are issued by counterparties that are less creditworthy, or if the demand for instruments being traded has faded.

The proper estimate of creditworthiness is a matter of credit risk. The likelihood that the price of a specific asset or liability will change is at the origin of market risk. Both are relevant in product pricing (as discussed in Chapter 1). Pricing, product appeal, timing, and creditworthiness correlate between themselves and with the risk being assumed. This notion is fundamental to damage control.

The concept of a quantitative analysis for damage control reasons is relatively novel. Several CEOs are now accepting that their institutions lack the proper balance between risk management and risk taking. A sound course of action in search of the best possible balance is to establish and frequently rethink and reevaluate strategic and tactical plans. Strategic and tactical plans tend to overlap with one another at midrange—i.e., sometime in the three- to five-year range. So keep in mind these key points:

- **The choice of goals and means of strategic plans must be conditioned by the environment(s) within which your institution operates, and they should support its long-term aims.**
- **The goals set forth and means employed by tactical plans should comply with those of strategic plans to which the tactical plans are always subordinate.**

Because the globalization of finance had unearthed new types of risks, at both tactical and strategic levels, there is increasing awareness of the need to create a new regulatory system that accounts for the fact that highly leveraged bets can disrupt normal economic processes and threaten otherwise viable business ventures. The more science and technology are integrated into the way business works (and therefore into the economic system), the more we need to develop sophisticated monitoring and control functions while paying full attention to fundamental strategic considerations such as the ongoing change in capital acquisition:

- The banks themselves have seen their credit ratings slip compared with those of their traditional customers.
- For large, AAA-rated industrial companies, the capital markets have become low-cost places to raise money.

Financial institutions that rely wholly or in part on the capital markets for their funding have less of a competitive advantage if they are not AAA-rated. The best-rated industrial companies can borrow more cheaply than banks. A dramatic example is Japan's long-term credit banks, which have lost their reason for being as a result of their vulnerability in the new economy and uncertainties regarding the way they could pull themselves out of trouble. These weaknesses are summed up into what is known as a "Japan premium."

As we saw earlier in this chapter, two of the Japanese long-term credit banks, which lent mostly to big companies and relied almost entirely on wholesale markets for their funding, were nationalized in 1998 to save them from bankruptcy. If we add to this the salvage of Credit Lyonnais by the French government, we get dramatic examples of how in Group of Ten countries the taxpayer acts as lender of last resort for bad risks, while in so-called emerging markets, the salvage of whole countries is done by the International Monetary Fund (IMF).

IMF money is, in the last analysis, taxpayer's money. The fact that IMF acts as a lender of last resort does not escape the attention of big banks and hedge funds when they establish their strategic plans. As a result, when they are more or less sure that the international fire brigade will come to their rescue, banks, hedge funds, and other investors take many more risks in lending to emerging markets than would otherwise be the case—and do so under the perspective of a short time horizon.

THE GLOBALIZATION OF FINANCE REQUIRES A LONG TIME HORIZON

As mentioned, one of the basic notions associated with an advanced economy is its vulnerability to unknown risk factors. Part of this vulnerability concerns novel concepts and systems that it uses in its operations and on which it depends. Different types of vulnerabilities are associated with different financial institutions and the instruments in which they trade. Some of them tend to correlate with long time horizons; others with short ones. Savings and loans, as well as retail banks that are strong in mortgage lending, are exposed to interest rate risk because they depend on deposits and savings—hence money with a short time horizon—to finance longer-term loans. The debacle of the S&Ls in the late 1980s is an example of this mismatch in maturities between deposits and mortgage loans.

Speculators typically have a very short time horizon. The time horizon of hedge funds is also short. By contrast, commercial banks have a longer time horizon in their lending. Classical texts on loans and investments stress that a long time horizon is a pillar in financial stability. However, there are prerequisites in adopting a long time horizon:

- Proof of creditworthiness on behalf of borrowers and trading partners.
- Financial staying power of the lender or investor, which permits it to face future adverse conditions.

These prerequisites require a critical analysis of counterparties, markets, and financial conditions, which facilitates documented decisions prior to making commitments—rather than being led into commitments without exactly knowing how to face the challenges that they imply.

Consumer and industrial confidence indicators are vital elements in this analysis. Both are characterized by significant volatility, as shown in Figure 11.4. Classically banks have provided for themselves the proof of creditworthiness by rating their clients. Globalization, however, makes this assessment more difficult, and it promotes the use of credit information provided by independent rating agencies such as Standard & Poor's (S&P), Moody's Investors Service, and Fitch IBCA.

With the 1999 New Capital Adequacy Framework, the Basle Committee has stated that the development of an internal ratings-based approach to regulatory capital is an important element in the effort to revise the 1988 capital accord through better documented prudential measures. For their part, regulators will most likely embark on a study of the banks' internal rating processes and supporting systems, evaluating the options for relating ratings to a regulatory scheme.

The concept is sound. The problem with this approach is that there is no single standard for the design and operation of a model-based internal rating system. While practically all banks use more or less similar types of risk factors, both their relevant importance and the way in which they are used differ from one institution to another. The commonality for nearly all institutions is that the forces promoting the new economy have:

- Significantly increased credit risk volatility,
- Led to the internationalization of credit risk, and
- Created credit derivatives as a new instrument of risk transfer.

Figure 11.4
Consumer and Industrial Confidence Indicators in Euroland, Based on
European Commission Business and Consumer Surveys, 1990–99

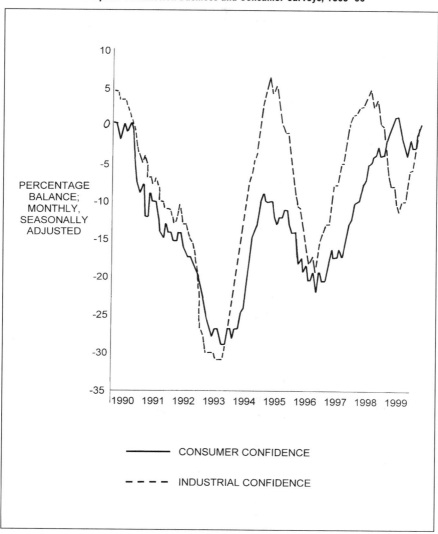

When a bank concludes a transaction, it assumes an obligation whose value will increase or shrink through its duration. This value may be positive and hence represent a reward. Or, it may be negative, in which case it points to an exposure. Ironically, if the transaction becomes more valuable, counterparty risk will grow. But when the value of the transaction moves south, market risk increases. Other things being equal, the following scenarios are true:

- **Longer maturities increase the likelihood that a certain price, rate, or market will move.**
- **But short maturities are associated with the problem that financial obligations become due in the near future.**

Short-term obligations may be poisonous. Few experts pay the needed attention to the fact that credit risk volatility increases as emerging markets boom, and their rapidly growing economies attract huge inflows of foreign capital. As trade barriers are reduced, capital crosses borders more freely. Institutional investors benefit by addressing themselves directly to emerging market countries and companies. But institutional investors have a short time horizon, while the uncertainties associated with emerging markets call for a long one.

Recent financial history teaches a lesson. By 1994, the capital markets' enthusiasm had carried most emerging countries and stocks to excesses that led to a long period of underperformance and eventually to the crash of 1997 in East Asia and of 1998 in Russia. Short time horizons saw to it that there has been a currency and market implosion of crisis proportions. Short-term euphoria could not last forever because the weaknesses of lenders and borrowers alike are unearthed in quick succession.

There is in fact no better example of risks associated with short-term horizons than the near-bankruptcy of LTCM (discussed in detail in Part Two of this book). As investors ran for cover following the Russian meltdown of August 1998, by early September 1998 all markets globally were oversold. This was the time of the crisis lows. But 10 months down the line, in mid-1999, practically all markets had recovered and appeared to be overbought. These ups and downs came in rapid succession and they are characteristic of planning for the short term.

Critics of short time horizons say that they are counterproductive; indeed they are exactly the opposite of what should happen in an era of globalization of finance and the advent of the new economy. By contrast, those who think that short-term horizon criteria are better fit to the present time suggest that globalization, deregulation, technology, and rapid innovation see to it that the future has become very much of our present. In the background of this school of thought lies the fact that, because of rapid innovation, the useful life of your products becomes shorter and shorter. As a result, some companies abandon a product or a process before it begins to decline. And/or, they don't invest scarce human and financial resources in defending what is part of yesterday.

There are good reasons behind this strategy. Indeed, institutions that follow it are among the best performing. But what is true of individual *products* and *services* is not necessarily valid for *investments* and *the economy* as a whole. When it comes to investments, the best-managed companies today are taking the long view. General Electric is an example. Over the past decade, it has weathered plenty of unforeseen events.

Any well-managed global company has become accustomed to some market somewhere either underperforming or overperforming, without getting nervous. Firms that have learned to operate in the new economy also appreciate what Federal Reserve Chairman Alan Greenspan says about the continuing inability to raise prices in a more competitive, global marketplace. This means that businesses must achieve earnings growth targets mainly through more intensive focus on innovation, productivity, and internal control. At the same time, practically every global player must understand that globalization, deregulation, innovation, and technology lead to the internationalization of risks.

Figure 11.5 shows where this brings us in terms of new instruments and regulatory controls. The senior management of a global company cannot permit itself to be upset by a change in fortunes. But high leverage might command otherwise if the institution has no more financial staying power to see it through in the long term. Therefore it cannot afford the luxury of asking itself, "Is this still worth doing?" prior to reaching a critical decision that impacts greatly on its survival.

RISK MANAGEMENT RESPONSIBILITIES OF THE BOARD OF DIRECTORS

From analyzing the wisdom of mergers to the choice of time horizons, the board of directors and the CEO must elaborate strategies and define major policies that greatly influence their company's future. These may relate to the management of credit risk, capital

Figure 11.5
The Forces of 2000+ Create New Market Opportunities and Major Risks

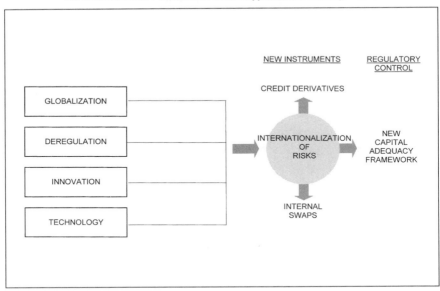

requirements, market risk and operational risk, investment positions, loans to be made, trade commitments, and other issues. Top management must also ensure that the following occurs:

- **Your bank should take all the steps necessary for monitoring and controlling exposure on an intraday basis.**
- **And a system of alarms should be in place to warn when corrective action must be immediate and effective.**

Because the board of directors is ultimately accountable for understanding the nature and level of risks assumed by the institution, it should be informed regularly of all types of risk exposure and of their possible aftermath. Steering may be carried out by an appropriate subcommittee of the board (similar to the auditing committee), which should have the following responsibilities:

- To approve board objectives, strategies, and policies governing interest rate risk, currency risk, loans, investments, and derivatives activities.

- To provide guidance regarding the board's tolerance for risk, ensuring that senior management takes steps to measure, monitor, report, and control all types of exposure.
- To ensure that there is transparency and that information flows are sufficient, accurate, and timely to allow assessment of the institution's risks and understanding of their aftermath.

Another key function of this committee should be to review policies, procedures, and limits by working hand-in-hand with the audit committee in periodically assessing compliance with board-approved policies and taking corrective action. It is in the best interest of all institutions to be vigilant, even if some need such a watchdog committee more than others because they have a greater appetite for risk, particularly with derivatives.

The risks to which I here refer are present intraday. The control of intraday exposure because of overleveraging (discussed in Chapter 1) goes way beyond the classical call of duty. It used to be that the board and senior management should ensure that the bank's operations were effectively managed, appropriate policies were in place, and procedures were established and maintained to ensure that resources were available to conduct the institution's activities in a safe and sound manner. While this is always important, it is not enough all by itself.

The board is accountable for overall exposure at any time, in any place, just like senior management has the responsibility for the daily direction and oversight of the institution's activities. This includes ensuring that adequate means are available to enforce the execution of risk management policies. An institution's risk management system should provide:

- Ways for measuring risk, valuing positions, and evaluating performance,
- Real-time control of risk limits and of their observance,
- A comprehensive reporting and review process, and
- An effective internal control system that is regularly audited.

Case Study: How Top Management at Credit Suisse Monitors Risk

Credit Suisse provides a good example of how to put in practice what I am suggesting, because it looks at risk management as an ongoing process starting with definition of business objectives, strategies, and policies; including identification and assessment; and providing for control of all risks associated with financial activities. Top management identifies as success factors for risk management:

- Clear policies, procedures, risk acceptance criteria, and risk measurement procedures, and
- A strong commitment by the board to an independent authority for risk management and control.

Risk measurement, Credit Suisse suggests, should take place across all products, business activities, and partner relations, with the aim to preserve the institution's capital base and optimize the allocation of entrepreneurial (regulatory) and economic capital to the individual business units and to the institution as a whole.

Credit Suisse emphasizes that the board of directors is responsible for the determination of general risk policy and strategic risk management including the appropriate organizational solutions. The board is also responsible for the definition of the Group's overall risk appetite. The Chairman's Committee (of the board) is accountable for reviewing the Group's risk exposure on a quarterly basis.

Because the five main business units of Credit Suisse Group have direct responsibility for implementation of their own risk management strategy within the Group's overall framework, each business unit has in place a specialized risk management structure. This includes a risk committee, appropriate systems and tools, and procedures and controls.

The risk management structure is independent of front-desk operations, as should always be the case. The idea underpinning such divisionalization of risk control duties is that while all business units are exposed to operational, reputational, and strategy risks, each major business unit has its own specific pattern of exposure:

- Market risks are concentrated at Credit Suisse First Boston,
- Credit risks are most important at Credit Suisse and Credit Suisse First Boston,
- Winterthur (the insurance company) is primarily exposed to insurance risks,
- Credit Suisse Private Banking and Credit Suisse Asset Management are faced with business volume risks.

CONCLUSION

As the Credit Suisse example and many others document, to manage in an able manner it is necessary to do all of the following:

- **Establish and maintain clear lines of authority and responsibility.**
- **Ensure that the bank's operations and activities are conducted by competent staff with technical knowledge and experience.**
- **See to it that available know-how is consistent with the nature and scope of the business unit's activities.**
- **Review periodically the institution's risk management system(s), including policies, procedures, risk limits, and technology.**

U.S. supervisors, like the Office of Thrift Supervision (OTS), require not only that lines of responsibility and authority be established and maintained in an able manner, but also that they be reviewed to ensure that they remain active. Institutions should identify the individuals and/or committees responsible for risk management and should ensure there is adequate separation of duties in key elements of the risk control process to avoid potential conflicts of interest. For this purpose, institutions should:

- Have a risk management function, or unit, that has well-defined duties and is sufficiently independent from position-taking functions, and
- Clearly identify the individuals and committees responsible for conducting risk management, including their structure, tools, methods, and accountability.

The risk management department must report directly to the board of directors, and it should be separate from, and independent from business lines. Large banks must have a separate risk management unit, particularly if their treasury is also a profit center. Smaller institutions with limited resources and personnel should provide additional oversight by outside directors to compensate for the lack of separation of duties.

CHAPTER 12

The Roles, Functions, and Responsibilities of Senior Bank Management

To paraphrase an old maxim regarding real estate property, the three most important things in picking the right company for investment are its management, management, and management. Other than knowing something of the company's track record and analyzing its balance sheet, the clearest indicator for a prospective investor is the quality of the board of directors, the chief executive officer, the CEO's immediate assistants, the company's internal controls, and the risk management system that is in place. This chapter describes the responsibilities of the board of directors and senior management of a financial institution and discusses policies, procedures, strategic planning, and management control.

THE IMPORTANCE OF STRATEGIC PLANNING

Both the board and top management should be concerned with strategy and tactics in the whole range of entrepreneurial endeavor. Furthermore, neither strategy nor tactics can be dissociated from risk control. The board's role is primarily in long-term establishment of business opportunity and in internal control. Senior management must concentrate on day-to-day operations from the development of business opportunities to effective control of risk. No organization can succeed in a competitive environment without strategic plans and their effective execution.

Strategy is the exercise of skill, forethought, and artifice in carrying out plans. Strategy is a master plan followed in making moves during the interaction of two or more persons or legal entities whose actions are based on certain expectations of moves by counterparties, over which the strategy maker has no control. In this sense, strategy is a master plan against an opponent. This definition contains three elements that set management strategy apart from other plans or moves:

- It states that strategy is a master plan, not just a list of individual actions.
- Strategy is against something. Hence, competition is involved as a basic ingredient in any strategy.
- There is an opponent—another person, group, or company(ies)—without which a competitive situation could not exist.

As a master plan, strategy has been applied to business, war, and propaganda, but fundamentally it is a much broader concept, having implications in politics and aftermaths in industry and commerce. In principle, strategy is not an objective in itself. It is a master plan for accomplishing objectives.

A vital characteristic of strategy is that the authority of knowledge is as legitimate as the authority of position. It takes skill to make strategy. Sun Tsu, Alexander, Caesar, and Napoleon (to name but a few great strategists) excelled in strategic moves, which was instrumental in their becoming foremost military commanders. Successful strategic moves are key ingredients in motivation. This is vital in finance, because the motivation of knowledge workers depends on being effective—on being able to achieve.

THE RESPONSIBILITIES OF THE BOARD

As noted, strategic planning is the first responsibility of the board of directors. However, within the framework established by the directors, strategic planning is also a top responsibility of the board of *management* (or executive committee). Let me explain these terms.

The board of directors is primarily composed of members outside the organization. In some countries (e.g., Germany, Switzerland) it is known as the supervisory board and, as this title implies, its foremost responsibility is supervision—hence internal control. This tends to preclude the chairman of the board of directors being the company's chief executive officer (CEO). Therefore, in this book, "the board" will mean the one who has executive responsibilities.

In central Europe, the CEO is the president of the board of management, which is also known as executive board, internal board, or executive committee. Its members are executive vice presidents of the company, each leading a major division or area of operations. Under these conditions, strategic planning is to a large measure part of their responsibility; the same is true of the management of risk.

This model contrasts to the so-called Anglo-Saxon solution prevailing in the United States and the United Kingdom, where membership on the board of directors is both external and internal. The chairman of the board of directors may also be the CEO. He or she may also hold the president's job. This model is more flexible but also, for better or worse, it leads to greater concentration of power, which can corrupt.

Recommended Size of the Board of Directors

There is no rule on how big or how small the board should be. Sharp financial analysts advise us to shy away from boards that are overly large (e.g., more than a dozen) or too small (e.g., fewer than six members). If there are too few members, the board is probably missing some crucial skills. It might also be a rubber stamp board. With large boards, meetings become little parliaments and it is difficult to reach meaningful conclusions.

Key Traits of Board Members

In the light of many collapses and alleged corporate fraud, it is rewarding to ensure that a bank has independent, nonexecutive directors who are both qualified and respected in their fields. Quite similarly, the board should know which managers working for the firm have a reputation for integrity, honesty, and business acumen (and which do not) as well as which managers are capable of hard, systematic work.

The strategic plans the board of directors and the company's top management must develop are made not only in terms of finance but as well of products, markets, technology, and human resources. Strategic concepts and strategic plans are brought forward and reach maturity only by high-level organizational solutions. They are made by people who have experience, intelligence, and ingenuity. All three of these personality characteristics are necessary—and constitute responsibilities of the board of directors and of the board of management together with effectiveness and accountability.

Other Required Traits and Experience of the Board

The most common qualifications for membership on the board of directors are the ability to preserve and protect the company's assets, keen financial and/or technical interests, honesty, effectiveness, and professional expertise. The members of the board are acting on behalf of the stockholders and therefore must safeguard the equity of the firm.

An irrational part of organizational life is the fact that in many cases the requirement of professional expertise is not clearly spelled out. A great deal of weight is placed on board members' abstract ability to bring to fruition a variety of skills and experiences, including legal and consultancy expertise as well as experience gained at the top management in other organizations and businesses.

Typically, board members are active in similar or complementary walks of industrial and business life—or, alternatively, board members provide expertise in legal matters and finance, as well as assure needed commercial connections. Though some people maintain that expertise in a given industry is not critical for board membership (or even for the CEO), my statistics and experience demonstrate that it can indeed be crucial. It is regrettable that most organizations don't take care to describe, much less define, what makes a good director though this would be a valuable guideline. Neither is it easy to find a written answer to the question, "What should our organization expect from people qualified for board membership?"

General traits can be misleading in a world characterized by steady and often profound changes, but at least one common denominator might be worth considering: the board member's ability to examine the critical factors that affect organizational survival, including the ability to forecast, introduce, and manage change.

Board members must have background and experience to estimate the direction of events. The effectiveness of implementing change depends on their qualification in leading the way, for which no theoretical models can be developed or instruments effectively used. The quality of management at board and executive committee levels is critical to every company, but it is not easily quantifiable, if it is quantifiable at all.

Together with analytically qualifiable personality traits and decision-making styles, a critical characteristic of board members should be their ability to live with their time. Computer literacy is an example. Equally crucial is the willingness to keep themselves and their skills in steady evolution; in short, board members need to remain active, be involved, and look after detail.

There are two reasons why I emphasize computer literacy: first, it is not usually found at board level, and second, because ours is an age characterized by technological progress outpacing anything we have known ever before. Technological progress has contributed to globalization and market dynamics. Every company, from the simplest to the most sophisticated, lives and operates in an environment of steady evolution. Therefore, no board can successfully manage its company's business if its members permit themselves to become obsolete or distance themselves from steady innovation.

Innovation happens in the market as it happens in the laboratory. The personalities of the members of the board, their knowledge, information, drives, decision styles, and, at the bottom line, the strategies and tactics they choose make the company tick. They also affect the life cycle of the organization.

Effective board members, the CEO, and the company's executive vice presidents have in common their ability to be conceptual enough to understand the big picture and analytical enough to reach the needed level of detail. This is precisely what is required by the practice of risk management at the top of the organizational pyramid.

Being an effective analyst of business opportunity and being a capable risk manager correlate. Both are a matter of training and practice or, more precisely, of a complex network of practices. It is a barbarism to say that practices are learned by practicing, but this is a fact. Keep in mind these basic management principles:

- **Practice is the key to competence.**
- **Virtue is the key to accountability.**

Key Functions of the Board

Overall, these are the primary functions of the board:

- **Internal control, risk management, and auditing are integral parts of the board's systematic work.**
- **All three are very important supervisory duties. The responsibility associated with them can never be delegated.**

An integral part of a board's mission is to have clear thinking and be able to set objectives that are realistic but at the same time far-reaching. Strategy, including risk management strategy, can be formulated only after objectives have been established. Strategic planning involves projection into the future and selection among alternative paths of action. Projections and forecasts help reduce the effects of the unknown, but they still leave elements of uncertainty. There is nothing certain in business, and this must be kept in mind when we exercise judgment. Prognostication and long-range planning don't deal with future decisions, but with the future impact of present decisions. Selection among alternative objectives and plans of action is a basic process, which you can use to optimize your opportunities.

Management by objectives makes sense if, and only if, you know your goals. The bad news is that most businesspeople don't, and many boards relegate their responsibility in setting objectives to lower levels in the organization. Show me a company where such relegation takes place, and I will show you a badly managed organization.

The setting of objectives is a strategic issue, but their execution calls for policy decisions. Quite often, people ask what is the difference between strategy and policy. The concept and nature of strategy has just been defined; policy is the means by which one avoids making repetitive decisions on issues that have already been elaborated and for which choices have already been made.

Here's an example. In 1994, after the huge losses suffered by industrial corporations, the board of directors of Kodak decided to get out of derivatives altogether. This was a *strategic* decision that was translated into the *policy* that Kodak sold its derivatives portfolio and never got into derivatives again.

Policies are elaborated by the executives of the bank. These are the members of the two boards described and some of their immediate assistants. Executives are policy makers. Some of these executives, particularly the internal directors and members of the executive committee, are also managers. Often in industry the terms *executive* and *manager* are used interchangeably, but also the exact meaning of each word is sometimes confused with the meaning of the other term.

INVESTMENT POLICIES, PROCEDURES, DEMERITS, AND MERITS

How Policy Helps Manage Risk

As noted throughout in this chapter, policy is a guide for thinking. It is a mental framework on which will be built the planning process. Company policies help to eliminate the making of day-to-day routine decisions on the same and similar issues. To be effective, policies must be dynamic and constantly reevaluated in terms of their adequacy and of the results they help to obtain.

Policies must be updated as market conditions change, new products are introduced, the culture of the institution evolves, or painful lessons are learned from failures. Formal statements giving the relationship between market conditions and resulting decision patterns help in highlighting certain issues vital to the institution. By being general statements, policies are never too specific—but they should be accurate and comprehensible.

To channel their decisions and actions in accordance with corporate policies, subordinates must interpret them. They must also integrate policy guidelines into their daily decisions and actions, by providing milestones against which to gauge the results obtained in the execution of their mission. In this function too SQC charts can help managers visualize trends and initiate corrective action.

There is a basic difference between the making of a policy and its implementation. Policies of companywide impact are established by top management and should be implemented at all levels of the organization, at any time and at any place. Risk management is a good example of a policy that must seep down the organization. The proper implementation of policies facilitates the following functions:

- Permits the coordination of all elements into a general framework.

- Supports the existence of prerequisites at operating level, such as establishing criteria for tactical moves, and

- Helps in exercise of a rather uniform ground for judgment, within a given pattern of activity.

Policy Leads to Procedures for Managing Risk—and Feedback Is Critical

Procedures should be confused neither with policies nor with plans. *Procedures* are means of action; they are the mechanism of a process that should be controllable. Within a risk management system, procedures should bring forward the profit, cost, risk, and leverage elements that we have discussed since Chapter 1. Remember that properly planned, risk can be taken as another major cost.

Feedback is a good example of an established procedural solution; it is also an example of an organizational prerequisite in a process whereby policies are translated into procedures. Feedback is one of the reasons why organizational systems are not linear. Its value is shown in Figure 12.1 through an example involving Plan-versus-Actual comparison. Keep in mind these key points:

- **The need for establishing a feedback mechanism is a policy decision.**

- **How the Plan-versus-Actual comparison should be done is a procedural decision.**

- **The implementation of feedback tends to make Plan-versus-Actual evaluations nonlinear.**

A company without a feedback mechanism is like a car going downhill without brakes. Once forecasts have been made and plans set, all managers should report regularly on progress toward their goals. In this effort, they should be assisted by models and computers, whose function is to interpret numbers, make comparisons, and visualize results for decision makers.

Numbers alone, however, don't tell everything feedback should contain. Therefore, managers need much more than reports to check on the execution of their order(s). They must go out themselves, examine results, look around, and hear opinions, thereby controlling both the execution of their orders and the way the feedback mechanism works.

Effective feedbacks are a good way to control the accuracy of the prognostications you make. Forecasts, plans, and feedbacks should be available online, seamlessly accessed by every authorized person with results presented in graphical form. A system of personal accountability must be in place to ensure that a course of action, such as risk management, is followed. Such systems should be enriched by merits and demerits.

Figure 12.1
Feedback Is Necessary to Ensure the Timely and Effective Execution of Plans

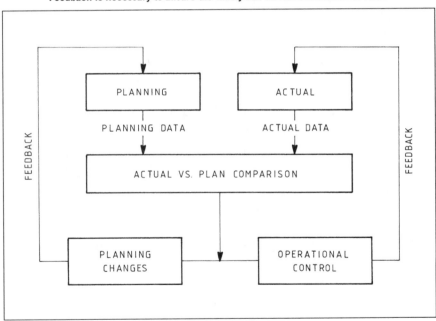

Using Merits and Demerits in Managing Risk

Merits are rewards paid for achievement. Sales commissions are an example, though recently sales commissions have been misused in connection to derivatives trades. They are subject to abuse as the cases of Kidder Peabody and NatWest Markets document. Here are two points to keep in mind when using merits to manage risk:

> • **A system of merits is based on assumptions, and the market often sees to it that assumptions go awry.**
>
> • **Another reason assumptions become obsolete is that the system of merits can be awfully exploited through leverage.**

Demerits are penalties, which should also be part of the system. Otherwise, merits alone would make the institution run wild. People are motivated by both the carrot and the stick.

Authority and Accountability in Implementing Policies and Procedures

The more dynamic the environment within which a bank operates, the better tuned should be your institution's system of merits and demerits. Also in such a situation, the bank's strategies, policies, and procedures should be evolving faster. This requires knowledge of:

- The strengths and weaknesses of your bank;
- The people who will be affected through your actions,
- The economic and social environments confronting your organization, and
- The goals to be achieved, including the goals of your competitors.

The emphasis on people reflects the fact that organizations are made up of individuals. In a financial institution (as in any other company), maximum utilization of knowledge and skills possessed by its managers, professionals, and other employees can be achieved through teamwork. The application of teamwork by management requires:

- Delegation of authority down to the lowest level of supervision, within the framework of agreed-on plans and programs,
- A good understanding of the nature of this authority and of its corresponding responsibility, and
- A basis of personal accountability, starting at the board and top-management levels and going down the organization.

An effective delegation of authority to lower levels of management and provision for the flow of accountability upward is accomplished by means of sound policies, clear directives, the supply of adequate skills, and timely, understandable information. This is true in terms of performance and observance of the agreed-on plans and programs as well as compliance to laws and regulations.

Good plans, sound policies, and valid procedures are established neither strictly top-down nor only bottom-up, but interactively. Their elaboration and execution require co-involving low levels of supervision in the process of making forecasts, plans, and programs. It also calls for trust in the ability of senior management to exercise timely control as well as of lower management to execute assigned functions.

In a similar manner, the evaluation of competition requires both analytical studies and sound judgment. Comparisons should be made from the viewpoint of clients, taking both your own bank and its competitors into account. No institution operates in a vacuum. Measuring yourself and your results versus those of your peers is a good way to keep in shape—provided you can move ahead of the curve.

THE TOP SIX FUNCTIONS OF MANAGEMENT

What are the functions of managers? The six outstanding responsibilities of managers are outlined in Figure 12.2. At the top half of the pyramid, decisions have to be made within an unstructured information environment, where there exist too many degrees of freedom in the way business and other events may evolve. Therefore, decisions are made on the basis of opinions rather than facts.

How Strategic Planning Facilitates Decision-Making

A fundamental contribution of planning is to help managers avoid making a decision that will tie their hands to a specific course of action without having considered all possible alternatives and their aftermath. Unpleasant surprises happen because there has been no prognostication and no evaluation of alternatives. Good planning helps to minimize risks in two ways:

Figure 12.2
The Six Basic Functions of Management of Every Enterprise

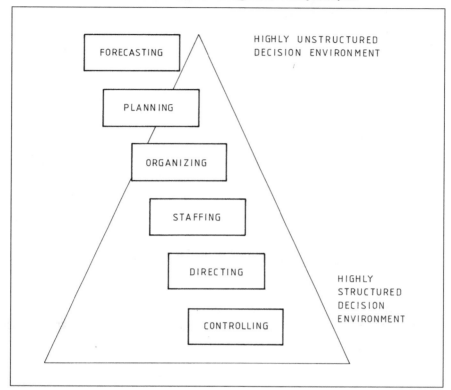

- By forcing you to consider alternatives to a certain plan, experiment with options, and examine results to be expected down the line.
- By permitting the organization to postpone making a crucial decision until a meaningful discussion takes place that reflects dissent.[1]

Peter Drucker explains nicely the difference between decisions based on opinions and those based on facts. He says that a decision is a judgment, a choice among alternatives. It is rarely a choice between "right" and "wrong." One starts with opinions. To determine what is

---

[1]Alfred P. Sloan, Jr., *My Years with General Motors* (London: Sidgwick and Jackson, 1963).

a fact requires first a decision on the criteria of relevance as well as on measurement: "The effective decision does not, as so many texts on decision-making proclaim, flow from a consensus on the facts."[2]

Therefore, the great leaders of industry have always encouraged diversity in opinion. They also promote dissent all the way to a clash of conflicting views among their immediate subordinates. They want to see a dialog between different viewpoints—and therefore a choice between conflicting judgments. Alfred P. Sloan was a master of this art because he knew well that effective decisions are not made by acclamation.

It is surprising that the majority of companies fail to appreciate that promoting different viewpoints and encouraging conflicting judgments—up to the moment when a decision is made—is indeed the board's responsibility. The board and the CEO also have the following responsibilities:

- To define the criteria of relevance that help in analyzing what is really at stake.
- To establish the boundary conditions within which action should take place.

To a very substantial extent, the dialog between the different viewpoints characterizes the high level of management functions: prognostication and planning. Dissent at these levels is salutary, but when it filters down the organization, it paralyzes any action.

As Figure 12.2 demonstrates, from bottom-up the fundamental functions of management range from relative certainty—which characterizes a structured decision environment—to uncertainty. At the lower half of the pyramid in Figure 12.2, the decision environment is structured; control must be precise. A structured information environment makes this feasible. Midway between the unstructured and structured environments, organizing and staffing are two activities that to a considerable extent reside in a semistructured environment.

For any practical purpose, a similar statement can be made about internal control, risk management, and auditing. At first sight, this may sound strange. After all, control is one of the six key functions of management and, as I just stated, it is part of the structured information environment. Yes, but internal control has a number of unknowns and to a large measure has more to do with organization and staffing than with accounting. Keep in mind these points:

---

[2]Peter Drucker, *The Effective Executive* (London: Heinemann, 1967).

- Auditing is closely related to accounting and it is part of the precise control structure.
- By contrast, compliance and risk management incorporate subjective judgments that must handle some of the existing fuzzy notions.

In conclusion let me add that the board has to select and appoint able people to carry out their assigned duties—people who measure up to the job. Staffing is the cornerstone to successful operations. But while authority is being delegated, responsibility can never be delegated. It always stays at board level.

SENIOR MANAGEMENT DECISIONS REGARDING INVESTMENT POLICIES

What we said about strategy and policy can be exemplified through the decisions made by the board necessary to effectively manage a portfolio of investments. Say, as an example, that the board has chosen a strategy of diversification for better control of credit risk and market risk. How can it be applied all the way down the line? What kind of boundary conditions should be set with it? What sort of controls should be exercised to ensure that the board's decisions are observed?

One argument usually heard in diversification of investments discussions is that financial markets can be found which compensate for price movements taking place in one another, as well as for likely weaknesses in some type of investments—for instance, stocks. It is suggested that diversification of investments will grow as a function of time, with less and less influence by market slumps. This is, however, theory, because of these principles:

- An equilibration of risks can happen only if two markets are negatively correlated and their correlation coefficient tends to equal minus one.
- In practice, such ideal conditions are not around. There exist, however, markets that are not positively correlated to a certain degree.

It used to be that positive correlations often happened among the Group of Ten markets and negative correlation between G-10 and emerging markets. Globalization sees to it that such negative correlations tend to disappear. Some sort of negative correlation exists today between market risk instruments (such as stocks) and credit risk instruments (such as credit derivatives). But this is not an absolute statement.

A different way of expressing the same concept is that until globalization changed the investment environment, increasing the positive correlation of financial markets by so much, financial analysts were searching for markets that were negatively correlated among themselves. If and when such markets are found, it is possible to decide on measures that up to a point might balance the risks. Basically, in terms of market risk, asset allocation should reflect correlations, volatility, and liquidity.

Volatility and liquidity are not the subject of this book, but they are critical inputs to the decisions the board makes. They also profoundly affect a company's risk management process. A self-respecting board should want to know whether the markets where investments are made are volatile, what kind of liquidity characterizes them, and what sort of legal risks are present. This leads to risk literacy, the alter ego of computer literacy, which, as mentioned, is a desirable skill for board members and senior managers.

No doubt the board should appreciate that the volatility of emerging markets is high because most of them are pushed up or pulled down by Western money flowing in and out at short notice. Contrary to the long-term horizon characterizing investments by commercial banks, institutional investors (i.e., managers of hedge funds, mutual funds, or pension funds) work for the short term. These money flows see to it that sometimes emerging markets are negatively correlated among themselves and with European and American markets. Theoretically, when this happens these emerging markets help in hedging. But practically, when a panic hits, emerging markets become positively correlated with the western markets.

Risk literacy is indivisible from market performance. Investment decisions by the board should consider the fact that in one year several emerging markets seem to be high performing, with 30% to 40% gains; but the next year they fall into negative territory with about the same amount of losses—which talks volumes about their volatility.

As these examples demonstrate, portfolio management is not a simple matter of routine action and preestablished procedural approaches. Able solutions must reflect the philosophy of investments which leads to strategic considerations heavily influencing policy decisions—for instance, an international diversification that aims to spread risk among different markets, instruments, and currencies but provides the board with real-time tools to manage such investments in a dynamic manner at all times.

An investment philosophy may or may not espouse the idea of global optimization; the board must decide. Typically, top management will have to elaborate a hedging strategy that will then be implemented by financial engineering. Say that the investment philosophy the board adopts is global asset allocation. This may involve investments in different markets, such as New York, London, Zurich, Frankfurt, Paris, and Tokyo. Good management would see to it that such investments are weighted in terms of reference currency and exchange. For instance, the board may decide that 50% of capital is invested at the New York Stock Exchange and in NASDAQ, with an edge in technology; or vice versa. Such an investment decision should also determine the amounts to be put in various currencies such as the dollar, pound, Swiss franc, euro, and yen.

Part and parcel of risk literacy is that no investment decision can overlook currency risk. The best approach is to decide on a basic currency (for instance, the dollar) and then diversify. It is critical also to decide about the amount of money to be put in different instruments such as equities, debt, and derivatives. Also, a sound investment strategy cannot forget about interest rate risk, whether we talk about loans, bonds, or geared investments through derivatives.

A sound investment strategy will be established under the best conditions when the board defines, in unambiguous terms, the company's risk profile. This will enable the bank's managers and professionals to know the level of exposure that should be taken in regard to the investment portfolio.

Setting a Policy on the Limits of Risk

The board's responsibility includes not only a policy on limits, but also their quantification. Limits set boundary conditions for both counterparty risk and each sort of market risk. Limits are dynamic and they need to be regularly reviewed with corrective action taken as soon as they are broken. All these steps are prerequisites to the able performance of risk management function. Limits have to be elaborated in regard to any counterparty and any instrument, as well as by any desk or trader, anywhere in the world.

Limits are tolerances and, as Figure 12.3 shows, they can be effectively controlled through statistical quality control (SQC) charts (which were introduced and discussed in detail in Chapter 4). As a reminder, the statistical quality control in Figure 12.3 is by variables. Widely used in the manufacturing industry, SQC charts are very helpful because they permit you to plot both quality control limits and tolerances. Therefore, they are now being implemented in banking. (See the reference in Chapter 4 to J.P. Morgan and GE Capital.) Typically, the tolerances are within the quality control limits. SQC charts are useful in managing risk for two reasons:

- The patterning of the quality of a product or process permits a bird's eye view of whether it might get out of control, so corrective action can be taken.
- SQC charts make it feasible to follow up the observance of boundary conditions at any time, anywhere, for any trader—and to do so without inordinate costs.

Figure 12.3
Statistical Quality Charts Are Powerful Tools with Significant Uses in Banking

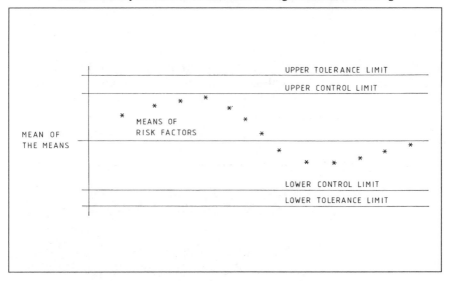

As boundary conditions, limits establish thresholds that contrast to the typical monolithic thinking of some boards who express their investment concept in extremes: "Minimum risk" or "significant return on investment"—which in practice means maximum risk. This coarse definition is not enough, as investment is not a black-or-white decision but features tonalities of gray. Therefore, much more is necessary in terms of strategic positioning and policy guidelines.

This lack of clear guidelines and of quantitative boundary conditions contributed a great deal to the downfall of Long-Term Capital Management, where the strategic decision seems to have been to pursue the highest ever return on capital. From what I heard on Wall Street, there was no limit on the risk to be assumed—and, as a consequence, on the amount of capital at risk. This made possible a more than 50-to-1 gearing and brought LTCM to virtual bankruptcy.

ORGANIZATIONAL PREREQUISITES TO THE MONITORING OF EXPOSURE

A significant amount of competence is needed to develop, implement, and maintain a strategic plan. Most crucial is the ability to do all of the following:

- Define long-term objectives,
- Develop the financial, human, product, marketing, technological, operational, and other plans, and
- Properly orient the research and development (R&D) effort.

Because innovation is crucial to the success or failure of an institution, the board must be keen on doing these functions:

- Establishing the right time frame for introducing innovative products to the market.
- Positioning the bank against the market forces that challenge its leadership, erode its share, or diminish its profits.
- Planning for risk management ahead of time to ensure the bank's ability to survive under worst-case scenarios, and
- Providing the proper organization and structure to keep the institution in control.

These four functions correlate—for instance, organization and structures with risk management.

Monitoring Risk

A modern financial institution has at least four markets that it should steadily watch and be able to read every signal—particularly when the signal shows that limits are about to be broken. Figure 12.4 identifies these four markets and suggests the range of activity in each one. Keep in mind these two guiding principles:

- **Risk is a wheel that turns all the time and, by so doing, changes the amount of exposure being assumed.**
- **Only real-time monitoring and tip-top policies can provide some confidence that assumed exposure to risk is in control.**

Figure 12.4
Four Markets to Be Watched for Exposure

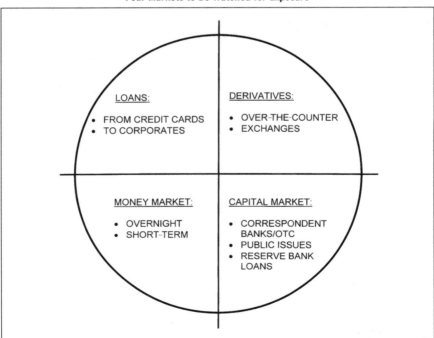

But neither real-time monitoring nor the control structure will stay put. Typically they will decay with time. To be ahead of the curve, real-time reporting must become faster and faster. As for organization, entropy sees to it that the only things that develop by themselves in a company are disorder and friction.

To counteract the results of entropy, which are part of daily life, the board must be ready to periodically restructure the firm, cut out the fat, redefine functions, and redirect communications lines. Restructuring calls for fundamental studies. It cannot be done on the run.

A thorough analysis must take account of current strengths and weaknesses. It must also rethink the channels of corrective action. In a similar vein, to support the bank's financial staying power, the board should study price structures, cost structures, and profit margins. It should direct senior management to steadily cut costs and consistently evaluate return on investment—as well as project cash flow in an accurate manner.

Fostering a Willingness to Change to Limit Risk Exposure

Another of the board's major duties is to find ways to overcome resistance to change. Failure to do so results in management inaction because resistance to change inhibits adjustment to new market conditions, a key performance criterion. In business, change is the only constant. Yet, most people fear change because of the unknowns that it involves and the risk of losing their current position and its perks.

The current position, however, cannot be supported at no matter what cost. The only way to ensure it is by accumulating, organizing, and applying knowledge and experience. This correlates to the functions of staffing: selecting, training, and promoting those who are effective, while letting go of the unable, unwilling, and unnecessary.

Hiring Effective Risk Managers

To dramatize this issue, Peter Drucker uses the example of George Marshall, who during World War II insisted that a general officer be immediately relieved if found less than outstanding. General Marshall flatly refused to listen to the argument, "But we have no replacement." "All that matters," he pointed out, "is that you know this man is not equal to the task. Where his replacement comes from is the next question."[3]

Marshall's example helps to demonstrate that to be effectively done, the management of change requires both patience and authority. It also talks volumes of the fact that staffing and directing correlate. Part of their interface is ensuring that the decision mechanism is open and in evolution, helping to avoid organizational arteriosclerosis. This is valid for all levels of management. A sound personnel policy requires these functions:

- Forecasting human inventory requirements, which provides lead time needed to develop knowledge resources.

- Ensuring that management skill is available to comprehend and simplify complex situations, but also to replace incompetent executives.

- Establishing priorities among competing goals in terms of human resources, their acquisition, training, and management.

Information Sharing Is Critical to Risk Management

Successful managers listen to all opinions, reach a decision after considering pertinent facts, and communicate their decisions in a clear, unambiguous manner. They also ensure organizational readiness in regard to the implementation of plans of action as soon as these plans have been formulated.

The best policy at the intersection of staffing and organizational structure is that of open channels capable of sharing problems. Bank One's former CEO John B. McCoy has a credo: "If you've got a problem, share it. Then we all have a problem. If you don't, and it grows, it's your ass."[4] McCoy lets managers visibly compete with each other. Every month, each one of the 200 Bank One units, including 74 controlled banks, must put its results on the corporate network. Deliverables are there for all to see, creating an atmosphere charged with bankwide visibility of risk and return.

---

[3]Ibid.

[4]*BusinessWeek,* April 9, 1990.

Here's another example: Softbank, one of Japan's go-go companies, is run as a network of 64 profit centers. Its founder, Masayoshi Son, came to this concept while the firm was still small and an illness prevented him from being in charge over a long time. Son capitalized on his inability to work and began decentralizing by organizing his workers into groups of 10, where each had profit-and-loss statement that would be updated daily, and those units who ran out of cash also ran out of luck.

"Son likes measuring everything," explains an executive of Softbank Holdings.[5] This environment is prone to espouse change. By contrast, banks operating under a veil of secrecy find many unpleasant surprises in their way. In February 1995, the Barings bank crashed because of secret accounts, like the 88888 of its Singapore operations, which (theoretically, at least) were not visible to top management. Similarly, in September 1995, the $1.1 billion loss revealed by the Daiwa Bank allegedly came out of a secret account kept by its New York operations.

Keep Management Flat to Facilitate Communication Regarding Exposure to Risk

In terms of organization and structure, another criterion the board should keep in perspective is *span of control*. This means how many managers report to the same boss. Information tends to flow more freely in flat organizations. Better coordination, a greater visibility of risk, and lower cost of operations are other benefits to be derived from flat structures. Too many management layers are ineffective, and the result is both cumbersome and costly.

A small span of control, at the level of two to seven managers depending on a single boss, means organizational fat. Equally disastrous is the case where managers tend to be given jobs as prizes rather than for what particular skills they provide the bank. This practice reduces responsibility and accountability while it rewards the politically oriented, the incompetent, and the inefficient.

In conclusion, organizational readiness is ensured through leadership and training, but also by means of an effective structure and personnel policies that reward the most able and manage change in

---

[5] *BusinessWeek*, August 12, 1996.

an effective manner. This information should be available to everybody. One criterion of good management is the way information flows through successive layers. Other things being equal, secretive organizations assume the greatest amount of risk.

FOUR STEPS TO EFFECTIVE RISK MANAGEMENT

In finance, as in any other business, planning is a process of choice. A planning problem arises when alternative courses of action are possible. A problem may have no solution, but typically if there is one solution there will be alternatives. Planning is based on forecasting, whose mission is to find out the most probable course our current decisions and actions might take—and, if possible, some other events. However, although prognostication and planning aim at the future, they do not deal with future decisions. Rather, their effectiveness as tools of management depends on *the way they can handle the future results of present decisions.*

Whether for risk control purposes or for anything else, management planning rests on a well-defined line of action. This presumes orderly execution of objectives, careful selection of the resources to be committed in meeting the objectives, studying the different stages our action will go through, and developing the most effective methods for attaining your goal. Keep in mind these key points regarding planning:

- **Planning means assessing the future, making provisions for it, and ensuring that established objectives can be met within acceptable time frames.**
- **A timetable for decisions, for action, and for the commitment of resources (human, material, financial) to control activity are the backbone of a plan.**

A management plan is made in stages, starting with the establishment of objectives set by the board (or proposed by the different operating divisions and departments) and confirmed by top management. When several objectives enter into corporate planning, it becomes necessary to sort out priorities. A sound policy would involve four key steps, described in the following sections:

Step 1: Establish goals in accordance with the general policy of the board and the chief executive.

Within the realm of overall objectives of the bank, specific goals must be elaborated by functional bodies such as divisional authorities. By providing the background capability to reach selected goals, the plan contributes to organizational accomplishments.

The planning process has by-products, but by-products are of little use unless the plan delivers its purposeful, designed main action. If the purpose of the plan is to protect the institution from a state of instability like the one in Figure 12.5, then it should definitely include limits (as discussed earlier in this chapter). Breaking them should trigger immediate management control to keep exposure under lock and key.

Figure 12.5
A State of Instability: The Ball May Roll Either Way Even with Minor Left or Right Input

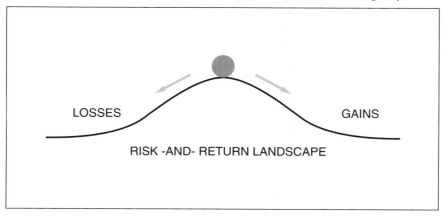

Step 2: Make choices among feasible alternatives to achieve goals, taking into account the bank's resources such as finance and intelligence.

Any institution has finite resources. Unlike what people may think, the most scarce resource is not financial but intelligence, talent, expertise, and skill, which must be properly allocated. Therefore, planning must be multidisciplinary, encompassing R&D, products, marketing, finance, technology, and human resources. Because the organization of the typical bank is departmental, it is essential that the planning mechanism ensures the necessary coordination between departments.

Step 3: Provide a mechanism to enable future decisions to be made rapidly and economically with little disruption of business course.

The interdependence of structures and resources characterizing financial activity can be expressed through plans. A formal plan leads toward the fulfillment of objectives, answering projected market opportunities as they appear. However, it is not counterproductive to plan once and freeze the plan forever.

Step 4: Establish techniques for effectively implementing the plan and following up on its execution.

The first principle for the implementation of any plan is that the people responsible for its execution are involved in its development from the beginning. Then, it will be their plan.

The second principle is the observance of timetables by everybody in a position of authority. A management plan consists essentially of timed objectives that must be reached within specific deadlines or the benefits will be lost.

The third principle, which we have already discussed, is feedback, which permits higher-up management to evaluate progress against objectives, identify problem areas, focus on salient problems, and take corrective action in a timely manner.

CONCLUSION

The concept of objectives set by management needs to be properly appreciated. An objective is an end, a result, not a task or a function. Long-term objectives both cover and help clarify short-range objectives. Within the framework of management planning, goals become planning statements. Major goals determine minor goals, and minor goals are usually the major goals' constituent parts.

Major goals normally evolve from concepts and ideas that aim to specify declarations of purpose. This can be done much more effectively if planning is based on sound forecasts. A plan will collapse if its forecasts are inaccurate, they are not made in time, or they are found to be seriously in error. Management must know in advance the answers to such questions as:

- How will the economy develop?
- What kind of markets will exist?
- What kind of products will these markets require?
- What quantity of sales can be expected?
- What kind of prices make the market kick?
- What might bend the bank's profit curve?

A central purpose of planning is to anticipate desired results to be achieved by proper management and the risks associated to reaching such results. This helps in devising the means needed to reach goals. Without planning, a financial institution is on a treadmill, reacting to events rather than influencing them, with the fire-brigade approach being the order of the day.

More to the point, a well-made plan makes control action feasible. Its clearly stated goals force managers, at all levels, to be alert to overall organizational objectives and policies. This is particularly important in large organizations where complexity or the lack of standards can be negative forces.

Finally, I would like to stress once more that plans must be regularly checked for compliance. This is the goal of the feedback mechanism shown in Figure 12.1. The cultural climate that makes business grow and science flourish is also a double-edged sword. On one side is an innovative, dynamic economy and on the other a cumulative amount of exposure.

Without the feedback mechanism permitting managers and the board of directors to evaluate the exposure taken with any counterparty, any instrument, at any time and any place—and to act on this information—the result will be an institution speeding out of control. This feedback mechanism is the operation for which the chief risk management office (CRMO) is responsible. Chapter 13 explains the functions of the CRMO.

CHAPTER 13

Staffing the Risk Management Department

Organizations are made of people and sometimes we can make neither heads nor tails of what these people do. A risk management department is no exception to this basic rule of human nature. It must employ specialists with background and experience permitting them to identify, monitor, mitigate, and control risk. But how much can it depend on these people?

The ongoing process of risk management, also known as production, has at least three prominent constituent functions:

1. Analyzing the performance of critical functions (including marketing, sales, loans authorization, investment decisions, and trading) as well as the way ongoing business affects the institution's financial staying power—This requires recording all transactions, evaluating their compliance to rules, marking-to-market or -to-model inventoried positions, investigating exposure, doing What-if analysis, and interactively preparing analytical, focused reports for senior management, preferably intraday.

2. Assessing uncertainty about future values of assets and liabilities associated with transactions and positions, and collaborating in the evaluation of limits—Limits act as the brakes that help to avoid runaway exposure. Their evaluation is a steady process which, to be done dependably, requires expertise in interactive computational finance, tools for sensitivity analysis, and means for real-time simulation from models to databases and computers.

3. Advising top management on timely corrective action necessary to redress the balances and when positions fall at the wrong side of the balance sheet; and taking such action under the board's or CEO's authority—Because of what they consider to be matter-of-fact trade-offs, most institutions tend not to monitor every critical function, at least not as intensively as they should. This is counterproductive because at the same time they take an inordinate risk whose magnitude often escapes top management's attention. Neither are the majority of banks today tooled for taking immediate corrective action; instead, they allow themselves to drift.

Another flaw in risk control practices is that to limit the dimensionality of risk assessment, some institutions make judgments about when certain types of market risk can be ignored and when positions in related securities can be aggregated together into a bucket. This reduces transparency and leads to situations where the bank suffers substantial losses from events not anticipated within a given time span or control framework.

Classical approaches to the management of on–balance-sheet and off–balance sheet risk are no good anymore because of conflict of interest prevailing among organizational units. Say, for instance, the International Division has marketing responsibilities. It cannot at the same time control the quality of counterparties.

A similar statement, albeit for different reasons, can be made about the Treasury, which most often handles derivatives. On the other hand, the Credit Department has a loans culture, which is not easily convertible to market risk, especially to derivatives. For its part, the Audit Department specializes in in-depth inspection, but it does not necessarily take the broader view necessary for global risk management.

Therefore, as Dr. Alan Greenspan suggested in his seminal article in *World Statesman* (Winter 1994), there is need for a top management officer able to take a rigorous but broad view of risk. He should do so by means of a real-time system assisted by qualitative and quantitative in-depth inspections. His position should be at the board-of-management level, reporting directly to the bank's chief executive officer. His function can be best described as that of the chief risk management officer (CRMO).

Managing the Institution's Exposure to Four Types of Risk

At the origin of risk is uncertainty. A less-than-certain outcome may concern the aftermath of a transaction, exposure associated with positions in your portfolio because of volatility, warnings about future earnings, or likely growth in liabilities. There may also be uncertainty regarding the behavior of counterparties in fulfilling their obligations. In financial institutions and in industry at large, uncertainty may be manifested through:

- Credit risk,
- Market risk,
- Operational risk, and
- Legal and other risks.

With the management of exposure based on models and computers, one of their "other risks" is model risk. Credit risk has been classically handled by financial institutions through functions assigned to the credit committee and the credit department. Every loans officer is made aware of credit risk during his training. This, however, is not true of market risk, operational risk, and legal risk. In fact, operational risk so far has been very poorly defined, with most approaches limited to payments and settlements.

Awareness about the broader perspective of operational risk is new. Its importance to the financial industry has been formalized with the 1999 New Capital Adequacy Framework by the Basle Committee on Banking Supervision. By contrast, legal risk classically has been the domain of the legal counsel (general counsel) and has been closely followed up by the chief executive officer.

Market risk started to really worry institutions only in the 1990s, because of leverage that had led to losses incurred with derivatives. A solution to bringing it under control has been promoted by the 1996 Market Risk Amendment by the Basle Committee. To catch discrepancies between exposure figures that are reported and those really prevailing, as well as to assist in restructuring their system of internal controls, some financial institutions now have independent units addressing risk management in a bankwide sense. They report directly to the CEO or the board. For example, Merrill Lynch set up this type of organizational unit after losing $377 million due to unauthorized trading in 1987. Other financial institutions have gone further, instituting a new executive entity: the chief risk management office.

This restructuring of responsibilities with a focus on market risk exposure became necessary because much of the banking system, including the American, British, continental European, and Japanese parts, is archaic in terms of global risk structure. It is locked in space and time, being oriented to practices that may fit small, weak banks but not global institutions. Keep in mind how the financial world has changed:

- **Traditional risk control systems were not made to keep a lid on exposure by sophisticated instruments and expansionist policies.**
- **Yet, today these sophisticated financial instruments and global policies have a dominating influence on the banking industry.**

There is great need for a risk czar who can combine courtesy and doggedness. But should he or she combine credit risk and market risk responsibilities? Should there be one or two organizational units managing the credit institution's exposure? If two, which one should be in charge of operational risk? Or, should a third unit look after this subject?

My research found no unique answers to these queries. But there are worries associated with the failure to find able solutions. Both the complexity of new instruments and the globalization of financial markets see to it that big players get bigger and more powerful as they compete on an international scale. At the same time, complexity tends to reduce transparency.

Because transparency is so important to risk control, top management should appreciate the absolute need to maintain a clear, sharp focus on all types of risks being assumed. It should also understand that sometimes major risks are lost from sight, at least temporarily, while even an intermittent eclipse can have disastrous consequences.

In the late 1980s, Walter Wriston, the former chairman of Citicorp, suggested that, as opposed to an old boys' club, the modern financial services business is very competitive.[1] When business opportunity changes as fast as it does today, organization and structure should change too in order to maintain one's competitiveness. The same is true of planning and control premises, which must become very dynamic.

---

[1] *The Wall Street Journal,* April 20, 1989.

In the domain of effective risk management, the interest in insti-
tuting a chief risk management office has been prompted by several
financial debacles and scandals and the huge losses they represented.
The following events of late 1994 were instrumental in pushing tier-1
institutions to improve the way they manage exposure:

- GE Capital lost $800 million, two months after GE's $1.5 billion
  loss in the fire sale of Kidder Peabody in October 1994.

- An Orange County, California, fund lost $2.1 billion in the
  300% leverage of its $7.5 capital through repurchase agree-
  ments and wrong bets on interest rates.

- Tesobonos (Mexico's equivalent of U.S. Treasury Bonds) left a
  gaping hole of $53 billion in Mexico's financial obligations,
  which had to be plugged with Group of Ten money.

Then in February 1995 came the Barings bankruptcy, bringing
home the message that every bank, every division, every policy, every
program, every activity should be controlled in a dynamic manner,
preferably through real-time simulation and stress testing. Old-fashioned estimates failed because as a rule they are underestimates and
exposure limits are breached many times over.

However, models bring with them a new type of risk that is particularly important with derivatives: model risk. A major factor behind
model risk is our assumptions. Therefore the chief risk management
officer and his assistants must test these assumptions against their own
estimates of risk and return. They must do so by means of a number of
critical questions to which they should receive well-documented answers:

- What is your mission?
- Is it still the right mission?
- Is it still worth doing?
- If we were not doing this, would we go into it now?
- What is the risk taken with this mission?
- Is the return significantly in excess of the risk we assume?
- What's the likelihood of the return? Of the risk being assumed?

These queries address the broader horizon of gains and losses.
Pinching pennies may be all well and good, but top management's
main problem is not only spending too much money. Indeed, there

may be things on which it should be spending more, not less—risk control being an example. The larger trouble confronting an institution could be that it spends almost randomly, trying to do everything imaginable without counting the risk taken.

HOW CAN WE IMPROVE MONITORING OF EXPOSURE TO RISK?

The need for sharpening the mind's eye for assumed exposure does not come only from derivative financial instruments. Nonperforming loans too can be deadly. The same is true of a number of other transactions. Sometimes, top management itself gives the signal that there are no rules, thus derailing risk control efforts. Consider these statistics:

- Losses from bad loans amount to about 50% of the would-be profits of banks, though there are exceptions to this statistic; and
- Exposure due to derivatives has reached astronomical proportions. Some banks have spent many times over their equity in pure derivatives exposure. As shown in Figure 13.1, three of the top six American banks have exposed more than 10 times their equity and one has at stake more than all of its assets.

Figure 13.1
Demodulated Derivatives Exposure Compared to Equity and Assets of Major Credit Institutions as of March 31, 1999 (in Billions of Dollars)

	EQUITY	ASSETS	NPA IN DERIVATIVES	DEMODULATED DERIVATIVES EXPOSURE*	RATIO TO EQUITY	RATIO TO ASSETS
J.P. Morgan	$11.3	$261	$8.861	$295.4	x16.1	1.132
Bankers Trust	4.7	133	2.563	85.4	x18.2	0.642
Chase Manhattan	23.8	366	10.353	345.1	x14.5	0.943
Citigroup	42.7	669	7.987	266.2	x6.2	0.398
BankAmerica	45.9	618	4.438	147.9	x3.2	0.239
Banc One	20.6	262	1.472	49.1	x2.4	0.187

*By a factor of 30.

Figure 13.2 gives a graphic snapshot of what is meant by so huge a level of exposure. Though Chase Manhattan is taken as an example, as we have already seen other institutions are not much better. Japanese banks have been just as severely hit by high gearing and have sought protection in massive mergers, though it is doubtful that two or three portfolios that went wrong make one that goes right. Neither are bad loans and derivatives exposure the only worry facing the management of financial institutions. Plain fraud is alive and well.

Figure 13.2
Some Frightening Statistics on Equity, Assets, and Derivatives Exposure at Chase Manhattan

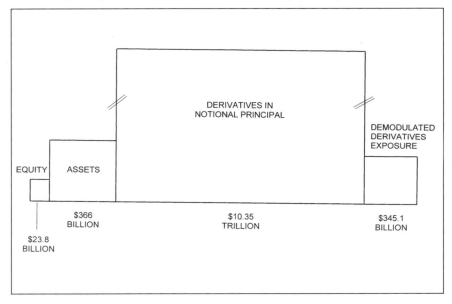

In the 1980s Robert Fomon, then head of E.F. Hutton Securities, was asked whether he should take some responsibility for an illegal check overdrafting scheme that tainted the brokerage. He replied, "No chief executive can be held accountable for any single thing that happens in a corporation."[2] But experts on ethics as well as many senior corporate officers say top management must accept full responsibility for whatever happens.

----

[2]*International Herald Tribune,* August 2, 1990.

This is not only the ethical way of looking at an issue of fraud or gross negligence but also the legal viewpoint. Even if top management does not know explicitly about the actions of subordinates, executives might be culpable if they have created a climate in which wrong-doing is condoned or even encouraged. The chief risk management officer has a very clear responsibility in this connection, which he cannot easily discharge. Keep in mind these two responsibilities:

- **Within the limits the law and regulators prescribe, the board should set the maximum allowed level of leverage of the institution as a whole, by product line and desk.**

- **One of the most important jobs of the CRMO and his assistants is to check for these limits to gearing and to sound the alarm to the CEO and the board when they risk being approached.**

SQC charts can help provide an estimate of exposure by graphically mapping the trend. They should be implemented and followed tick-by-tick. The upper half of Figure 13.3 shows a control chart by variables: $\bar{x}$ is the mean of a group of transactions, the limit to be set by the board expresses the tolerance—or pain—the institution decides that it can afford. But while each transaction may fall within the limit, their cumulative exposure might break the company rules. The cumulative plot in the second half of Figure 13.3 is there to sound the alarm.

This application requires a policy decision rather than mathematical skills, because the mathematics were well established 60 years ago and have been successfully implemented in the manufacturing industry. More than one CRMO told me that a problem with risk management is that traders, salespeople, and often their managers care only about making a deal, but not about the damage that deal might cause afterwards to the institution. To complicate matters even more, authority on the trading floor heavily depends on how much money a desk is making. The CRMO and his staff do not have the right to interfere with deals in the making.

Policy decisions should establish that prudential limits established by the board are the watchdogs during trading. The problem is that most banks lack the sophisticated technology to catch in real-time the breaking of limits by trade, desk, instrument, counterparty, and region. This contributes to the mounting exposure the institution is taking on.

Figure 13.3
A Tick-by-Tick Follow-up on Exposure by Means of Statistical Quality Control Charts

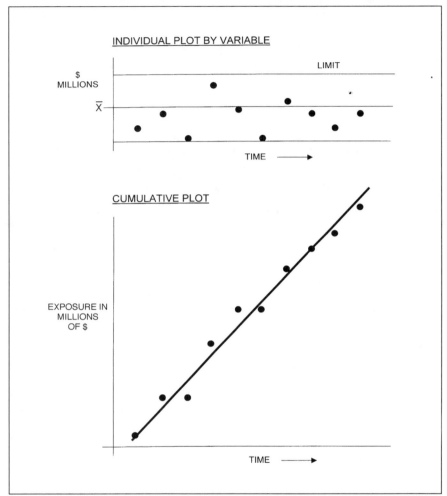

Some of the CRMOs I met also suggested that there is an asymmetry in the allocation of advanced skills. The best quants employed by the institution work for trading desks. This makes more difficult the task of catching mispricings. Let's face it. Some derivative financial instruments are marketed more for the fat margin they carry along than for their suitability to the bank or to investors. Here's the reality in many financial institutions:

> - **Corporate managers and key employees are paid substantial option packages that have no immediate impact on the bottom line as an expense but will weigh on future profits.**
>
> - **Part of the challenge in keeping the balances straight is that companies and analysts are overly preoccupied with short-term results and less focused on longer-term profitability.**

The able management of risk (particularly of high-risk products) has prerequisites. These are the ability to consider both the short and the longer term, clear-cut responsibilities, and high technology support. Your bank would like to earn a good fee as trader, broker, and assets manager—all risks counted. It would not like to be the speculator subject to major swings and lose its capital. This calls for the ability to control risk in a timely manner by means of a complete management system that encompasses these functions:

- Establishing both analytical and aggregated approaches to risk measurement,
- Building user-friendly interfaces for online database access and experimentation,
- Providing for minute tick-by-tick follow-up of all high-risk products and geared counterparties.

The CRMO should also pay significant attention to human failures. More often than not, bank failures have as a common background the people in the system, particularly those who run it (or are supposed to do so). Equally important is to rethink and reevaluate policies and procedures, proposing to the board and the CEO necessary changes. Many bankers believe that old policies cover new risks. This is patently false. In risk management as in any other case, the biggest fool is the man who fools himself.

TOP MANAGEMENT SHOULD BE ACCOUNTABLE FOR RISKS THE BANK IS TAKING

"Senior management should be held accountable for unethical actions if they have put severe pressure on their employees and have not emphasized that these goals should not be achieved by cutting ethical corners," says Kirk O. Hanson, a professor at the Stanford Business School and president of the Business Enterprise Trust, a nonprofit institute that examines issues of business ethics. He and other experts suggest that today's pressures on companies to improve performance pose the special risk of questionable behavior. Consider these scenarios:

- **In some institutions, top officers put forth performance goals with the message "I don't care how you do it, just do it."**
- **In other financial institutions, senior executives deliberately turn a blind eye to wrong-doing or even implicitly agree to it, but remain shielded from blame.**

The message both points carry applies by all evidence to the way LTCM was run, leading to its downfall. "I think that top management has the responsibility to create a climate where that kind of behavior never arises," says Richard M. Rosenberg, former chairman and chief executive of BankAmerica. "That's maybe a naive statement, but I really believe it." So do I.

To ensure that everybody in the organization is accountable for his or her actions as well as observant of the policies established by top management, the duties of the chief risk management officer must be much broader than bean counting. While information on risk is valuable, its analysis is just as important.

Look Out for Extreme Events and Maintain a Broad Focus

The CRMO should carefully watch for spikes, which are usually produced by some extreme event. The plot in Figure 13.4 is a special case of that in Figure 13.3. The exposure taken by a certain desk seems to be within the limits, but then a spike leaves it out of control. Immediate corrective action rights the balances, bringing the system under control again.

Spikes may present themselves at any desk, with any instrument, at any time, anywhere in the world. For this reason, the CRMO should operate worldwide—wherever the bank is present—and the person in charge must be a member of the executive board so that he or she has equal status to the other divisional managers (as discussed in detail in Chapter 12). In fact, in several banks, the CRMO reports directly to the chairman—a sound solution because it permits the institution to establish and follow an independent risk control channel. Consider these recommendations:

- **The CRMO functions should not be limited to off–balance-sheet products; instead, they should include all types of trades and portfolio positions.**
- **While the CRMO department should focus on derivative contracts (most specifically on over-the-counter deals), it should also integrate loans exposure.**

The reason for this broader focus is that the value of both the trading book and the banking book can fluctuate significantly as a result of credit risk, market risk, and other risks. Depending on the composition, gearing, and duration of the investments, the capital at risk may considerably vary even on small movements in stock, bond, and currency prices or in interest rates.

Figure 13.4
Spikes Are Particularly Dangerous Because They Leave Exposure Out of Control

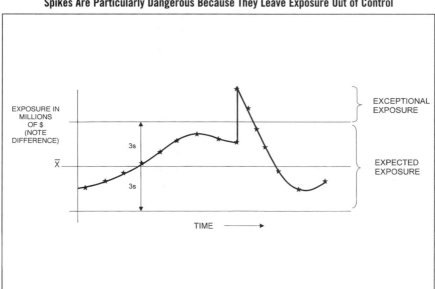

The able monitoring and measuring of market and credit exposures in a portfolio must be transaction-specific. It should also represent a realistic view of the bank's true risk with a given counterparty at any point in time. Typically, to obtain a realistic appreciation of current risk, we must go beyond historical data and statistics, recording exceptional market events and leading ourselves toward solutions by means of rigorous scenario analysis. This is particularly necessary because a typical portfolio may contain a bewildering array of assets and liabilities, including:

- Exposure due to fixed- and floating-rate debt,
- Sophisticated swaps that switch among currencies,
- Securities lending and repurchase commitments, and
- Structured notes and other exotics.

The range of issues to which the CRMO must bring its attention is theoretically limitless. But the following list covers some of the main risks confronting a financial institution:

- Consolidated exposure to global risks
- Credit risk
- Liquidity risk
- Currency risk
- Volatility risk
- Interest rate risk
- Country risk
- Legal risk
- Transaction processing risk
- Sales conditions risk
- Position risk
- Funds transfer risk
- Operational risk
- Fraud risk
- Settlement risk
- Event risk
- Underwriting risk

(Notice that some of these risks overlap with one another, making it difficult to follow them individually.)

There are very few cases of banks that, when faced with a complex position, know what their trading book and banking book are worth at any given time. Even more rare is the knowledge of what sort of exposure is involved and whether the institution has the financial staying power to sustain such exposure. Financial history shows that in a number of occasions, the following scenarios occur:

- **Profit snowfalls and panics are not only twins but also self-feeding processes that revert to one another.**

- **Such a switch happens because market sentiment sometimes reverses itself to its exact opposite.**

Unearth Weaknesses and Ask Tough Questions

Barings executives found out too late that the ability (as well as the willingness) to ask tough questions when times are good is the wisest policy. Even if penetrating questions make some people unhappy, there is no alternative to steadily testing for weaknesses. The asking of tough questions when times are bad comes too late to be of any value in redressing a situation that has gone out of control.

Risk position tracking, modeling, and experimentation on assumed exposure are integral parts of the job not only of the CRMO but of every member of the board of directors and of the management board. The inability to unearth weak points and positions and redress them when there is still time to do so ends in misuse of personal responsibility and in trading scandals.

Several executives have pressed the point that not all financial institutions and all people are willing and able to go to the heart of the matter, exposing hidden risks and taking corrective action. This does not necessarily mean they are unable—they may in fact be shy! Others are not able to bring themselves together to face reality, hoping that things will take care of themselves in due course.

But problems don't just resolve themselves in due course, and plenty of evidence suggests that half-baked measures are counterproductive. Invariably, suppression of bad news and delays in corrective action prove to be the worst possible course as well as evidence of poor management. Paraphrasing an old trading adage, "There is no such thing as a bad risk. Only bad pricing and bad management." Good management is usually a blend of organization, structure, and personalities of people entrusted with critical duties.

SELECTING THE RIGHT MANAGER FOR RISK CONTROL

Because organizations are made of people, personalities count. However, before considering desirable personality traits, institutions should recognize that effective personnel selection is an important issue that should be high in the priorities of every board member.

When the board is presented with a high-level appointment (and the CRMO is a high-level position), its members should always ask themselves these questions:

- Does this person have strength in at least one major area?
- How vital is this area to her new responsibilities?
- Is that area really important to the risk management job?

The underlying concept is that if the candidate achieves excellence in this one area, at least she does not start everywhere from scratch. Of course, it would be best if the candidate has strengths in all areas of importance, but such people are not easily found if they are found at all.

The board should not suffer from the delusion that the CRMO job can be split between different people. Two or three mediocrities never achieve as much as one competent person. In fact, two incompetents achieve less than one incompetent as they get in each other's way. Some institutions, however, have organized various committees to support the CRMO. For example, at Credit Suisse, the board of directors has delegated some of its risk management and control responsibilities to the group chief risk officer (GCRO) and the Group Risk Coordination Committee (GRCC). The GRCC meets at least quarterly and defines overall Group risk policies, approving general instructions as well as standards and processes concerning risk management at business-unit level. It also reviews the Group's capital management process to ensure financial staying power.

GRCC meetings are usually followed by a meeting of the Group Executive Board's Risk Management Committee. This concentrates on the evaluation of new projects and products from a risk perspective. It also deals with risk-relevant compliance issues. Both the Risk Management Committee and the GRCC are led by the group chief risk officer. Risk Committees at the business-unit level are established by the chief executive of the business unit. But it is the task of Group Risk Management (GRM) to harmonize risk management approaches across the various business units.

Speaking from experience, I can ascertain that it is possible to find a first-class person to fill the CRMO's shoes, but there is a likelihood that his current boss will say, "I cannot spare this man." There are only a few explanations why a superior considers a subordinate to be indispensable:

- The indispensable person's strength is being misused to bolster a weak superior who cannot stand on his own feet,
- His or her strength is misused to delay tackling a serious problem or even conceal its existence, or
- He or she is really incompetent and can only survive if carefully shielded from demanding tasks.

Peter Drucker suggested these explanations and goes on to say that in every one of the aforementioned situations, the indispensable person should be moved anyhow and soon. Otherwise whatever strengths he or she may have will be destroyed, because incompetence of the boss breeds incompetence in the subordinates.[3]

As a good example on how to staff the opportunities rather than feed the problems one is faced with, Drucker takes George Marshall's policy during World War II. Marshall insisted that a general officer be immediately relieved if found less than outstanding. To keep him in command, he reasoned, was incompatible with the responsibility of the U.S. Army. General Marshall was right! In fact, it is incompatible with the accountability of top management in any organization.

General Marshall refused to listen to the argument "But we have no replacement." "All that matters," he pointed out to his assistants, "is that you know that this man is not equal to the task. Where his replacement comes from is the next question." But Marshall also pressed the point that in the majority of cases to relieve a man from

[3]Peter Drucker, *The Effective Executive* (London: Heinemann, 1967).

command was less a judgment on the person itself than on the commander who had appointed him.

"The only thing we know is that this spot was the wrong one for that man," George Marshall argued. "This does not mean that he is not the ideal man for some other job. Appointing him was my mistake, now it's up to me to find what he can do." Out of this policy, Drucker suggests, came the future generals of World War II who were still junior officers with few hopes for promotion when Marshall became the boss of the U.S. Army.

WHY MODELING AND SCENARIO WRITING ARE HELPFUL

First and foremost, the personality of the CRMO makes or breaks the job he is expected to perform. The people working with him must think much of him and his perceptual capabilities; indeed they should be impressed. A company's CRMO should be widely viewed not just as clever, but as able to exercise independent judgment and as unwilling to say what he thinks his superiors want to hear unless he truly believes it.

In addition, to these personality traits, however, come analytical skills. Risk management demands accuracy in both qualitative and quantitative terms. The usual approach to experimentation associated with quantification of market risk is to estimate the overall effect on a portfolio if rates change even by small amounts—for instance, 1, 2, 5, or 10 basis point changes in interest rates. To assess this risk:

- **The CRMO needs to not only detect volatility and determine corresponding risk figures, but also elaborate a worst-case scenario.**
- **Worst-case scenarios can be instrumental to proactive risk management, provided they are based on sound hypotheses and correct computational procedures.**

Monitoring, mapping, and evaluating correlate. Just like accurate risk estimates are a prerequisite to realistic modeling solutions, modeling is crucial to risk measurement. The appreciation of changes in risk factors and the way these affect exposure is done through scenario writing. Modeling and scenarios, however, must benefit from information that is both accurate and current. (As documented in Part Two, LTCM and its partners were famous for neither).

In a well-managed financial institution there should be no room for lying by using models. For example, recall how Chapter 9 described how UBS received from LTCM on a monthly basis a number supposed to represent a sort of the hedge fund's intrinsic value. However, at least on the UBS side, nobody quite understood what this curious number stood for, except that it was received in Zurich just once per month. Yet UBS, which had bet more than $1 billion of LTCM's fortunes, used this unreliable and obsolete number in its daily computation of VAR—a computation that is a regulatory requirement.

Reliable risk measurement, modeling, scenario writing, and reporting are integral parts of the CRMO's methodology, and they are vital components of the bank's risk control framework. Once management identifies and quantifies its credit risk and market risk exposure, it needs to ensure that they are actively and appropriately managed.

The identification and measurement of different types of risk are critical to the entire process of keeping exposure under control. In addition, top management must appreciate the need for policies that permit a financial institution to accurately and effectively keep its business under steady supervision, on an ongoing basis intraday, in real-time.

Accurate and effective risk measurement is especially challenging because the control of credit risk and market risk is, as already stated, both quantitative and qualitative. Variations in quantitative issues are easier to measure, including the aggregation of individual transactions into portfolios and the computation of recognized gains and losses for reserve and capital allocation purposes. Both quantitative factors and qualitative issues can be nonlinear.

Nonlinear functions entering into country risk include devaluations, export controls, inflation, bailouts, and meltdowns. To a large measure, these examples identify political risk. The steady management of credit exposure as well as limits adjustment for market risk involve ancillary topics. Examples are transaction motivation and willingness versus ability to pay.

Financial institutions must always guard against underestimating and overestimating exposure because both can lead to erroneous decisions and a misallocation of resources to face assumed risks. The development and use of realistic estimators is an integral aspect of the risk management process and hence of CRMO's responsibilities.

The CRMO must be able to heighten the board's awareness of the changes that affect the market, the instruments, and the counterparties, given the fact that the business environment is in full evolution. It is his duty to explain to the members of the board, the CEO, and all executives that because of globalization, deregulation, innovation, and technology there are more surprising dips and curves in modern business life than there have been in the past.

It is no less the CRMO's job to document that the essence of being conservative in trades, loans, and investments is to look at the downside more than the upside and, whenever possible, to monetize the risk taken in case of a downside. As I have explained, the monetization of risk rests on the idea of a risk premium that acts like an insurance premium. The goal of risk monetization is to:

- Include risk in product pricing, trades, loans, investments, and other instruments, and
- Ensure that to all transactions is associated capital at risk; no return is risk-free.

In a manner best exemplified through RAROC, the monetization of risk is done in the sense of a premium commensurate with the level of exposure being assumed. That's the way the actuaries work. This premium can be applied in the trading book in an accounting sense, and it can be instrumental in increasing everybody's sensitivity regarding exposure.

The need for such practice will become commonly known when management policies specify the following requirements:

- Insurance premiums on risks must always be applied,
- Allocated limits must be observed,
- Accurate and timely risk measurements must be made, and
- All information should be databased and then data-mined, a job to be done interactively, ad hoc, in a seamless manner.

When the amount of capital at risk and its insurance premium have been defined, the goal becomes one of computing return on risk capital (RORC). Consider these recommendations:

- **Establish risk premiums as if they were insurance premiums.**
- **Apply them by instrument, desk, and trader as well as market and counterparty.**
- **Steadily make detailed real-time reevaluations of assumed exposure.**
- **Develop powerful models to explore database contents and do simulation.**
- **Use agents (knowledge artifacts) for exception reporting in 3-D color graphics and also in real-time.**

These points constitute the technological side of the equation of which the CRMO must be a master. There should exist as well a procedural side that heavily rests on the system of checks and balances that we call internal controls. Yet, in my professional work I am surprised by the number of institutions lacking a rigorous internal control system. Companies without one take startling liberties with the facts of business life.

RESPONSIBILITIES OF THE CHIEF RISK MANAGEMENT OFFICER

Globalization, deregulation, innovation, and technology see to it that the foremost responsibilities of the CRMO and his assistants are of a global scale. This requires flexible concepts, adequate policies, and high technology support. A valid way to define global risk management is the ability to simultaneously administer and control the risk embedded in the client relationship and in the bank's own portfolio.

This must be done without the usual constraints of time and space. Within the broader perspective of global risk management, the concept and tools of quality control borrowed from the manufacturing industry (see Chapter 4) ensure that in the process of financial services the security valves operate perfectly, supporting a fast turnaround of information and know-how.

Even the most talented CRMOs must keep within what their functional description requires. They are not responsible for setting limits to counterparty risk, interest rate risk, currency risk, country risk, or any other. Their duty is to build and maintain a system able to observe the limits set by the board, and to set alarms when these risk being broken. Alarms are usually actuated by triggers. This is the chain of events:

- **The bank's trading system will continue to function even after a trigger event has occurred.**
- **But the CRMO must immediately bring to the CEO's attention deviations for timely corrective action.**

For this reason, much of the CRMO's responsibility has to do with measurement, information, and experimentation—not with operational decisions that overlap with the functions of operating departments. For instance, from a credit risk perspective, the CRMO tracks transactions to ascertain if traders indeed deal with counterparties of high rating. Once again, bear in mind what the CRMO's responsibility really is:

- **The CRMO has no responsibility for establishing credit rating.**
- **The CRMO's duty is to control in real-time if the bank's norms are observed.**

In performing this and similar duties, the CRMO has to use simulation to help focus on risk exposure generated by transactions. A simulation typically will be based on thousands of statistical runs in estimating the aftermath of certain hypotheses and/or selected inputs. An example is a credit loss distribution function.

Experimentation on exposure done by the CRMO can provide valuable information on expected and unexpected credit losses, the reserves and capital required to support the outcome of different scenarios, possible market liquidity problems, and likely evidence that an assumed volatility smile has been misjudged by those who did options pricing.

The CRMO must also have access to sophisticated models able to monetize risk. The monetization of risk helps in applying a sort of reinsurance and it can be implemented not only with derivatives but also with loans—as it is done with Risk-Adjusted Return On Capital (RAROC). What we are essentially targeting is the definition of capital at risk (CAR) which we accept a priori, whereas value at risk (VAR) is a postmortem calculation.

Sometimes this capital at risk is stated explicitly as in the case of Salomon Brothers, Merrill Lynch, and other financial institutions. Their problem has been that, having lost their AAA status, they are no more sought-out derivatives partners by correspondent banks. Hence each one of these entities set up a fully owned subsidiary and endowed it with a capital of $500 million, which is practically capital at risk.

In other cases, the capital at risk is more subtle. Bankers, treasurers, and investors hope that they are not betting capital in the deals that they make. They only look for a return. Yet, the concepts of risk and return are indivisible. Barclays Bank, for example, calculates for each risk and for all exposures what they amount to compared to the whole portfolio of the institution. This computation is done at a 99% level of confidence.

It is essential that the level of risk your bank assumes is commensurate to the payoffs you target. Risks should never exceed projected payoffs by any margin. Regarding which model should be used for analytical studies of the type I am suggesting, opinions differ. Books on this issue diverge in regard to the prescription they promote:

- Some address modern methods of risk management, including variance, covariance, historical simulation, Monte Carlo, Greek ratios, volatility, correlation, and other statistical tools.

- Some specialize in such pricing methods as present value, Black Scholes, and binomial trees and provide guidelines as to which of the above methods should be used for which instrument.

- Some concentrate on the regulatory environment and address risk management through a review of options and swaps, the composition of a portfolio, credit risk issues, and techniques that should be employed to ensure effective understanding of exposure being taken.

From my own experience, I have found all three sets of methods and tools are useful. The wise CRMO will not depend entirely on any one specific approach or trend, but will balance the strengths and weaknesses of the different methods.

CHAPTER 14

Why Superior Organization Supports the Risk Management Function

Organization is regarded as the establishment, with necessary authority and associated responsibility, of coordinated relationships between persons assigned to perform specialized missions. These missions, duties, or tasks (such as risk management) are necessary for the achievement of the institution's objectives.

Organization leads to structure, and structural relationships by which a bank is bound together form a framework. Individual efforts within this structure are coordinated by a higher-up manager to whom individual units report. Here some important organizational issues should be considered:

- How should different activities be grouped?
- How close should their supervision be?
- How much authority should each unit have?
- How can responsibility overlaps be avoided?

The answers to these questions cast light on the nature of the framework of command and control. Typically in well-run organizations there are principles that can be used as guides to decisions, keeping in mind that most management problems are derived from human and material factors as well as from traditions. Many of these problems cannot be solved with one simple answer.

One problem relevant to the control of exposure to risk is whether there should be one or two organizational units looking after damage prevention and repair: one for credit risk, the other for market risk. A departmentation of risk control is largely the consequence of historical reasons: Classically there has been a central credit risk department. More recently a different organization has been created and assigned the market risk mission.

Some institutions, such as Credit Suisse First Boston (CSFB), merged the two departments into one. Later on, however, CSFB reverted to two separate risk control organizations. Yet, there are merits in the existence of a unified line of command.

Every institution faces this problem of a choice between two separate risk departments or a single one. Those who persist in having two risk departments cite as reasons cultural differences between the people who manage credit risk and those addressing themselves to market risk. But there are also common elements, such as these factors:

- Behavioral control connected to the observance of limits and other guidelines, and
- The rapidly increasing use of mathematical models for both market risk and credit risk.

There are also other crucial organizational issues that need addressing. Major among them are the degree of centralization or decentralization and the subordinate–supervisor relationship. An effective definition of the mission to be performed takes the form of responsibilities, indicators, and objectives shown in Figure 14.1. The responsibilities should be given in headlines and be few and clearly stated. Indicators help to explain what these responsibilities mean. Both responsibilities and objectives change rather slowly. By contrast, objectives are dynamic. They should be established, reviewed, and met every year as well as changed during the year as the situation warrants.

CENTRALIZATION, DECENTRALIZATION, AND INDEPENDENT BUSINESS UNITS

The organizational solution to be chosen will necessarily reflect the culture and structure of the financial institution. A hierarchical, centralized firm will follow different decision-making and execution lines than one that is decentralized and leaves the choice of alternatives at the level of the profit center or independent business unit. This is true of every activity, not only of risk management.

Figure 14.1
The Effectiveness of Organizational Relationships and Execution of
Assigned Missions Requires Clear Directives

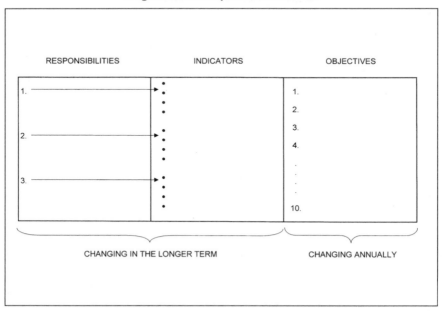

The argument between centralization and decentralization is as old as human society itself. The centralized entity can provide more tightly knit plans and a straighter line of control, but size limits its effectiveness. The wave of mergers in banking works against central-ization, yet there must be in place forces keeping the organization together. Another constraining factor rightly or wrongly linked to centralization is organizational fat. Highly centralized institutions tend to have a small span of control (with only a few managers report-ing to a boss) but many layers from top to bottom, which makes plan-ning, directing, and controlling inefficient.

A flat organization with few management layers is more cost-effective than a tall pyramid with many layers, but it can be nearly as centralized in terms of command and control. The next question therefore is what should be the degree of decentralization (or even relative independence) of organizational entities? The answer is that the independent business unit idea has evolved as a means to keep organizations manageable because of globalization, necessary speed of response, product diversification, and changing customer orientation and complexity.

Independent business units are usually focused on a subject. The earliest approach in specialized responsibility was the division between staff and line management, which originated in the military and migrated into business with the Industrial Revolution.

Line responsibilities in financial institutions concern the operating units such as lending, trading, investments, and private banking. Divisions can be made based on product, area of operations, or other criteria. But departmentation reveals the need for coordination. Among the prerequisites for decentralized management are:

- The implementation of a global strategic plan,
- Policy statements that are generally observed,
- Limits that are centrally established and controlled,
- Regularly held evaluations of risk and exposure, and
- A deep sense of responsibility and accountability.

A basic organization principle is that coordination and control action must be ensured in spite of the fact that management strategy is never written in its details, because otherwise strategic plans become inflexible and obsolete. Keep in mind these principles regarding strategy:

- **A master plan against an opponent will be more effective if management can explain objectives in an interactive and convincing manner.**

- **This unwritten management strategy is a cornerstone of any successful enterprise, because it provides a sense of direction to all its units.**

Not all credit institutions understand that even the best strategic plan will fail if there is no corresponding control action. To achieve objectives, a financial institution or any other organization needs to create at the top management level an environment in which responsibility and accountability flourish. This, too, is part of the strategic plan.

The most recent organizational concept promoted as a solution to more effective communication and action in an enterprisewide sense is a federated organization. As shown in Figure 14.2, a federated organization differs significantly from the more classical decentralization; federated and decentralized organizations are opposites of each other:

- With decentralization, authority flows *from the center* to the periphery.
- By contrast, in a federated organization the authority of the center comes by delegation *from the periphery*.

For example, the Swiss Confederation shows how independent business units can collaborate by delegating part of their authority to the center. The Japanese *keiretsu* reflects the same principle. With federated organizations, the center primarily has the functions of planning and control including risk control. Clear-cut control lines and functions are necessary to ensure that the organization does not break apart because of centrifugal forces, and that exposure to risks is kept under lock and key at all time.

Figure 14.2
Federated Organizations versus Decentralized and Departmentalized Structures

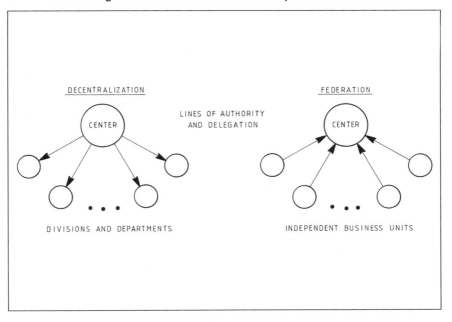

Whether for risk management or any other operation, planning and control is a way of business life, not an annual paper exercise. The organizational concept of a federated solution, and its independent business units, are not doing away with the need for rigorous management. To the contrary, they strengthen that need. The underlying principle is that of centralized planning and control connected through real-time systems to the periphery—that is the independent business units.

Centralized planning and control provides common purpose and direction, while also ensuring that the right thing happens at the right time, and avoiding decentralization turning into disintegration. Federated solutions address organizing, staffing, and directing in a decentralized way permitting better adaptation and much greater flexibility.

CASE STUDY: THE RISK MANAGEMENT DEPARTMENT AT MERRILL LYNCH

Just as trading, loans, investments, and personal banking can be independent business units, risk management is a staff function that could also be served through an independent business unit.

At Merrill Lynch, risk management is handled by the Global Risk and Credit Management (GRCM) department, which is organized into units overseeing market risks and credit risks. The Market Risk Division and Credit Risk Division are run by a single head of risk management, who is a member of the Executive Management Committee.

The risk management organization at Merrill Lynch has the authority to set and monitor firmwide risk levels related to counterparty credit limits and trading exposure. It can also veto proposed transactions because many deals are subject to prior approval from GRCM, including:

- Underwriting commitments of equity,
- High-yield and emerging market securities,
- Real estate financing and bridge loans, and
- Most derivatives and syndicated loans.

To solve the problems associated with the coordination of control activities, risk management and representatives from other control units (e.g., Auditing Operations, Law and Compliance) approve new types of transactions as part of the new product review process. Senior people from GRCM and these other control units take an active role in the oversight of control of exposure through the Risk Control and Reserve Committee (RCRC).

The Risk Control and Reserve Committee provides general risk oversight for all institutional trading activities. This includes setting quantitative limits for market and credit risks and developing guidelines for the approval of new products. This committee reports to the Audit and Finance Committee of the board of directors, and is independent of Merrill Lynch's business units.

The Reserve Committee is chaired by the chief financial officer (CFO). It monitors valuation and certain other risks associated with assets and liabilities, and reviews and approves companywide reserve levels as well as changes in reserve methodology. This committee meets monthly to perform the following functions:

- Review current market conditions,
- Act on specific issues,
- Examine specific risks and exposures, and
- Evaluate aging, concentration, and liquidity.

Underpinning the functions of the Reserve Committee is a range of planning and control activities. All well-run organizations see to it that there is a formal system of planning and control that focuses on accountability and, through it, permits delegation with commensurate responsibility. The system of checks and balances must do the following:

- Bring senior management's attention to key issues, both at the central level and in the periphery,
- Keep management informed of progress by coordinating and unifying action, and
- Flash out exposure, not only periodically but also in real-time as thresholds are crossed.

Figure 14.3 shows a model to track these duties. Each financial institution has its own factors to add to this presentation. There are no stereotypes of the one best solution. A successful control activity can be organized in a variety of ways, but efficiency must always be kept in mind. There is no better example of this statement than the functions of the CRMO (described in detail in Chapter 13).

Figure 14.3
Management Must Be Informed in Real-Time About the Bank's Operations Anywhere in the World

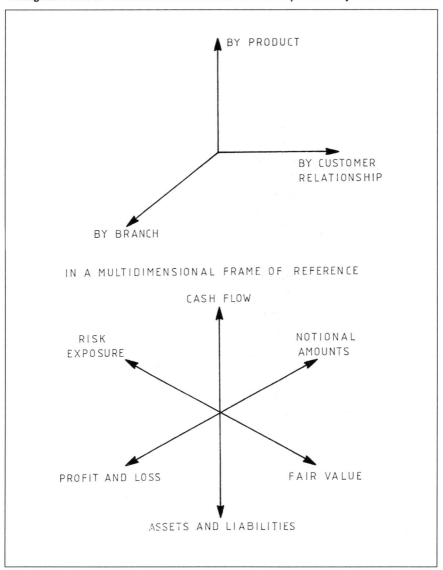

Group management must encourage its independent business units to take the lead in setting annual objectives and to agree on broad strategies. It must ensure that operating units are responsible for developing their own plans, but are committed to achieving the corporate target goals. And it must facilitate the exercise of control assisted through a real-time information system on an organization-wide basis.

A suitably designed risk management control system offers substantial benefits by performing the following functions:

- Focusing management attention on key decision areas,
- Controlling the delegation of authority,
- Tracking risk at any time in any place, and
- Facilitating the assessment of individual performance.

However, no control structure can make strategic decisions. Because control activities can involve strategic issues, top management must still set aside time for evaluations. Furthermore, control information must be easily accessible, accurate, and frequently updated. Its quality depends on the soundness of the basic data and the models used to generate it.

To ensure effectiveness, a control system should rigorously identify the key components of risk and return within operational plans, develop sensitivity analyses of each key element of risk, and rank each in terms of impact on the survival of the institution. The role and functions of the Chief Risk Management Officer should be seen in this perspective, and the same is true of definition of responsibilities for front desk, back office, and middle office.

Is There a Crisp Distinction Between Back Office and Middle Office?

If the buildup of a market-risk–oriented control organization is a phenomenon of the 1990s, largely due to top management starting to appreciate the inordinate amount of exposure taken with derivatives, how was control exercised prior to the advent of a new department? The answer is that up to a point, particularly at a low level of the financial transactions food chain, this was done by the back office.

Sometimes market risk management was nonexistent because it was left to the front office to control itself, which, of course, is nonsense. A major organizational weakness in the case of Barings has been the violation of the principle that the same individual should not be in charge of front desk and back office. With Barings, there also were attacks on the concept of matrix management, senior executives having both regional and functional reporting lines. This tends to dilute personal responsibility and accountability by creating alibis. It also blurs the lines segregating front desk and back office functions, to the detriment of both.

Any senior executive worth her salt should understand the importance of clearly defined lines of responsibility and accountability covering all activities under her control. Financial institutions should maintain an up-to-date organizational structure clearly defining who is accountable for what, which are the details of risks taken by this person and how these risks affect the overall exposure of the institution.

Let me briefly bring some functional issues into perspective. Traditionally, a bank has been executing its transactions at the front desk and registering them at the back office. However (depending on the type of bank), the nature of the front desk and the structure of back office operations may vary. In a retail bank, by and large the customers conduct their business at the tellers' window. In an investment bank, the traders are the main front desk, whether they deal in foreign exchange, interest rate instruments, derivatives, or any other product. Here's how the functions should be separated:

- **The general model is that front desk executives execute transactions and the back office writes the transactions in the books.**
- **The principle is that those who deal and those who register executed transactions should not report to the same boss.**

Well-managed institutions appreciate that there should be a wall separating front desk and back office so that there is no conflict of interest. However, this principle of separation of duties is very often violated, resulting in huge losses to the bank because the traders, the loan officers, the investment specialists, and other professionals have escaped prudential control.

The separation of duties and of the reporting structure is valid not only in regard to front desk and back office but, as well, in regard to other activities critical to the correct functioning of an institution. Figure 14.4 presses this point by suggesting that front desk, back office/general accounting, auditing, risk management, and information technology should be separated by logical and physical walls. Each must report to a different member of the bank's executive board, and every precaution should be taken to avoid conflicts of interest.

Figure 14.4
Separation of Duties Is a Good Safeguard Against Conflicts of Interest and Fraud

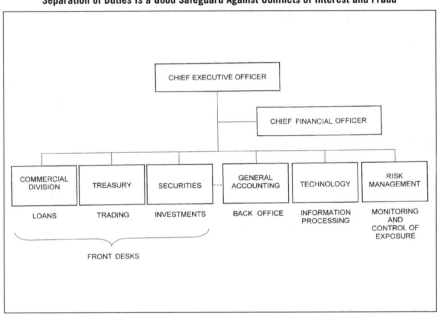

In business practice such separation is more logical (and hierarchical) than physical because competition and technology see to it that information penetrates every wall. This is only one of the reasons why computer support should not be centralized but distributed around the workplace—with the databases remaining a corporate resource, like the institution intelligent network. These distributed databases are not "owned" by the end user, as is sometimes suggested. Instead, they are corporate property, and they should be regularly audited by the audit department.

Purposely, Figure 14.4 features no "middle office" even if we are talking about it in this section. I prefer the term *risk management,* because it is more precise. But in the text I will be using *middle office* largely to identify what is wrong with the current organization, job definition, and information technology support regarding those people entrusted with the responsibility to control exposure.

How the Back Office Should Function

Going back to the fundamentals, classically banks have used their back office as an information processing engine. Because the data volumes were heavy, they equipped it with accounting machines, a fact that is sound at the origin of organizational attachment of computers to the accounting function from the 1950s through part of the 1970s. The back office can function in an able manner as an information processing and reconciliation outfit if it receives the bank's data streams on time and if it has the facilities to handle them. This leads to some principles of operations (for instance, the need to facilitate data entry, ensure the correctness of trades, check the accounts of counterparties, as well as control amounts and conditions).

Trading date, time, and every element identifying the transaction must be entered automatically by the system and it should be impossible for the trader to alter them. The system must see to it that each trader can enter transactions solely under his own identification number. If the trader deviates from specified norms when registering transaction data, this must be controlled by the system and captured by the back office. In my mind, middle office operations don't enter into these functions.

Late trades concluded after the back office has closed recording for the day must be marked as such and included in that day's positions with a late-trade slip passed immediately to a party unconnected with the traders. Rules should as well specify if trading outside the business premises is admissible within the scope of an express ruling by management identifying:

- Authorized individuals,
- Purpose and volume that are acceptable,
- Rules for notification and confirmation, and
- Type of review and evaluation to be exercised by senior management.

What I have just stated fits well with the most general view of the back office's role: handling the business documents obtained from front desk transactions, checking in-house input against counterparty correspondence, and confirming commitments. It is a back office duty to write the necessary confirmations and contract notes, also attending to other processing formalities such as maturity control and payments. The principle characterizing back office operations is that all transactions must be subject to constant checks. In particular, checks must be made to ensure that:

- Business documents are complete and up to date,
- The nature and scale of transactions are within the scope of business activities and limits,
- Information provided by loan officers and traders is correct and complete and matches the data in the confirmations,
- The clauses of all transactions conform to market terms that have been agreed upon, and
- Deviations from specified norms are sanctioned, whether these regard amounts, master agreements, delivery instructions, methods of payment, or other issues.

How Risk Control Becomes a "Middle Office" Function

As contrasted to these activities, the role some institutions have thrust upon the middle office is risk control. Let me repeat that when risks were less complex and more limited, this function too was performed by the back office. But as an increasing number of financial institutions have found out, it becomes necessary to institute a new unit to look after risk and exposure.

One of the negatives of the middle office, as originally conceived, is that its functions and responsibilities are not very clear. Particularly fuzzy is the control action it can exercise when an anomaly is detected, let alone the fact that finding out a malfunction in risk management has not always been easy because both the rocket scientists and the high technology are at the front desk, and typically the middle office has not had their skills.

Another handicap of the original middle office idea is that, in the majority of cases, this unit is not an integral part of the bank's internal control if and when such a system is in place. This has created problems of coordination, with many unwarranted risks filtering through the gaps. In all fairness, I should add that the risk management unit too is not always integrated with internal control. This is a severe mistake because risk management and internal control are, to a very large extent, indivisible.

But while technology provides a great deal of assistance, only rigorous internal control can ensure that accounting records clearly show at all times the individual transactions broken down by type of business, maturity, and counterparty. Also, the positions taken by the institution per currency, interest rate, and instrument, as well as the trading results that must be reconciled regularly with the traders' figures.

ORGANIZATIONAL GUIDELINES SUPPORTING RISK MANAGEMENT

Since risk management is at the top of the back office/middle office food chain, one cannot repeat too often that the measurement and control of every type of exposure is critical to deployment of capital within the framework of rapid convergence of the financial markets. However, the solution you adopt must respect organizational principles; it should also be adapted to the type of institution your bank is with respect to your customers, products, and employees.

This helps in the division of responsibilities between back office and risk management. When their functions overlap, this evidently weakens bankwide control activities. The question is who finds the discrepancies, clarifies them, documents them, and reports to the appropriate authority. Such definitions are instrumental to the creation of a rigorous market risk management organization.

The separation of duties should not blur the fact that there are also similarities between the information requirements of back office and risk management (or middle office). Part of the back office duties is that any discrepancies are to be noted and clarified immediately. Trades subject to a netting agreement must be individually documented, recorded, and processed as individual transactions. Where direct recording and settlement systems are used, there must be controls. Some of the sophisticated software back office and risk management need may be quite similar. Keep in mind these guidelines:

- **Knowledge artifacts should be employed to reconstruct at any time which trader, loan officer, or other professional carried out which functions and when.**
- **Other agents should search for existing mismatches; still others for discrepancies that have happened in the past and may happen again.**

Short of sophisticated software enhancing the information services, the CRMO and his assistants must do all of the following functions:

- Combine risk measures from disparate systems.
- Express input parameters coming from heterogeneous platforms.
- Make approximate adjustments.
- Convert disperse metrics into others more homogeneous that are needed by various computations of exposure.
- Translate risk measures into a common language.
- Combine data streams to approximate the bank's portfolio structure in a comprehensive way.

This complicates significantly the risk controller's mission. Inputs and outputs to and from different systems must be checked, and decisions need to be made to adjust for any differences in valuation methodologies without altering data content. Invariably, this effort toward greater homogeneity leads to the need of explaining to the traders:

- Why they did not make as much money as they thought,
- Why the positions were incorrect on their original report,
- How and why money was lost due to volatility in market prices and different pricing failures.

Plenty of cases demonstrate that when working with low technology, neither the back office nor risk management can perform its function in a diligent manner. For example, one major bank was to mention that auditing identified 10,000 transactions that were not processed over a whole week and, as a result of this lapse, some rotten traders had created quite significant losses for the institution.

The roles of both the back office and risk management are greatly enhanced through high technology, with all transactions recorded immediately online and procedures actuated in parallel for clearing and bookkeeping. Subsidiary agreements on transactions that are not themselves trades but create trading positions should likewise be recorded online by the accounting system.

Real-time processing must focus on both events and nonevents (for instance, uncompleted transactions that are, as a matter of principle, recorded in subledgers at the time they are contracted, like a memorandum of accounts). Upon completion, knowledge artifacts must see that the completed transactions are booked in the general ledger and in individual accounts with value-date recording. AT&T mentioned another type of nonevent it wanted to have a record of from its experience with credit cards: Cardholders who used their credit very rarely and then only for small amounts.

Far from being a side issue, the supporting services that I outlined are a pivot point both for management accounting and for risk control. Control of exposure is not limited to market risk and credit risk. Indeed, one reason why developing a comprehensive risk management system is complex is that it has other constituent parts, including asset risk, legal risk, and operational risk.

All exposures must be managed in unison using fairly homogeneous methods and tools. Today, this happens only among tier-1 institutions. Organizational and cultural reasons account for some of this disconnected state of affairs both in banking and in insurance. In the insurance industry, for instance, asset risk and operational risk are typically managed by two separate departments using distinctively different tools:

- Actuarial science is used for asset risk, and
- Financial economics is used for operational risks.

Understanding the reasons why risk management strategies are lacking, as well as the trade-offs, is further complicated because there exist different means by which risk is measured throughout the insurance industry—for example, volatility of surplus, downside risk of surplus, volatility of return on equity. The better-managed companies now employ models in trying to reconcile these approaches, seeing to it that entrepreneurial risk and capital management are used to evaluate trade-offs and outcomes of various financial and operating decisions. These are based on the insurer's measures of business success and assumed exposure.

The message from these examples is that whether in insurance or in banking, some traditional lines of departmentation hinder the proactive control of exposure. Again, technological incompatibilities, which to a significant extent have historical reasons, add to the problems faced in managing credit risk and market risk.

The CRMO also has to translate market terminology for back office clerks who need to know if something was restructured in the input and who is responsible for material aspects of reports and operations. Because back office and risk management share some responsibilities, they should understand the same things in the same way and be able to justify their numbers. Members of the risk management team must also spend time explaining trading products to account officers. Such explaining is instrumental in:

- Integrating the reporting of credit risk and market risk exposure, and
- Calculating market-risk–dependent credit exposure adds-ons.

In conclusion, the control of exposure is often handicapped by overlaps and lack of common standards by back office and risk management (or middle office). This situation is made worse by weak technology, which itself is responsible for many inconsistent risk control practices and for delayed management action.

A properly established risk management organization should encompass all aspects of exposure including goals, definitions, limits, procedures, rewards, and identification of appropriate level of technology. It should stress clear mandates; look out for awareness by traders, loan officers, investment specialists, and accountants; and underline discipline—both internal to the institution and market discipline.

A USEFUL LESSON IN RISK CONTROL: INFORMATION MUST BE RELIABLE

Released in June 1999 as a discussion document, the New Capital Adequacy Framework by the Basle Committee on Banking Supervision strongly emphasizes market discipline, which it sees as a pillar in the management of risk. The Commission Bancaire of the Banque de France underscored these points:

> • **Market discipline essentially means reliable public information and therefore transparency.**
>
> • **And reliable information should characterize both the institution's own (internal) and the public (external) data.**

It would indeed be detrimental to everybody's interest if we lose sight of the fact that risk management is basically an open information problem. There are, however, many technical and business issues to overcome in making reliable financial information transparent, including:

- The poor quality of legacy data processing,
- The lack of consistency in cross-disciplinary and cross-country information,
- The ability to develop and maintain user-friendly interfaces that permit effective communication,
- And, perhaps more than anything else, the policy of keeping financial data close to one's chest.

The need to be able to quantify and qualify risk will be served if we can identify areas where the institution has not been careful in the quality of its data collection, computing, storage, and retrieval for long-term serviceability. Five, 10, or 20 years down the line this information must still be reliable to enable us to use data histories that can reveal significant risk patterns. Therefore, useful lessons can be learned from reliability engineering.

Let me give a historical hindsight. In the 1950s, the aerospace, nuclear, and weapons systems industry faced risk control problems similar to those encountered today in banking. The reasons at the root of these problems were organizational because the then-new reliability function had to be cross-departmental. Some problems were also analytical because reliability models and methods were new and untested.

Reliability concepts and methods by now have half a century of history. They are tested and secure—and they are very useful in the control of risk. The reliability of data streams, for example, can be ensured in an able manner if, and only if, the board and top management become literate both in rigorous risk control and in advanced technology. This means that they have to fully appreciate the overriding need for a completely flexible system which has the following features:

- **All data and models used or generated by the bank and its branches must be captured and filtered and become available in real-time.**

- **It must be possible to check any position by any conceivable scenario, and to experiment on expected risk, unexpected risk, and extreme events.**

This means much more than just having available some basic indicators and trends, such as trading volume, average ticket size, number of open items, volatility betas, replacement values, risk equivalents, and other information regarding positions. Experimentation, particularly real-time analysis and simulation, requires lots of preparatory work, including these tasks:

- Infrastructures have to be built,
- New data types need to be integrated,
- Models must be developed and tested,
- Visualization solutions must be custom-made, and
- The whole system must operate in real-time in the most dependable way.

Solving technological challenges is not the CRMO's job, but it is his responsibility to see to it that the institution's risk management system does not remain an uncertain prototype but goes into full production, remaining flexible and adaptable without any interruption in its operations. Commenting on these requirements which superficially look as if they lead to a function conflict, some years ago a senior executive of BankAmerica said, "It is like changing the wheels while the car runs full speed."

Even When Information Is Reliable, Risk Managers Need to Watch Out for Human Errors

One of the most important lessons reliability of weapons systems can teach to risk management in finance is the need to search for reasons underpinning unreliability. Put bluntly, in 99% of all cases, the number 1 reason for unreliability is *human error* amplified by defective or lax management practices.

One example of unreliability in the banking industry connected to instruments and counterparties was the huge market losses from derivatives under stress of a market panic following the meltdown of East Asian tiger economies. A risk within this risk has been the unexpected credit exposure resulting from unreliable partners whose frame of mind is "heads I win, tails you lose."

But was the South Korean counterparty unreliability truly unexpected? In October 1993, four full years prior to the South Korean meltdown, I wrote a report to the board of a western money-center bank following a study of prevailing risk management practices among major Japanese institutions. (Notice that South Koreans still are way behind the Japanese in the control of exposure.)

Entitled "Good News and Bad News about Risk Management" and based on a factual documented study in East Asia, my report brought attention to the fact that, like any other reserve bank, the Bank of Japan was taking a very close look at derivatives trades and seemed quite preoccupied by the prevailing exposure figures. The report added, however, that the system of checks and balances for off–balance-sheet financing, which other central banks have put into place, was not yet working in Japan. The Bank of Japan was in the process of developing new norms for off–balance-sheet risk management. The interest was present. But the results were not yet there; hence it was not possible to say how successful this effort was.

Other East Asian countries had not even started an honest effort to control risk. The report added, "From what I have learned during this research, as compared with other national banks—as, for instance, Federal Reserve, Securities and Exchange Commission, Deutsche Bundesbank and Bank of England—the Bank of Japan is way behind. Some Japanese city banks and brokers seem to be in control of risk management concepts and procedures, but the majority is awfully lagging in this effort."

Though in every country there are financial institutions that are relatively ahead and others that are relatively slow in adopting appropriate organizational and procedural solutions, Japan's wide gulf between "haves" and "have nots" was unique—the more so as we talk of major financial institutions. Here are some other examples:

- Mitsubishi Bank, Dai-Ichi Kangyo Bank, and Nomura Securities were ahead.

- Nippon Credit, Long-Term Credit, and Sanyo Securities (which since went bankrupt) were laggards.

It seemed to me that all three financial institutions named in the second bullet (and many more I do not mention by name) were not in a position to control their off–balance-sheet risks. Their people seemed to be totally disoriented and dispirited in regard to risk management. They did not have a valid risk control concept, and it seemed as if they had felt that being in the "poor risk management" class was not so bad after all.

RISKS INHERENT IN MANAGING RISK

Risk management policies and practices have been horribly weak and ineffectual in some financial institutions. And although many ills are organizational and a lot of others have to do with missing skills, the common thread among all of them is weak or nonexistent policies on internal control, limits, and corrective action—starting with policies at board level. Here's the crux of the situation:

> • **One major problem with risk management is that because many board members don't understand technology, they fail to see the need to tune the means to the complexity of tasks.**
>
> • **Another major challenge comes from the fact that board members know very little about derivatives. Therefore they seriously underestimate assumed risks.**

Dr. Murray Weidenbaum, chairman of the Council of Economic Advisors under President Reagan, claims that too many companies may be looking to derivatives as a deus ex machina sweeping in from the sky to save them from currency and interest rate changes: "I have a hunch that some of the less sophisticated businesses are jumping on the derivatives bandwagon. I am not knocking derivatives, but some companies just don't really know what they are getting into."

This is no time for complacency. In the short span of less than two decades, the market in derivatives has exploded, growing at a reported 30% annually. The risk has never been so high. Current estimates are that in year 2000, in notional principal amounts, derivatives exposure will be well in excess of $200 trillion, though official figures will likely stand at 80% that figure. Even if that estimate is conservative, it is so high and the exponential rise is so steep, that it should give nightmares to investment bankers, commercial bankers, and regulators.

Just like firewalls do not protect against all types of penetrations in a security sense, it is wrong to assume that hedging takes care of all exposures. In fact, the effect might be quite the opposite as hedging can create new risks. Theoretically, but only theoretically, off–balance-sheet instruments assist in hedging risk. Practically, very few companies use the derivatives market to hedge risk. The large majority of players do so to speculate.

Here again exists a similitude with reliability engineering: Unreliability may be built into a machine or system at the drafting board because of cost reasons, fuzzy goals, and/or faulty design. At the root of this wrong strategy is a huge misconception that finds its parallel in banking. If they think the cost is reasonable and if they believe they can manage the execution side (which most of them think), companies will find a way of dealing with derivatives in a speculative way. Keep in mind these pitfalls:

- **One major drawback with off–balance-sheet instruments is their inherent complexity.**
- **A bigger concern is that derivatives make leveraging difficult to resist.**

Compounding these issues are weak disclosure rules that prevail in most countries in one form or another. Derivatives do have a role to play in the economy; the problem is that too many players are not keen in controlling off-balance risk. They will do so only when the law obliges them to move in the direction of risk control, as does the 1996 Market Risk Amendment.

This is not to say that risk management does not itself have its risks. Here are some risks of risk management:

- Currently used pricing models and control procedures are too linear.
- The hypotheses we make are uncertain.
- Laws and regulations tend to be static.

Years ago, an economy-friendly interest rate policy should have placed higher interest rates on high-risk speculative financing, such as derivatives and lower rates on lending for medium- to long-term investments in infrastructure and production. This was not done. By now, the world's financial system has become so inflated that to raise interest rates on the bubble will primarily blow up the bubble. This lag in forward-looking measures is another risk of risk management.

Of course, a two-tier interest rate system is not that easy, because financial markets traditionally don't work that way. Some economists have suggested emulating the higher interest rate through special taxation at the source, applicable to leveraged deals. Today exactly the opposite occurs. It is the dividends that are doubly taxed.

Neither is it easy to regulate cross-border and most particularly cross-current money flows. Yet, this may be necessary. Since April 1995, when the Bank of Japan took emergency measures supported by a worried Clinton administration and the Federal Reserve, the financial markets live in the fear that a Japanese collapse could bring down with it the entire financial system of the world.

The most discussed scenario of a possible meltdown starts with the fact that the Japanese government, private banks, and insurance firms hold over $500 billion in U.S. Treasury securities. Were Japanese banks or the government forced to liquidate a sizable part of that amount, it would precipitate a crisis globally beyond anything seen after the Crash of 1929.

I present these facts because a good part of the Chief Risk Management Officer's job is to evaluate the most likely catastrophe scenarios and come up with a coherent strategy of countermeasures. Financial earthquakes should stand at the top of his worries. Do we have the financial staying power to survive a painful recovery period? Do we know in advance the plan of action so that even worst-case conditions will not catch us unprepared?

In conclusion, the worst risk of risk management is the unguarded door. Too much linear thinking does not allow a view of the unlikely, the unexpected, and the unpredictable. Few people are truly able to challenge the obvious. The aftermath of the failure to do so is usually devastating.

CHAPTER 15

Managing the Transfer of Risk Between Different Instruments

Many people still debate whether market activity is a zero-sum game. In other terms, is it true that what one player loses, the other gains, and vice versa? If not, which pattern might best describe risk and return in market activity? What's the time horizon of such pattern, if there is one?

The answer is not simple. Yes, some trades look zero-sum, but in the general case markets are not necessarily this sort of proposition. When they go into positive territory, all investors seem to gain—at least on paper. But also they may all lose when the market goes down. There are fundamental reasons why market activity does not add up in netting pluses and minuses.

Credit risk is one of the key reasons why a zero-sum hypothesis does not hold. The existence of credit risk sees to it that a bank or an investor may lose, in spite of being able to overcome market risk. Furthermore, even if by classical market standards someone seems to be a "sure winner," such gains are conditioned by events beyond his control, which, in the short term, may turn the tables on even the best planned market moves.

For zero-sum with market risk, a great deal depends on the investor's time horizon. No two bankers, treasurers, or investors have the same time horizon, but they tend to cluster within certain groups. Arbitrageurs have a very short time horizon. Central bankers as well as bankers whose institutions are giving long-term loans have a long time horizon. As Figure 15.1 suggests, underwriters, position takers, and other players fall in between.

Figure 15.1
Growing Levels of Risk As the Time to Maturity of an Instrument Increases

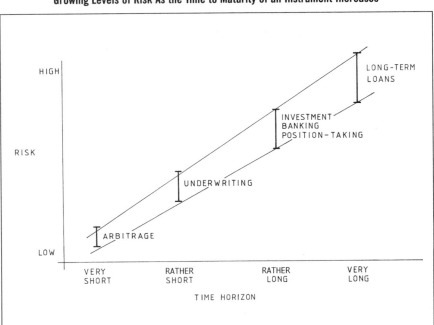

Furthermore, the zero-sum argument might make sense if the cost of money, growth of gross national product, inflation, and other economic factors are left aside. This is not a valid sound approach, however, and it should never be used in the short term. True enough, some individual trades might look zero-sum. An example is forward rate agreements entered by two counterparties. But other deals do not follow this algorithm—a statement valid for all financial instruments that have to do with wealth creation, such as currency exchange operations, bonds and their derivatives, and the equity market as a whole.

Based on an original idea by Professor Yves Wagner of Banque Générale de Luxembourg, Figure 15.2 shows risk factors affecting an investment portfolio that, under certain market conditions, neither individually nor in unison add up to a zero-sum game. The trading culture that justifies this statement is also the one that creates an innovative and dynamic global economy, where zero netting is a mirage.

Figure 15.2
Risk Factors That Do Not Add Up to Zero-Sum

CURRENCIES	BONDS	STOCKS	DERIVATIVES
A basket of currencies under different weights	Credit quality	Buy/sell recommendations	Leverage and its aftermath
Currencies managed as a block	Interst rate	Highlighted stocks	Hedging activities
Inter- and intrablock allocation of funds	Duration	Index trading	Reverse repos
Base currency as reference	Convexity	Inventory risk	Capital at risk

In Figure 15.2, highlighted stocks are those that move faster than the lot in price/earnings ratio and market value. An example of the late 1990s is Internet stocks. The reverse repo agreement is not zero-sum either, and a similar statement can be made about a lot of other financial vehicles discussed in this book.

These concepts are important on their own merits; they are even more critical in a discussion of risk transfer because if risks were netted out as some people believe they are, there should be no reason to transfer them among institutions and investors.

As the market changes, so does the impact of different means available for risk transfer. There is as well another factor to consider. In a dynamic economy, no matter how good a financial product may be, chances are it is only a couple of years from becoming obsolete.

THE ROLE OF FINANCIAL INSTRUMENTS IN RISK TRANSFER

Not long ago, a senior Swiss banker with whom the issue of transfer of risk was debated stated flatly, "If one brings credit risk into play—and therefore the possibility of bankruptcy—no trade can be zero sum." Another financial expert contributed this thought: "As bankers we issue instruments and gain a premium for that. This premium will cover imperfections, presumably including the fact that no financial market is really netting winners and losers." Keep in mind these key points:

- **Whether we appreciate it or not in our trading decisions, financial instruments are a means of buying and selling risk—and they are not a level ground.**

- **Used in an able manner they can contribute to market liquidity and provide protection against exposure, but what one party loses is not always what the other party wins.**

It is essentially the imperfections that make the market tick. Without them, the financial pulse will attenuate. Imperfections also see to it that financial instruments are a means for making profits. The better profits are made when business opportunity is widened but risk is kept under control through a combination of management skill, sound policies, accurate information, a valid methodology, and high technology.

Chapter 7 described the function of management, the skills it requires, the nature of banking strategy, and the concept of policies and procedures. In every enterprise, management skill is fundamental in ensuring that the financial instruments being used are properly chosen, are well managed, and provide protection against the shifting market values and risks associated with such shifts.

The more complex the business scene and the less known the instruments, the more is required in terms of sophisticated management functions. The business environment constantly changes, and this further accentuates the need for know-how, skills, and flexibility. A similar statement can be made about innovation in banking as well as the changing regulatory environment.

The business environment changes because of both innovation and legislation. Until the Great Depression of the late 1920s and early 1930s, commercial banks could engage in all sorts of investment banking and underwriting. Then, from the early 1930s until the early to mid-1990s the banking system in many countries was surrounded by a legal ring that prevented nonbanks from owning banks as well as commercial bankers from undertaking securities underwriting.

But by the late 1990s the business environment changed again under the weight of deregulation, globalization, and technology—and with this came the need of different skills and know-how. At the same time, while this change enlarged business opportunity, it also created greater risks requiring an even higher level of skill to be managed. Leverage magnifies the impact of changes and skews the distribution of values. Keep in mind these points:

- **Derivatives are used to take a position on a future price change of currencies, interest rates, equity indices, agricultural products, and other commodities.**

- **But because off–balance-sheet instruments are geared, they offer a much greater market exposure for a smaller outlay than do the more classical financial products.**

Derivative financial instruments give a new dimension to the distinction between counterparty risk and credit risk, which is, quite simply, that counterparty risk includes credit risk; counterparty risk also overlaps with market risk. Credit risk is classically associated with the other party's ability to perform. Into counterparty risk comes the other party's willingness to perform (which is dented with huge losses due to leverage) as well as country risk and other factors. The counterparty may be willing and able to perform, but new capital flow controls and/or exchange controls may not allow it to do so. Keep in mind the difference between perception of risk and the reality:

- **Typically, bankers, treasurers, and other investors think that through derivatives they exchange market risk for credit risk.**

- **In reality, a good deal of market risk remains, as both country risk and currency risk are market risks.**

After the South Korean meltdown in late 1997, the Morgan Bank was faced with an unexpected $480 million in sour derivatives because its counterparty, SK Securities, refused to perform due to its allegedly precarious situation. The virtual bankruptcy of South Korea and its conglomerates stemmed from market risk which rekindled counterparty risk in its wake. That much about the transfer of risk.

When these notions were explained at one of my London seminars on risk management, one participant asked, "Why do banks go for derivatives?" The answer is "In search of business and profits." Implicit in this answer, however, is the fact that for off–balance-sheet instruments to become risk transfer agents, an institution must see to it that it has both a new dimension in risk management and well-defined Chief Risk Management Officer functions.

To appreciate this statement, remember that with the deregulation starting in the late 1970s, the decade of the 1980s was not kind to the classical product lines of commercial banks, which came under attack by nonbank competitors. For their part, by 1990, many investors, bankers, and corporate treasuries were using derivatives beyond hedging by betting on the most likely market trend in interest rates, currencies, and other commodities. Bear in mind these statistics:

- **Between 1988 and 2000, the number of derivatives deals mushroomed, and, with it, gearing and assumed risk.**

- **In the middle of this period, in the 1993–94 time frame, more than 25% of the client base of major commercial banks were new users of derivatives services.**

Most of these players have not been well acquainted with the nuts and bolts of risk transfer, particularly in regard to leveraged instruments where exposure is magnified. Neither do they appreciate the evolution of risk in the function of critical parameters. As an example, Figure 15.3 presents four trend lines to keep in mind when evaluating risk and return.

THE UNKNOWN CONSEQUENCES OF RISK TRANSFER: HIDDEN HUGE LOSSES

Because the public can invest its savings in all kinds of government bonds and money markets, the role of a bank as the deposit institution accumulating money for loans and investments is no more what it used to be. The role of the intermediary has changed, and regulators take the (correct) stance to not forbid derivatives transactions, but they oblige the banking industry to establish a sound risk management policy and infrastructure.

Because leverage increases both market risk and credit risk, however, one of the biggest challenges facing bank executives today is that exposure is larger than it has ever been prior to the advent of derivative financial products. Unknown to many, there exists the threat of a small mistake that, when amplified through gearing, can topple large institutions.

Figure 15.3
Risk Trends in Instruments, Markets, and Counterparties

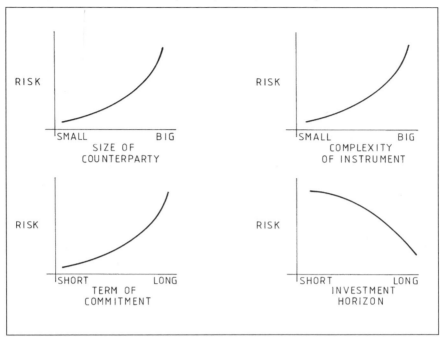

High leverage is a sort of inflation the economy can ill sustain in the long run. Consider just one example, from a thousand years ago. The Chinese had experimented with every form of money—copper, alloys, stones, shells, silk sheets—before they came to paper, but when emperors combined paper with printing to yield paper money, that move led to hyperinflation and the fall of dynasties. The Sung dynasty (960–1126) was the first on record to issue paper money. Before long these notes were off on a course nobody could control. After Sung collapsed in an inflationary implosion, the Mongol dynasty succeeding it also burned itself in a folly of hyperinflated paper currency. Then Kublai Khan's dynasty faded away in a blizzard of useless paper money.[1] These events are often forgotten and no lesson is derived from them regarding the limits of risk transfer (though the hyperinflation of the Weimar Republic is still remembered up to a point).

---

[1]Theodore H. White, *In Search of History* (New York: Harper & Row, 1978).

What once attracted bankers, treasurers, institutional investors, and private investors to off–balance-sheet instruments is the fast profits that could be made. But as more players joined the derivatives market, the once wondrous profit margins started shrinking fast. There have also been multimillion dollar hits taken by corporations and institutional investors—in America, Britain, continental Europe, and Japan—providing more proof that the market is no zero-sum game.

These losses have induced the regulators into action. The fear that banks may be taking inordinate risks has forced them into a critical reevaluation of their position, but they have kept shy from forbidding financial institutions to participate in derivatives because the prevailing opinion is that such a prohibition would weaken the banking industry. Much of the classical banking business might dwindle away to other institutions devoted to saving and investing money, such as:

- Pension funds,
- Money market funds,
- Life insurance companies, and
- High-risk–taking hedge funds.

This possibility is very real in the new financial environment and is also full of unknowns. Systemic risk can be triggered through synergy of many causes rather than only because of one king-size failure. Therefore the CRMO will be well advised to study the synergy of risks in a rigorous manner, by tracking and analyzing actual historical performance of counterparties and instruments. Counterparties whose volatility is greater than average are said to have high risk divided into two components:

- *Systematic risk,* which, for instance, tells how much a company's shares are geared to general market movements, and
- *Specific risk,* which has to do with individual characteristics of the entity, from its management to its products, markets, and finances.

An analysis of financial staying power of counterparties should always consider the case that companies create themselves specific risk because of ill-advised trades or investments. An example is Yakult's derivatives losses. In March 1998, this Japanese yogurt company announced losses of $810 million in undisclosed derivatives trades over the previous four years. The fact that an unsophisticated yogurt firm could lose that much in derivative products should be a good lesson to all entities that venture into financial engineering—whether senior management authorizes such silly trades or they are done down the line by eager beavers because internal controls are substandard and the CEO is deprived of risk visibility.

Skewed investments in growth shares can also lead to specific risk. Growth shares on low yields carry along higher risk because, while they can rise more in a bull market, they drop further than others in a bear market. In the long term, if the company's business is growing, the reward will be greater; but buying at the wrong time under geared conditions can be deadly. Nobody really knows the best timing in spite of claims to the contrary.

The increasing popularity of leverage even among companies and investors who don't really know what it means, and the existence of so many unknowns with possibly disastrous consequences, makes steady vigilance more mandatory than ever. Risks must be continuously monitored, evaluated, and controlled through a comprehensive process. Scientific tools help in this mission, as we will see in the next section of this chapter.

BANKERS, ROCKET SCIENTISTS, AND THE SYNERGY OF RISKS

Following on the track of risk and reward, academics develop and use theoretical models in addressing problems of modern risk management, while market professionals discuss issues of pricing and risk control in connection to the marketing of advanced derivative products. Rocket scientists explore the use of derivatives to dismantle and restructure capital markets instruments and to uncover anomalies that could provide opportunities for profits (though the search for anomalies is itself a risky process, as seen in Part Two of this book, in connection to LTCM).

The crucial role of pricing in bank profitability is widely recognized, but there is no general consensus on what really constitutes the right price; nor do all institutions appreciate the need to monetize risk and include it in the instrument's price. Research and develop-

ment (R&D) laboratories at leading financial institutions try to learn
about pricing exotic options, tackling the problems of measuring
volatility and of understanding differences between various option
pricing models. Here's a quick overview of modeling:

- **Modeling approaches aim to provide a framework for
appreciating how, for instance, currency exchange risk might be
managed using forwards and futures, debt, swaps, and options.**

This too is a risk transfer mechanism. Most banks are still learning how to design it and how to use it. Only tier-1 institutions appreciate that there may be unexpected (and unwanted) consequences
and therefore try to put in place some firewalls for the worst case.
Here's one benefit of modeling:

- **Through modeling, rocket scientists attempt to push forward the
frontiers of state-of-the-art knowledge of risk and return
regarding derivatives and other financial instruments.**

One aim of a rigorous analytical approach should be to bring to
attention hidden factors. For instance, a focal point may be the study
of when and how to employ currency options and option-related
derivatives such as range forwards and differential swaps, in connection to projected risk and return; or the assessment of merits characterizing newer, exotic derivatives such as barrier options, average rate
options, and quantos.

Whether the instruments are simple or complex, the synergy of
their risks cannot be effectively studied unless we analyze the market
factors into components. This is one of the goals of analytical studies
by rocket scientists. An example is provided in Figure 15.4 with equities. There are two parts: one addresses industry sectors; the other
focuses on currencies. In this two-dimensional evaluation system, vari-
ation in one dimension may affect the other, but to study the volatility of each we must construct a more general model. This model
should include market confidence, gross domestic product, current
account deficits, exchange rates, interest rates, market psychology,
and a host of other sensitivities. In sum, modeling facilitates better
risk management:

- **Globalization has introduced complex modeling requirements that have to be analyzed.**
- **New instruments make the demand for accuracy greater than it ever was.**
- **Modeling accuracy is important because it permits greater business opportunity and more effective risk control.**

When we talk of the exposure assumed by the bank in its transactions, we will be well advised to distinguish between intentionally assumed risks and those resulting from routine daily business activities. Risks are intentionally assumed through proprietary positions and trading lines that may provide greater profits than fees and commissions but that might also become nonperforming, turning your balance sheet on its head (for example, the Yakult derivatives losses mentioned earlier).

Figure 15.4
Class Equities, Patterns, and Sensitivity Conditions

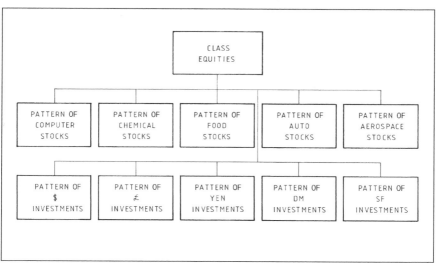

Increasingly, rocket scientists apply theoretical and empirical research to the practical problems of modern risk management by investigating whether and when firms should hedge selectively or as a herd. In so doing, they are considering the contribution of minute movements in the bank's exposure. But while such studies are most useful, they risk remaining an intellectual exercise until and unless the board takes the appropriate risk management decisions. Therefore, under no condition should analytical finance be done for its own sake. Instead, it should happen as part of risk transfer and risk control.

A basic decision to be made by the board of directors in connection to market risks, credit risks, their synergy, and the nature of analytical studies is the maximum level of exposure that can be assumed by the treasury in four specific investment categories: derivatives, foreign exchange, equities, and debt. The determination of these levels is usually a compromise between the following factors:

- Return on capital,
- Return on equity,
- Return on assets,
- Cash flows,
- Liquidity requirements, and
- Solvency targets.

One of the best means of control is to focus on the upper limits of open positions (for instance, positions taken by currency dealers). Rocket scientists can elaborate on a catastrophic scenario reflecting the probability of a single very negative event that endangers the solvency of the institution. Another target study should be the occurrence of several negative events and their cumulative impact on trading book and banking book.

There are other challenges in analytical studies targeting risk transfer, including these:

- Policies and procedures to be used for measurement of economic as well as accounting exposure.
- Dynamic control of risk embedded in each and every position.
- The aftermath of hedge accounting.
- The use and misuse of exotic option-based products.

Both individual items and their synergy must be brought into perspective through interactive computational finance.

The reason for studying risk synergy in an analytical manner is to better understand the advantages and limitations of active risk transfer including the possible compound effects. This cannot be done by hand. Therefore, the bank needs sophisticated estimators and forecasting models, steadily improving the results to be obtained from their use by tuning the hypotheses on which these models rest. Making the original hypotheses and testing them is the job of senior bankers, not of the rocket scientists.

UNDERSTANDING RISK AND RETURN IN THE MACROMARKETS

Both top management and the members of operating groups into which the bank is divided must understand and appreciate the tricky aspects of risk transfer in the financial business. If modern banking requires tough management to fend off competitors, it also calls for computation of appropriate funding requirements. Such understanding is fundamental in ensuring that the institution remains solvent. The experience with financial debacles—such as Herstatt in the 1970s, Continental Illinois in the 1980s, and Barings and LTCM in the 1990s—demonstrates how and why it is absolutely essential that the members of the board comprehend the nature of all activities of the institution and its commitments, including the most complex instruments and their execution. After all, they are directly responsible for the bank's performance and for its survival in the long term.

When it comes to risk and return, derivatives literacy is no static notion—whether we talk of literacy in foreign exchange markets, interest rate commitments, equity indices, or other products. As I cannot repeat too often, risk transfer is challenging because new financial instruments and global markets are in full evolution, and the players in this field must run fast just to keep the position that they already hold.

Globalization and technology have seen to it that one of the latest concepts in business opportunity is the macromarket; it includes both the more classical products and all sorts of exotic derivatives. Though these instruments are diverse, they have in common their macrodimension and the fact that the macromarkets feature an extraordinary amount of risk for the potential return they offer, and are large enough to accommodate many investors with ferocious appetites.

Cognizant analysts on Wall Street and in the City think that, before too long, credit derivatives will develop into another major instrument of the macromarkets; the same is true of weather derivatives and other insurance-oriented products. The dimension of a credit derivatives market can be enormous. So can the scope of credit derivatives' requirements, including:

- The know-how not only to understand the instrument but also to model it and control it properly, and
- The sophisticated ways in which securitized corporates can be analyzed, packaged, marketed, and generally manipulated.

In June 1999, Banca di Roma became the first Italian bank to securitize and sell off a portion of its nonperforming loans to the bond market. It took all nonperforming loans of the old Banco di Roma and Rome's Saving Bank, wrote them at 50% of face value, added some sugar coating, and had Standard & Poor's, Moody's, and Fitch IBCA rate them. Under this euro 1.18 billion ($1.25 billion) transaction, Banca di Roma reduced the ratio of its nonperforming loans from 12 to 8% of its total loan portfolio.

Private placements to interested parties reached about 50% of the offering. Another 25% went on public sale. Banca di Roma kept for itself the more risky 25%. This permits to recover about 37.5 cents to the dollar of nonperforming loans while another 12.5% transits from liabilities to assets. With this securitization, Banca di Roma created one of the highest ratios of nonperforming loans in Europe and exploited its advantages:

- The legal system in Italy is in good shape,
- There are institutional investors flexing their muscle,
- Credit derivatives start as a way to diversification, and
- Investors begin to appreciate they can make more money by taking credit risk than market risk.

The messages carried through these points in regard to risk transfer are valid not only for credit derivatives but as well for other macromarkets. In the macromarkets top management, operating executives, and auditors (i.e., all authorized persons) should be able to look at risk and exposure not just through summary figures but in detail, by means of database mining and visualization. Management should be able to do so not casually through batch reporting, but interactively, ad hoc as commitments are taking place. Detail means all the way down to:

- Counterparties involved in the transaction,
- Desk level and, from there, trader level,
- Every single financial instrument and its atomic parts,
- Currency in which the transaction was made,
- Interest rate that was applied,
- The deal's duration and other conditions,
- Any possible legal risk, and
- Market where each transaction has been executed.

These eight dimensions are represented in the radar chart in Figure 15.5. The higher the risk in a market in which the deal is done (and this characterization surely fits the macromarkets), the more care top management must show in establishing limits corresponding to the outer periphery of exposure. Each deal should be mapped into the radar chart versus these limits. Consider these guidelines:

- **What-if scenarios in risk transfer must be examined interactively, assisted through database mining and increasingly sophisticated models.**
- **Such strategy underlines the need for simulation and experimentation in regard to the level of risk being assumed and its evolution over time.**

In terms of a technological solution, the board of a global institution that is active in the macromarkets should accept nothing less than the best currently available. Institutions that address the macromarkets through old technology should prepare themselves for deception and trouble. Even the most able managers will fail if they cannot capitalize on real-time technology in controlling exposure. High stakes don't allow complacency of any sort, because failures can be of tragic proportions.

Figure 15.5
A Radar Chart for Mapping the Key Dimensions That Control the Acceptability of a Trade

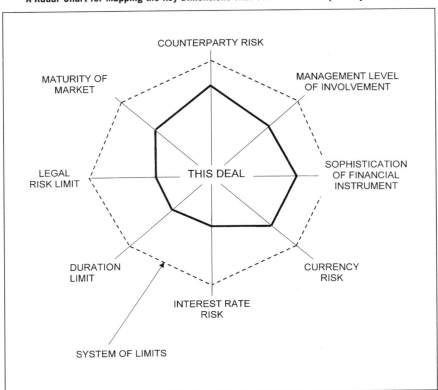

Tuning Capital Adequacy to Derivatives Exposure

The market is a tough critter. Bankers now complain that their predicament is being made worse by bank supervisors' response to the deteriorating quality of their loan book and the amount of risk in their trading book due to derivatives. Capital requirements, however, are the most traditional way of risk transfer. Through capital adequacy, a credit institution improves its financial staying power by creating a cushion in case adversity hits.

In the early 1990s and again in 1998, the collapse in stock market capitalization of some leading money center banks to less than half their book value suggested that the supervisory response to internal risk transfer had yet to take the full measure of real estate lending and derivatives problems. In facing the challenge to maintain liquidity through capital adequacy, some institutions forgot these basic principles:

- **An appropriate level of capital requirements is not a new worry; it is as old as banking itself.**
- **What is new is that globalization has seen to it capital adequacy became a universal subject with high visibility.**

What the Basle Committee essentially did in 1998 was to review and normalize the subject of composition of tier-1 capital. Subsequently, it focused on whether innovative instruments should be assigned to the prudential concept of core capital. Ten years later, in October 1998, during the meeting of the International Conference of Banking Supervisors (ICBS) in Sydney, the Basle Committee agreed on a set of guidelines subject to which innovative instruments (including contributions to the capital by silent partners) may be assigned to the core capital.

Under these guidelines, up to 16% of core capital may consist of innovative components. But the study that led to this position also concluded that some countries were not in compliance with the rules. This statement does not include the Group of Ten countries, yet it is no secret that American, French, and Japanese banks have been particularly hit by the capital requirements resulting from the 1988 Basle Accord. The irony is that by 1990 the Japanese banks' capital was further shrinking as a result of the collapse in the Tokyo stock market and mounting problems in real estate.

The sense of the events after 1988 (some still continuing) is that radical approaches are needed if the international financial community is to avoid being caught in an old-fashioned liquidity trap. This notion is amplified because of what the macromarkets add to capital adequacy worries.

Not only must a new financial architecture pay full attention to the transfer of risk and, therefore, the derivatives market, but also it must remain sufficiently flexible to adapt to changing conditions. The derivatives market is steadily changing. In 1995, as a result of well-publicized 1994 losses, demand plummeted for exotic derivatives contracts (those that are most lucrative for dealers but often carry significant risks). Many customers decided to limit themselves to conservative derivatives deals, which involve the better known instruments. But the "safer" deals are also the least profitable for dealers, even if they create headaches in terms of capital at risk.

Because the ups and down are getting more pronounced, capital adequacy to effectively face the evolving credit risk and market risk is a pressing issue—and it cannot be solved once and forever. Nobody suggests that either counterparty risk or derivatives exposure will go away. To the contrary, financial analysts expect derivatives activity to continue to expand at a significant pace. They also say that with corporations and investors time and again licking their wounds, the days of high profitability are over.

The essence of this discussion is that the market for options, futures, forwards, swaps, mortgage-backed bonds, financial products based on various stock indexes, and credit derivatives will keep on growing, but at the same time global investment patterns are changing. Investors, money managers, and traders who participated in surveys made the following predictions about their investment strategies in the coming years:

- Their activity in traditional investments, stocks, bonds, and currencies will increase slightly from current levels.

- In contrast, their use of derivative instruments will soar, but not among products that have the fatter margins for brokers. (The opinions I heard in the course of my research were divided in terms of which instruments will fill this market).

The one significant convergence of opinion I found here is that, at least for the time being, the macromarkets (described earlier in this chapter) will remain the province of hedge funds and of the more aggressive credit institutions and investment banks. In fact, many banks and institutional investors participate in the macromarkets by financing hedge funds, which gives a new perspective to the concept of capital at risk.

Whether a player is directly or indirectly active in macromarkets, exposure must be managed cross-border, in many currencies, and under different regulatory and legal conditions. This makes the issue of capital adequacy more broad and complex. These facts, of course, have not escaped the attention of the Basle Committee, resulting in the June 1999 New Capital Adequacy Framework, which includes:

- A revised notion of regulatory capital requirements,
- A strengthened definition of measures for credit risk,
- Steady supervisory review of capital adequacy,
- A role given to credit rating by independent agencies,
- The concept of market discipline and its implementation,
- An internal-rating–based (IRB) approach to the measure of credit risk,
- Greater transparency and reliability in financial reporting, and
- A reference to operational risk formalized by regulators for the first time.

The new framework takes account of a wider range of actual and potential exposures faced by the commercial banking industry than any previous regulation or directive, though not by hedge funds. At the same time, it tries to cope with incompatibilities in national accounting, legal, tax, and banking structures that tend to create differences among national markets—thereby impacting upon a bank's behavior in regard to its exposure, which is rising every year. Confronted with mounting risk, the wise thing to do is learn and then apply what you learn.

OPERATIONAL RISK AND CORE COMPETENCIES IN A BANKING ENVIRONMENT

Globalization makes it mandatory not only to have a first-class risk control system but also for top management to be in command through deep knowledge of the processes underlying the instruments on which its own bank invests and trades. Financial institutions often say that they are assuming an operational risk. This is correct but imprecise because operational risk is not one monolithic event, but should be analyzed in several constituent parts:

- Board risk,
- Senior management risk,
- Professional skills risk,
- Transaction risk,
- Execution risk,

- Payments/settlements risk,
- Fiduciary/trust risk,
- Legal risk,
- Security risk, and
- Technology risk.

My bet is that in the coming years operational risk will cover every corner of the operational environment in which management of other risks takes place, because it infiltrates into these other risks, even if for no other reasons than the following:

- The skill of managers and professionals, or lack of it,
- The ever more present aftermath of technology, and
- Execution risk, which enters into any transaction.

For example, Barings crashed due to failure of market risk management within a failure of operational risk management. It is easy to project a similar interaction of operational risk with credit risk. This leads to the concept that even the best credit risk and market risk control systems exist by necessity within an environment of operational risk control. Regulators are justified to want capital requirements for operational risk. The problem is that there are not yet clear ideas about the method while each of the aforementioned risks is composed of several parts, each with its own characteristics.

As we saw in Chapters 13 and 14, technology risk itself consists of several component parts, including these:

- Risk of falling behind in software and hardware,
- Risk of obsolescence in skills,
- Risk of slow time-to-market,
- And vendor failure risk.

Few financial institutions have so far been able to cope with technology risk in a commendable way.

Other risks too can be broken down into more elementary components. For instance, part of senior management risk is that executives too often stay bound to the home office rather than traveling to supervise other offices. In a multinational financial institution, senior managers must frequently visit the overseas offices where trading is done and talk to traders, relationship managers, back office managers, risk managers, auditors, and other staff about their activities and their appreciation of risk and return.

Central directors' gaining intimate knowledge of local operations is a two-way educational process. By riding horses rather than comfortable armchairs at their desks, board members and senior managers regain the salt of the earth of operations, something often lost at high organizational levels. At the same time, front desk and back office operators on the periphery come to appreciate that they are not alone.

Barings is far from the only bank that suffered an absolute failure of internal controls where there was confusion among the upper layers of management and where geographically remote operations were allowed to run wild. While real-time systems are a must, they are a complement, not a substitute, to senior managers' (the commanders') first-hand analysis and appreciation of the prevailing situation.

Alfred Sloan, the pioneering chief executive officer of General Motors (GM) in the 1930s, created a caste of general managers whose main job was to gather information from the shop floor and the market and then to use it as a basis for allocating resources. The Sloan model of management has become a pillar of industry. Though it is getting a bit obsolete, much has been learned in the meantime on the functions of management and the background reasons of assumed risk.

The most important requirement today is that banks concentrate on developing core competencies. These represent the flexible skills that allow them to produce a stream of distinctive products that cannot be easily imitated by a rival, but also permit them to estimate exposure associated with these products and set the limits accordingly. Core competencies reside in human capital and in less obvious things such as critical mission statements and high technology.

Cultivating advanced skills means putting efforts into recruiting, leading, and training well-performing employees to avoid professional skills risk. But star employees should not be given a blank check because this greatly increases operational risk. There is a need for a balance between exceptional performance and obeying the rules and checks implied by internal control. Otherwise an institution becomes unmanageable.

Pareto's law is a good guideline to use in management inspection and to contain transaction risk and exposure associated with risk transfer. At the end of the 19th century, Vilfredo Pareto found that a small part of variable A accounts for a big chunk of variable B when he established that 1% of the Swiss population controlled 35% of national wealth. In a similar manner, here's how Pareto's Law pertains to banking:

- Less than 1% of orders going through the London Clearing House and Payments System (CHAPS) represents 95% of value.
- Deals done with about 1% of the clients of a company correspond to 30% to 40% of its business.
- A small number of traders, salespeople, loan officers, and investment advisors bring in-house a big chunk of both profits and exposure.

An asymmetric distribution of financial risk prevails within each bank in connection to its most important clients and its most productive people. Therefore, while necessary, it is not enough to make some summary figures available to the board and senior management. Economic assessment should be factual and documented, based on a thorough methodology. The block diagram in Figure 15.6 presents, in a nutshell, the methodology I helped to establish in a credit institution for trading book purposes.

Figure 15.6
Sound Practices Require a Sense of Balance in Risk Management

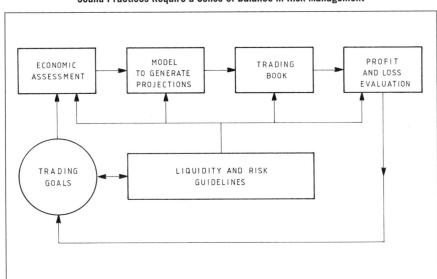

Knowledge artifacts and therefore high technology should be used extensively to cut operational risk. An example is setting alarms in connection to the follow-the-sun overdraft that exists internationally in the securities markets, with the result that risk is being imported. Internally, in each bank an overdraft exists with all accounts whether at the level of the trading book or the banking book.

Part and parcel of needed homework is the fact that time stamps and other supports are not among the current features of bank information systems, not even of the exchanges. Because the majority of credit institutions lack specific preparation in operational risk containment, they find it nearly impossible to properly identify destination of funds, untangle done settlements, and roll back a sour transaction.

For instance, Barings' settlements and treasury departments in London seem to have done nothing to clarify whether the sums traveling through its network, London to Singapore, were for client trading or Barings' own house trading. No wonder that, time and again, much of the financial industry's criticism concerns itself with these problems:

- Management failures,
- Nonexistence of internal controls,
- Lack of core competencies, and
- Little regard for operational risks.

Top management should be wary when one individual fields all questions about an activity and/or that person is consistently a star performer. At Barings, Nick Leeson appeared to be consistently generating large profits from activities such as arbitrage, suggesting that the business he was doing was essentially free of risk. This goes against the rule in investment banking that risk and reward are inextricably linked.

While the supervision of operational risk is still in a state of flux and there is plenty that needs to be done to structure the subject, there is no lack of critical queries that have to be answered. For instance, in the event that something goes wrong, who is liable? How can we reevaluate and reestablish the concept of financial integrity in the banking trade? In those simple sentences is embedded a great deal of operational risk.

CHAPTER 16

Accounting for Potential Risk Exposure in the New Economy

Institutions with experience in risk management appreciate how helpful it is to be able to distinguish between potential exposure, (which is also known as deemed risk, time-to-decay risk, and presettlement risk) and actual exposure (which may be referred to as mark-to-market risk or replacement cost). Potential exposure highlights the importance of being proactive, which in turn requires both analytical skills and accuracy in our evaluation of risks.

We must also be able to prognosticate future exposure because of current commitments and those at the negotiating table, measuring our resources against what we project as a worst-case scenario. This is most important in view of rising credit risk and a leverage factor built into our financial system. A study by Merrill Lynch suggests that annual growth of 4% appears to require a 12% increase in annual sector debt and a 30% increase in financial sector debt.[1]

Worst-case analysis can be done through either of two methods. One is case studies focusing on financial entities that a few years ago rode high, but their bad loans and high leverage in derivatives brought them to the edge of the abyss. The other is by simulating future events, including outliers, which permit a pre-study of things to come. We want to know whether some of these things might turn our institution belly up.

Both methodologies—case studies and simulation—can greatly contribute to a proactive strategy of internal control. The prerequisites to a simulation approach include a properly functioning accounting

---

[1] *Global Research Highlights,* October 8, 1999.

system, high technology, and rocket science. Potential exposure should be dimensioned in a way corresponding to the size of the institution and the complexity of its business. Keep in mind these guidelines:

- **Proactive credit risk estimates must be approached on an individual basis, by major client, and on a consolidated basis.**
- **Estimates of potential exposure due to market risk should capitalize on long time series and include extreme events.**

The measurement of risk and management of potential exposure must be fully documented tick-by-tick: by transaction and position. Auditing of both credit risk and market risk estimates must be done regularly. This auditing of present and estimated exposure (as well as the models on which estimates are based) should be reported to a board-level Auditing Committee to ensure that there is no conflict of interest aggregating model risk or in making the results transparent. Similarly, senior management must pay attention to the envelope of maximum exposure.

Estimates of maximum potential exposure help the board and senior management to evaluate whether the activities of the institution are in line with those described in its charter, whether the responsible executives are in charge of exposure being assumed, whether rewards justify risks being taken, and whether the financial staying power of the institution is intact. Furthermore, auditing should regularly ensure that the institution's internal control system functions in a dependable manner.

HANDLING MISMANAGEMENT AND SCANDALS

Top management must realize that the only way to stem the tide of financial calamities is by fundamentally overhauling the way the bank (or the treasury department of an industrial company) deals with risks. The way to bet is that disasters don't happen accidentally. Calamities usually accumulate over a period of time and come to the fore when the explosion point has been reached.

The CEO and the members of the board must recognize that the effectiveness of their internal control system and of their risk management strategy can determine whether their institution flourishes or withers and dies. This requires comprehensive, companywide programs that target the entire array of risks, not just derivatives.

This being said, it is necessary to train in new financial instruments—which with derivatives come up practically every day and engulf traditional lines such as loans and bonds—all people working for the bank in managerial and professional positions as well as the bank's clients who have to deal even remotely with the new instruments. Let's face it. Derivatives have gotten into the daily practice of organizations, and this has happened without the appropriate revival of ethical values, cultural change, and upgrade in know-how.

A revival of ethical values and a redefinition of financial responsibility (including a basic element of personal accountability) are indispensable for survival reasons. Management must be always on the alert in evaluating assumed exposure. Figure 16.1 presents in a block diagram some of the components a sound methodology should include.

The Daiwa Bank Bond-Trading Scandal

The keyword underpinning Figure 16.1 is transparency. Disasters happen when people and companies hide the facts. On November 2, 1995, federal and state banking regulators kicked Daiwa Bank out of the United States, ordering the Japanese institution to close its American operations in 90 days as punishment for concealing losses in a $1.1 billion bond-trading scandal. The Federal Reserve Board, the New York State Banking Department, and regulators in five other states said all U.S. banking operations of Daiwa must end by February 2, 1996, although an extension was feasible to permit an orderly departure. The bank had operations in 11 states in North America.

The reaction to these events by Japan's Finance Ministry was too little, too late. Postmortem, it urged Daiwa's management to make public a plan to improve its internal control and risk management practices that failed to prevent a trader from running up $1.1 billion in losses in New York on (allegedly) unauthorized deals. Japan's government sources said the Ministry of Finance was prepared to punish Daiwa for the scandal, which sparked harsh criticism of the bank. For its part, the U.S. Department of Justice stated that it would bring criminal proceedings against Daiwa and its managers accused of covering up the losses.

Daiwa was one of the best examples of what happens when top management rides desks rather than horses. As explained in Chapter 7, the risk that remote operations can run wild is particularly acute with money-center banks, because of their dependence on bought money, which means they don't have deep roots abroad. Therefore, they need much more rigorous internal control, real-time information networks, and database mining to some members of the board and the CEO.

Figure 16.1
Evaluation of Assumed Exposure and Equilibration of Results

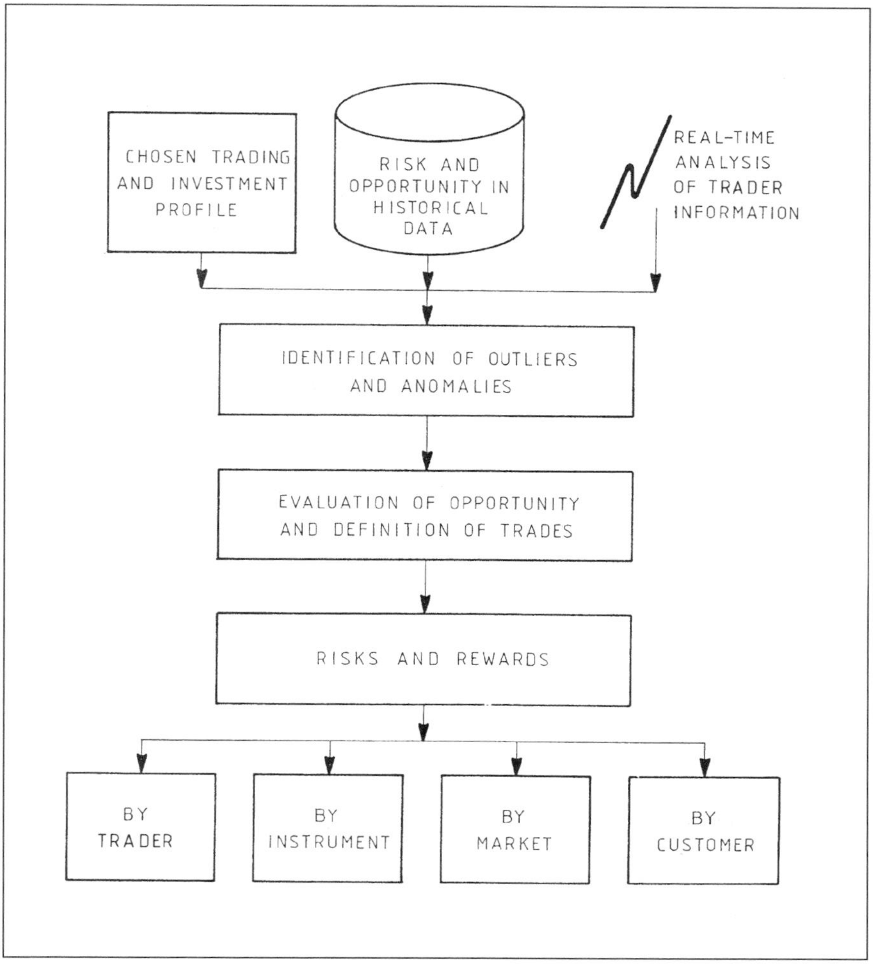

Managers Need Greater Understanding of Derivatives

Direct interactive access to databases with ad hoc queries is part and parcel of the proactive attitude required in modern finance to keep exposure under control and avoid bad surprises. The cultural change starts with derivatives literacy, but few organizations give this subject more than lip service. In September 1995, I was lecturing on derivatives risk management in Jakarta, Indonesia, to 55 Asian bankers including several bank presidents. Practically every bank represented in the conference room did derivatives trades. Yet, when I asked how many participants knew derivatives, only two raised their hands.

Top management should thoroughly know the breadth of products offered, their complexity, and risk assumed in the global market. Short of this know-how, it is not possible to establish a valid system of internal control. New financial products make sophisticated solutions an absolute necessity. The maintenance of old-style slow-going practices is wrong.

The CRMO should play a proactive role in this restructuring and he or she should be a master of sound, documented risk-mitigation techniques which are:

- Thoroughly evaluated through stress testing,
- Benefiting from dynamic limits adjustment, and
- Being subject to real-time reporting and transparency.

Because global operations and innovation in financial instruments involve so many unknowns, the CRMO should use Monte Carlo simulation as routinely as in old times an engineer used the slide rule. Simulation is one of the most powerful approaches in experimenting with dynamic risk management policies and the adversities any financial organization invariably has to face. One example of proactive use of technology is the contribution of database mining and pattern analysis in combating organized crime. Another example is the CRMO's contribution in facing the enemy within the organization, scandals that can wreck the bank's reputation.

Little attention has been paid so far on the role the CRMO and his people should play in combating the penetration of the bank's business by organized crime. Yet, this is a very important issue whose impact can be demonstrated through an August 1999 example concerning the $10 billion scam at the Bank of New York.

Billions of dollars were channeled through the Bank of New York in the 1998–99 time frame in what is believed to be a major money laundering operation by Russian organized crime. An estimated $4.2 billion were whitewashed in more than 10,000 transactions, passed through one account through an ingeniously conceived scheme. On account of information collected by U.S. federal authorities, it has been estimated that as much as $10 billion may have flowed through the bank in that one and related accounts. Investigators publicly said that these transactions added up to one of the largest money laundering operations ever uncovered, and vast sums of money may move in and out of the bank in a single day.

With the collapse of the Russian financial system in the summer of 1998, the flight of money out of the country accelerated, and investigators have been on the lookout for activities they suspect are money laundering operations. While the tracking of organized crime per se is not one of the CRMO's responsibilities, the rigorous analysis of transactions and of their pattern for reasons of exposure is one of his major duties. There is a synergy between these two functions.

REPORTING PRACTICES AND THE AUDITING OF SALES TRANSACTIONS

The example of unreliable insurance contracts underwritten and sold to customers unaware of the risks involved finds its clones in banking and in brokerage. Reverse repos are an example. Sometimes these instruments hit their issuer with a vengeance (as the huge losses by NatWest Markets and Kidder Peabody helped document), but usually customers and investors get the worst part of the deal.

In addition to the MetLife example, Prudential Insurance Company of America (the largest American life insurer) and New York Life (the fourth largest) have also settled cases involving wrong sales practices. Sales practices that lead to disasters are not alien to the job of CRMO, particularly when they involve volatility smiles and/or leveraging—and therefore potential disasters.

One of the most important means of analysis would be the CRMO's appreciation of the nature of leveraging and its effects. As noted, leveraging is nothing more and nothing less than geared debt. From this simple reality comes a multifold magnification of exposure that leads institutions and their customers to shoot themselves in the foot.

The fact that the CRMO and his assistants should try proactively to uncover and squash unwanted or outright harmful sales deals reflects in no way a negative attitude to sales. Sales is the red blood cell of business, but excesses can lead to disasters. The CRMO must be among the first in the organization to realize that the window of business opportunity is open only briefly. Therefore, because traders don't have the time to meditate long on a contract, everything should be in place for a go/no-go decision on commitment.

Proactive approaches to marketing and sales are welcome because the best risk management procedures work before the fact. Accurate analysis should be available in real-time during the negotiation and before commitments are made. As noted, risk takers and risk controllers should use the same models. What should differ is their hypotheses and their viewpoints.

In my practice I find it helpful to provide both traders and risk managers with templates that help in orienting their appreciation of risks. A template based on industry statistics, like the one in Figure 16.2, is helpful. Even better is one based on your bank's exposure, involving a much more detailed list of instruments than the three taken as an example in Figure 16.2.

- These statistics are based on a sample of risks assumed per instrument, over a 2-year time frame.
- Once a methodology is in place, it can be used intraday, allowing management to exercise much better control over exposure.

Not only should risk management be working on split-second capitalizing on database mining and real-time analysis of proposals, but also the models and systems for risk control must be activated through agents. The CRMO should be instrumental in devising a systems solution that prods to action, exploiting to the maximum the potential usefulness of information as it becomes available.

Compliance is an issue on which the financial industry has not yet made up its mind in terms of specific responsibility. Observance of regulatory reporting rules eases the CRMO's job. Disclosures recommended by bank supervisors may not be directly relevant to shareholders, but the way to bet is that they assist in evaluating risks.

Figure 16.2
High/Low Levels of Capital at Risk with Three Different Instruments

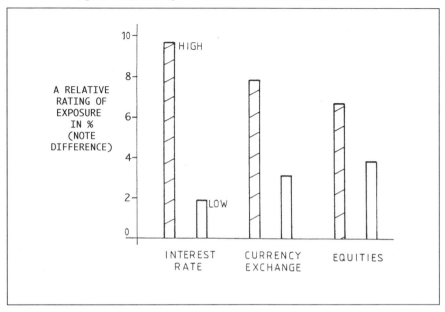

Both internal controls and supervisory chores are handicapped when banks don't apply in a uniform manner reporting formats established through regulation. As an example, Figure 16.3 presents how 10 banks applied in 10 different ways the framework on daily exposure to derivative instruments formalized by the 1996 Market Risk Amendment. Matters are made sometimes worse by the fact that members of the board and senior management have not been trained to understand the meaning of a statistical inference. Figure 16.4 focuses on only one aspect of differences outlined in Figure 16.3: confidence intervals. Consider these statistics:

- **A 97.5% confidence interval will represent less market risk than a 99.0% interval, and the market risk at 95% and 90% will be even less.**

- **However, barring extreme events, the computed amount will be exceeded only 1% of the time at a 99% level of confidence, but 2.5% at 97.5%, 5% at 95%, and 10% at 90%.**

Figure 16.3
Major Assumptions and Associated Differences Underlying Value at Risk Estimates
Presented in Annual Reports to a European Regulatory Authority

	BANK A	BANK B	BANK C	BANK D	BANK E	BANK F	BANK G	BANK H	BANK I	BANK J
Confidence interval	99%	99%	99%	99%	99%	98%	97.7%	97.5%	95%	95%
Holding period	10 days	10 days	10 days	10 days	30 days	1 day	1 day	30 days	1 day	1 day
Aggregation method	Corre-lation	Simu-lation	No corre-lation	NA	Corre-lation	Simu-lation	Corre-lation	Corre-lation	Corre-lation	No corre-lation
Maximum daily VAR	471	121	80	NA	118	47	30	1090	21	6.9
Minimum daily VAR	389	64	20	NA	63	19	10	366	4	3.2
Average daily VAR	415	81	NA	280	100	34	23	NA	10	4.4

NA = not available.

Figure 16.4
Market Risk Factor with a Historical Volatility at About 17% at Three Levels of Confidence Intervals

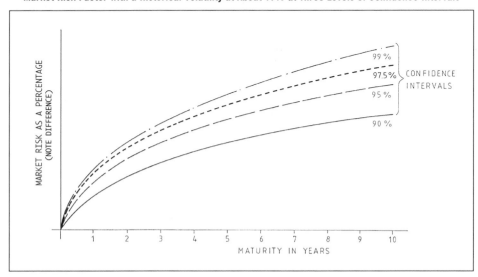

By choosing a lower lever of confidence for internal reporting than that specified by the Basle Committee on Banking Supervision, commercial banks are kidding themselves. Given that information on risks is vital in understanding the impact of financial instruments on the bank's position, standardizing the level of confidence has become a vital element in communicating information on exposure.

The structure and standards to be observed in connection to interactive reporting brings another issue into perspective. While mathematical analysis is vital to the CRMO's job, banking experience is just as crucial. And because organizations are made up of people, the CRMO should also double as a psychologist and analyst of egos. Some managers panic when confronted with accumulated risks. Others refuse to admit that they have a problem. Keep in mind the affect on risk of these personality factors:

- **Big egos and stonewalling are a destructive force in risk management.**
- **Inability to understand the complex nature of some risks also plays a role in defensive attitudes.**

KEEPING AHEAD OF NEW REGULATORY DEVELOPMENTS AROUND THE WORLD

"Our analytical tools have to be increasingly sensitive to asset values and balance sheet valuation," Dr. Alan Greenspan said on August 27, 1999. This statement should be the guiding light of every financial institution executive because it describes in a nutshell the essence of coming regulation. New materials need new tools. First-class analytics are necessary to address the following risk factors:

- Exposure associated with multinational securities deals,
- Mismatch risk due to interest rates,
- Volatile foreign exchange rates, and
- Placing and partner risk as well as fraud.

The downside is that risk evaluation for global operations is still in its infancy, though progress is slowly being made. The new, powerful analytical tools to be developed must be both tactical (of a what-if type) and strategic (sophisticated simulators). There are policy questions to be examined relating to major events such as:

- New global regulation from the Basle Committee,
- Regional regulation from the European Union executive,
- And national regulation brought up to strengthen the banking industry through better focus on assumed exposure and capital requirements.

The process of bank supervision has been strengthened for good reason. No more than a few days after taking office in May 1997, Gordon Brown, the chancellor of the Exchequer, freed the Bank of England from government control over the power to set short-term interest rates. Then, two weeks later, he moved the supervision of the banking industry away from Bank of England and into a new integrated entity, The Financial Services Authority (FSA).

This has been a major phase shift because, among the G-10 central banks, the Bank of England was the more liberal in terms of supervision. Its policy was largely laissez-faire, which has its rationale. The new supervisory policy promises to be most rigorous. Changes in regulatory policies is one of reasons why under no condition the CRMO can be indifferent to supervisory policy shifts.

Gordon Brown's model in regard to bank supervision has been that of upgrading the Securities and Investments Board (SIB) to stamp out fraud and deliver more proactive regulation. The Securities and Investments Board is London's chief markets watchdog. What if the FSA's new supervisory policy is at par with the toughest supervisory strategies among G-10 central banks?

To properly study this particular what-if, the CRMO needs to be versatile in political give-and-take, which invariably influences the evolution of regulatory rules and duties. This will help him to better appreciate the supervisory strategies of central banks in the other G-10 countries and how these relate to financial stability policies. In the UK, under the new system, the Bank of England still has the duty to maintain financial stability. To do that effectively, Eddie George, the bank's governor, says it will need to continue monitoring banks. In Germany and in Switzerland, however, bank supervision is not one of the functions of the central bank, but of a special authority as it is now in the UK.

Both Germany and Switzerland keep their bank supervisors separate from the central bank, though monetary policy officials and supervisors do collaborate. In France, the functions of Commission Bancaire are, so to speak, co-authored by the Banque de France and the powerful Ministry of Finance and the Economy.

True enough, in America, the Federal Reserve is responsible not only for monetary policy but also for a large part of bank supervision. But there are two more supervisors of nationally chartered banks: the Office of the Controller of the Currency (OCC), which is a branch of the U.S. Treasury; and the Federal Deposit Insurance Corporation (FDIC). At the same time, state authorities also have a say in bank supervision.

In America banks also have to watch out for supervision by the Securities and Exchange Commission (SEC) which comes into the process of controlling financial institutions because banks are public companies. Their stability and well-being is of prime importance to investors—hence SEC's need to control how well public institutions manage their risk and return to keep themselves out of bankruptcy.

Furthermore, with operational risk capturing the attention of supervisors, it is only normal to expect that oncoming regulation will emphasize skills and technology that banks need to bend the curve of operational risk—hence human capital. This includes both qualifications of operations executives and auditors and the means put at their disposal to analyze operational risks. One of the necessities for good management outlined by the regulators is that skills and tools must be commensurate with the problems posed by the following factors:

- The size of the bank,
- Its domain of financial activities, and
- The instruments it promotes.

The more exotic the instruments with which a bank deals, the more refined should be the analytics and risk management skills, because the greater is the threat of a global financial meltdown. No wonder bank regulators in America, the UK, continental Europe, Japan, and elsewhere are increasingly nervous about the lack of rigorous risk management techniques for credits, derivatives, the capital markets, and money markets.

The board should appreciate that better risk management will allow business opportunity to flourish and cut the odds of an international financial crash when the inevitable excesses occur. As already stated, better risk management does not start with models, though models have a key role to play. It begins with thoroughly studied strategies, policies, and procedural solutions necessary to build a culture and practice of sound risk control.

Figure 16.5
Overlapping Concepts Underpinning Different Kinds of Risk

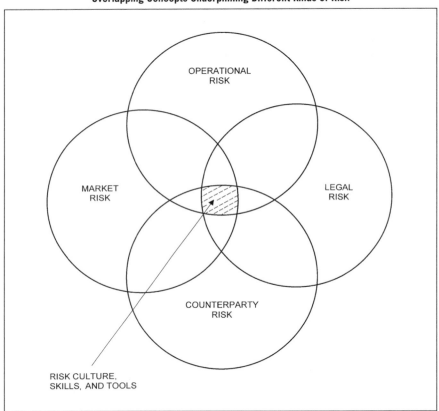

As Figure 16.5 suggests, the concepts underpinning different risks overlap. At their core we find the risk culture, tools, and skills needed to control them. Lack of first-class skills and substandard internal controls correlate. This correlation is a basic reason for banks veering toward bankruptcy. At the same time, an incoherent, unsystematic and low-technology approach to managing risk cannot face the increasingly complex and perilous financial markets of the 21st century. Risk management responsibility becomes:

- Too spotty and too narrowly focused, thereby escaping senior management supervision.
- Too fragmented in different departments and affiliates of the financial organization.
- Too disorganized because it follows largely unwritten, incomplete, contradictory, and imprecise policies.

Unless and until the board of directors and the board of management take a firm stand on the control of exposure, internal controls are considered by many of the bank's managers and professionals to be too much of an impedance to their daily activities. They put the brakes on free-wheeling treasurers and traders in terms of their profits, losses, and commissions.

Because regulators are moving to close the gaps in most of the domains mentioned in this section, the board, the CEO, and the CRMO will be well advised to take a proactive stance. The classical charts, graphs, and economic analyses will be of little help in coping with new regulatory requirements in the coming years. Having done serious work in the past is no guarantee of success in the future because compliance to new regulations will include many new concepts—hence the wisdom of proactive stance.

ADOPTING MORE POWERFUL RISK METRICS FOR RISK EXPOSURE

The development of new product lines has been necessary because in deregulated financial environments, credit institutions have to compete for public savings with money management (mutual) funds, pension funds, and life insurance companies. In many countries, savings through a pension fund has important tax advantages over savings accounts in a bank, though this may be changing.

New proposals keep coming in front of the U.S. Congress to further encourage saving and investment. Their objective is to generate rates of return compelling enough to stimulate many people who have not taken full or even partial advantage of the other forms of tax-incentive savings, such as the traditional individual retirement account (IRA) or company-sponsored 401(k), to get into the savings habit. Legislation should always aim to encourage more people to join the saving and investing population.

Investments and savings, however, compete with one another. In the United States, investments by, so to speak, the man in the street have become a trend that, over the past dozen years, has swept over the landscape. It continues to grow at the expense of classical savings and bank deposits as well as at the expense of more classical investments such as real estate.

As far as credit institutions are concerned, on the lending side too the situation is in full evolution. Lending has become more complex for commercial banks, as companies use investment banks as advisors to the issuance of commercial paper. Lending on easy-to-liquidate collateral is diminishing, and this hits the banks' bottom line.

Lending money has also become a service provided by financial institutions competing with the classical banking industry. Pension funds and life insurance companies are examples of institutional lending, while a significant exposure in investments is taken by professional risk takers and speculators. All kinds of specialized investment funds act in this role. Consider these recommendations for lending institutions:

- **It is not enough that the regulators ask banks to mark-to-market their lending portfolio.**
- **The same policy should be followed with nonbanks. Otherwise the control of exposure is skewed.**

As an example of current regulation of nonbanks, American pension funds are reporting to the Internal Revenue Service (IRS) and U.S. Department of Labor. But current reporting standards are archaic and the government takes two years to compile the information it receives.

The standards must not only be updated and dynamic. They should also account for the bends and twists in the way business is done. For instance, with transborder lending by banks and institutional investors booming, both are increasingly involved in long-term agreements where there is no quick way out. One reason behind this is that commercial banks no longer have a monopoly in lending at home or, for that matter, in the securitization of lending.

There are also other changes to notice. Whereas in the past, credit institutions established a counterparty rating for their clients and lending was based upon these ratings, in a large measure the task of evaluating counterparties in a global sense is now taken over by independent credit rating agencies. This facilitates the process through which big industrial companies that have good credit standing can borrow directly from the market without the intermediation of a bank. Standard & Poor's, Moody's, Fitch IBCA, and other rating agencies provide the market with credit information on the banking industry itself, on large corporations, and on smaller industrial companies.

The information revolution sees to it that the results of analyses, professional references, news flashes, and even rumors are now widely diffused. In the past, many banks considered credit information to be absolutely proprietary, since it had to do with their financial power. But keeping vital information close to one's chest is not that easy in our age. Keep in mind how the financial industry is changing:

- **Ratings by independent agencies about other banks are equally available to banks, nonbanks, treasurers, speculators, and investors.**

- **This significantly changes both the way business is done and the products being offered, obliging a strategic reevaluation of our bank's position.**

In my judgment, although credit risk rating is very important, market risk information, should also be normalized in a way that is generally understood and used for decisions. Capitalizing on the fact that position risk is becoming part of management culture, we can both rate market risk and integrate the ratings into a meaningful framework. For example, we can use three metrics to evaluate risk:

- *Average expected market risk*—This is potential exposure based on maturity of financial transactions and the expected movement in market prices because of prevailing volatility. The word expected is used in the sense of expected value (or mean) of a statistical distribution. Assuming that this can be approximated by a normal distribution, we can compute different levels of confidence (shown in Figures 16.3 and 16.4).

- *Expected worst-case risk*—This is potential exposure based on maturity of the transaction and the worst-case market movement, connected to leveraged financial instruments. With derivatives, worst case will be a function of market movement of the underlier. This essentially concerns market risk but the magnitude of the shock can also have credit risk characteristics. Other things being equal, the higher the level of gearing, the higher will be the worst-case risk.

- *Unexpected worst-case risk*—This represents potential exposure due to outliers that impact on the movement of the security and, in the case of derivatives, of the underlier—all the way to extreme values. This is the largest of the three classes that account for exposure embedded in a portfolio of trading transactions. Unexpected worst-case risk can be divided into two parts: not-leveraged trading transactions and leveraged trading transactions.

The need for new risk metrics is propelled by the fact that growth in financial aggregates exceeds money supply and leaves physical output far behind. As shown in Figure 16.6, the virtual economy and the physical economy have been, so to speak, uncoupled. Therefore, old norms and metrics originally made for money supply can no more map accurately the risk embedded in the virtual economy—particularly worst-case exposure.

A similar case can be made of loans, from underwriting to securitization. Both loans and derivatives should be examined as parts of the restructured business of investment banking and of the need to be ahead of the curve in estimating risk.

As the lending market increasingly attracts consultancy by investment banks and resulting fat fees, it is no wonder that major commercial banks in Europe (particularly in Germany, Switzerland, and the Netherlands) have become envious of Wall Street's long-time dominance of the global investment banking business. By buying British investment banks and, more recently, U.S. investment banks and by setting up shop in London and New York, continental European banks are rushing to catch up, and they are targeting the next wave of privatization, mergers, and other megadeals.

Big commercial banks' switch toward investment banking partly compensates for the fact that in terms of a steady train of business, what is left for the banking sector are the riskier transactions. With plain vanilla products, the margins are becoming smaller and smaller.

On the other hand, with exotic financial products, the board and the CEO should expect a greater exposure to risk.

In the course of the research that led to this book, some commercial banks suggested not only that their classical lending business is in doldrums but also that the loan rates they charge their clients are too low, given the level of competition. Yet, the risks a credit institution bears have not diminished.

In fact, credit risks are increasing, while at the same time risk calculations and pricing are not of a standard commensurate to the demands posed by new financial instruments. Alert officers now appreciate that the policies and tools used in gauging risk must be ahead of the complexity of the transaction the financial institution undertakes. In real life, nobody can avoid taking risks. Nevertheless, keep in mind these recommendations:

- **The assumed exposure and its likely evolution should always be calculated.**

- **And the aggregate of worst-case, expected, and unexpected risks should not exceed established limits.**

Figure 16.6
The Rapid Growth in Financial Aggregates Exceeds Money Supply and Leaves G-10 Countries' Physical Output in the Dust

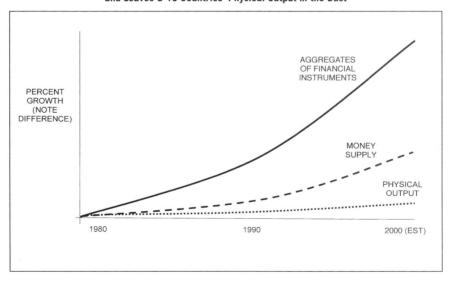

Let me repeat, in brief, the lessons from the meltdown of LTCM. Risk can be better controlled if we evaluate the counterparty's senior management, analyze the quality of the counterparty's track record, and pay attention to ethics and performance in dealing. We should definitely require much greater transparency, appreciate the importance of stress testing, practice collateralization with dynamic haircuts, and steadily study the likelihood of both systematic and systemic risk.

In conclusion, the risk management solutions we apply should become increasingly sophisticated. The same is true of systems developed to follow up on monitoring, testing, and corrective action. The most fundamental concept I heard in the course of my research is to not push new ideas for their own sake, but to induce people to think of better ways to control risk. Quality programs must be initiated at the top before real improvements can be made by the people operating below.

Accounting for Different Types of Risk and Their Impact

"**S**uccess is measured by economic output. There appears to be no close relationship to human achievement," said John Kenneth Galbraith in his 1999 lecture at the London School of Economics. Right? Wrong! It is difficult to find a statement which is more unsound than this one. The size of a company is measured through its turnover; profit is no measure of size, neither is capitalization. Keep in mind these three general principles regarding business success:

- **Profits, cash flow, and capitalization are measures of a company's success.**

- **Success and size don't necessarily correlate. They respond to different criteria and are subject to different metrics.**

- **Success can never be judged independently from human ambition, drive, the will to get results, and the failures made in the course of various actions.**

There are also other contradictions in Galbraith's statement. In the virtual economy in which we live, if success were measured by economic output, then having passed the $170 trillion in notional principal amounts, the derivatives market would have been the greatest success story ever in human history—especially since, according to some estimates, this market is headed for the astronomical $1 quadrillion mark. Risk managers are asking these questions about the new economy:

- How are the experts reacting to this $1 quadrillion forecast that will presumably characterize the new economy?
- What are the risks associated with it, and what are their impacts in the short, medium, long terms?
- Can these risks hit the derivatives industry like a thunderbolt? Can they destabilize the global economy?

Nobel prize winner Dr. Merton Miller suggests that derivatives have made the world a safer place (though he does not explain how and why). But George Soros (who is no theoretician but is a practicing financier) warns that, quite to the contrary, derivatives will destroy society. Both are overstatements.

As far as I am concerned, the greatest risk with derivatives comes from the fact that very few people can see through to their limits. Yet boundaries exist with any process and with any instrument, even if we have no hint of where the limits are, or how far the damage would go if the market crashes. The financial market might implode (as so often happens with bubbles), exposing the gap between some theorists' rhetoric and facts stemming from the real world. But it does not need to implode, if the following market conditions are met:

- If there is a correction that permits the market to find a new, consolidated base, and
- If prudential risk control is exercised at all times by financial institutions, the treasurers of other companies, and the regulators.

If the market implodes, what then? "While bubbles that burst are scarcely benign, the consequences need not be catastrophic," said Federal Reserve Chairman Dr. Alan Greenspan on June 17, 1999, before the U.S. Congress's Joint Economic Committee. Echoing his December 1996 "irrational exuberance" warning, he added that the Fed may take preemptive actions that "can obviate the need of more drastic actions at a later date that could destabilize the economy."[1]

Greenspan made another interesting point in his deposition: "Bubbles generally are perceptible only after the fact." Therefore, if we hope to take proactive action in connection to the new economy, we must prognosticate coming events, particularly those relating to our own transactions and inventoried positions—a job befalling everyone.

[1]*EIR*, June 25, 1999.

Longer-range planning and controlling activities do not deal so much with future decisions as with future impact of current decisions. There are four types of risks that the board, the CEO, and the chief risk management officer should be carefully watching:

1. The risk of asset loss because of credit risk—This is largely exposure taken because of likelihood of counterparty default. For instance, mortgages, corporate loans, and bonds may go sour. The banks that loaned $58 billion to Daewoo, gearing the company above its head, should not be feeling so comfortable at this moment. Credit risk is also present with trading transactions. As mentioned, J.P. Morgan still has not recovered the $480 billion owed by South Korea's SK Securities out of derivatives deals—which, with the excuse of the late 1997 East Asia meltdown, does not want to meet its obligations.

2. Losses due to interest rate, currency exchange, equity, and index swings—Market risk, in simple form, is loss resulting from movement in market prices or rates. It exists because commodity prices connected to a given transaction or inventoried position, or underpinning a leveraged derivatives instrument, are volatile. If there was no movement of substance in market prices, there will be no concern over market exposure. This is, however, the sort of *if* no serious person would put his name to.

A different *if,* however, makes sense. Amadeo Giannini, founder of Bank of America, expressed it beautifully when he advised his friends, his clients, and his associates never to use borrowed money to gamble in the stock market, but to invest only the funds they had available. What Giannini essentially was saying is "Don't leverage yourself. Without gearing, you have nothing to fear but fear, when stock prices drop."

3. The risk of a bank's wrong pricing its own products and services—This may be due to plain error. The reason may instead be adverse volatility. Behind wrong pricing may also be greed, commissions, or other factors. There are many types of pricing insufficiency, starting with the hypotheses we make as to which way the market may go.

The causality of price risk, like that of capital gains and losses, has not been thoroughly analyzed; neither has it been meaningfully addressed by supervisory authorities. If it had been, then we would not be faced with so many cases of volatility smiles in pricing options and other instruments.

4. Operational risks, which so far have received a rather scant attention—Yet operational risks can be severe. They are many and quite diverse from one another. The list of operational risks is long, starting with mismanagement at all levels—from the board and CEO to lower supervision. The quality of professional personnel is an operational risk in the new economy where skill and know-how are king, and so are issues connected to organization, the front desk, and the back office.

Execution risk, including the handling of transaction, debit/credit bookkeeping, and confirmation, as well as payments/settlements and fiduciary activities are in the operational risk domain. Legal risk, documentation, and infrastructural services are also operational. There are also operational risks associated with less known or less appreciated factors because of novelty and the unknowns of the new economy.

All four domains of risk require contingency reserves, with norms applicable on a global scale. The 1988 Capital Accord, 1996 Market Risk Amendment, and 1999 Capital Adequacy Framework by the Basle Committee on Banking Supervision targeted these issues. The 1988 Capital Accord addressed only credit risk; the Market Risk Amendment dealt with market risk, and The Framework introduced the need for operational risk reserves. (The Framework was subject to a comment period which ran to March 31, 2000. A revised accord will be phased into national laws in 2002.)

What the regulators specify as prudential capital reserves is a general solution that heavily reflects the appetite for risk of the financial industry as a whole. Regulatory guidelines are welcome, but they are not the whole story. Within the perspective set by this general solution, each particular bank must do its own homework, keeping in mind these key points:

- **Individual solutions require rigorous analysis, seamless database mining, accurate modeling, and real-time experimentation.**
- **This is the essence of analytical computational finance practiced only by tier-1 institutions—hence the inequality existing between technology "haves" and "have nots."**

Risk management officers worth their salt appreciate that in the new economy, analytics are so important because risks may be compound. In managerial and professional terms, there is a likelihood of missing your risk and reward goals associated with tracking a moving target in highly dynamic markets. To calculate the risk inherent in a banking operation, we must:

- Identify fundamental risk factors,
- Determine linkages and establish metrics, and
- Take measurements and reach conclusions.

To improve risk management, we must

- Establish an elaborate risk management system with corrective capabilities that include feedback,
- Take decisive action every time danger signals are flashing,
- Experiment on limits for risk control,
- Monitor the observance of these limits without any loss of time,
- And make sure that orders regarding the level of exposure being taken are executed in a timely fashion.

Without steady follow-up, the likelihood that top management's orders will not be executed is nearly equal to 100%.

It is not sufficient that the board or CEO decide on "something" for this to be done. When Ike Eisenhower was elected president, Harry Truman said, "Poor Ike; when he was a general, he gave an order and it was carried out. Now he is going to sit in that big office and he'll give an order and not a damn thing is going to happen."[2] Big offices in large financial institutions suffer from exactly the same defect of command and control.

Enforcement procedures in the Oval Office of the White House and the executive offices of corporations seem to be based heavily on the common sense of subordinates. But common sense, a proverb says, is the most widely spread human characteristic, which is why each one of us has so little of it. An enduring contribution to risk management requires not just common sense but also clear policies and timely execution reports. These call for the proper infrastructure, which can be built only when expert bankers and first-class technologists closely collaborate to establish the means for a sound pursuit of

---

[2]Peter F. Drucker, *The Effective Executive* (London: Heinemann, 1967).

business opportunity commensurate with manageable risk. As we saw in Chapter 1, help in developing new financial instruments open up new business opportunities and help to control risks of different origins and kinds.

The contribution of rocket scientists to risk management functioning is important inasmuch as a steady transition through different states has become the modern means of doing business. Because this transition is fairly rapid, modeling and experimentation are balancing acts. Like regulation and legislation, analytical solutions aim to bring the system under control without killing the goose that may lay the golden egg. Rather than being a constraint, regulation is, so to speak, the flywheel of the modern economic and financial system—and therefore of the new economy.

Index

352

Index

Long-Term Credit Bank (LTCB), 211, 212, 299
Losses, 134

Management, decentralized, 283
Management accountability, 268, 269
Management by objectives, 237
Management controls, 71, 73, 75
Management control structure, 65
Management plan, 208
Management planning, 254–56
Management risk, 69
Managers, responsibilities of, 242, 243
Market and credit exposure, able monitoring and measuring of, 270
Market risk, 3, 13, 125, 151, 165, 167, 209, 228, 230, 260, 275, 303, 308, 320, 322, 347
Market risk, average expected, 341
Market Risk Amendment, 191, 209, 260, 301, 333, 348
Market risk information, 341
Market risk management, 289
Market risk management, failure of, 322
Marron, Donald, 155
Marshall, George, 251, 252, 283, 274
McCoy, John B., 252
MeesPierson, 23
Membership on the board, qualification for, 235
Mergers, 214–19, 227
Merits, 240, 241
Meriwether, John, 87, 95, 101, 146, 153, 161, 162, 185
Merrill Lynch, 18, 52, 91, 154, 155, 260, 279, 285, 286, 326
Metallgesellschaft, 100
MetLife, 331
Microsoft, 219
Middle office, 291–93
Miller, Merton, 18, 19, 87, 94, 153, 346
Ministry of Finance (MOF), Japanese, 52, 53

Ministry of International Trade and Industry (MITI), 61, 62
Mitsubishi Bank, 299
Mitsui Chuo Trust, 66
Mizhuo Financial Group, 212
Model failure, risk of, 121
Modeling, 275, 312, 313
Model risk, 262
Models, 167, 338
Modigliani, Franco, 18, 19
Money-center banks, 210
Monitoring, real-time, 250, 251
Monte Carlo simulation, 119, 330
Moody's Investors Service, 224, 316, 341
Morgan Bank, 307
Morgan Stanley Capital International, (MSCI), 38
Morgan Stanley Dean Witter, 126
Mortgage-backed financing, 71, 77
Mullins, David, 153, 154
Mutual funds, 123, 156

NASDAQ, 4, 193, 197, 198, 247
National Bank of Iceland, 208
NatWest, 21, 22, 63, 241, 331
NatWest Markets, 185
Net replacement value (NRV), 100
Netting, 100
New Capital Adequacy Framework, 3, 22, 186, 190, 209, 260, 296, 320, 321, 348
New economy, 3, 7, 64, 105, 207, 345
New instruments, complexity of, 261
New York Federal Reserve Bank, 183, 193, 202
New York Life, 331
New York State Banking Department, 328
New York Stock Exchange, 4, 121, 247
Nippon Credit bank (NCB), 64, 65, 212, 213, 299
Nippon Mortgage, 47
Nomura Securities, 299
Normal distribution, 21
North American Free Trade Agreement (NAFTA), 6